William Marshall

The Rural Economy of Norfolk

Comprising the Management of Landed Estates...

William Marshall

The Rural Economy of Norfolk
Comprising the Management of Landed Estates...

ISBN/EAN: 9783744750318

Printed in Europe, USA, Canada, Australia, Japan

Cover: Foto ©Suzi / pixelio.de

More available books at **www.hansebooks.com**

THE
RURAL ECONOMY

OF

NORFOLK:

COMPRISING THE

Management of Landed Eſtates,

AND THE

PRESENT PRACTICE of HUSBANDRY

IN THAT COUNTY.

By Mr. MARSHALL,

(Author of MINUTES OF AGRICULTURE, &c.)

RESIDENT upwards of Two Years in NORFOLK.

IN TWO VOLUMES,

VOL. II.

LONDON:

Printed for T. CADELL, in the STRAND.

M,DCC,LXXXVII.

A D D R E S S

T O T H E

R E A D E R.

IN regiſtering the practice of this Diſtrict, I purſued a two-fold method.
Such eſtabliſhed rules of management as are
generally obſerved in common practice, I
committed to a SYSTEMATIZED REGISTER,
as they occurred to my obſervation. But
ſuch particular operations, and peculiari-
ties of management, as required an accurate detail of circumſtances ;—alſo ſuch
complex obſervations, as included a plu-
rality of ſubjects ;—alſo ſuch inſtances of
practice and opinion, as I found peculiar to
individuals ;—I reduced to MINUTES, in
ſeries, with thoſe on my own practice.

In

In preparing thefe materials for publication I was defirous, on the principle of fimplicity, to have united the two regifters: that is, to have incorporated the MINUTES with the fyftematized matter. But this I found entirely incompatible with the fimplicity I was feeking. Many of the individual minutes pertaining to a variety of diftinct fubjects, would not affimilate with any *one* of them; while others were, in ftrictnefs, foreign to the fyftem of practice prevalent in the Diftrict; being upon incidents in my own practice, and upon obfervations and reflections on fubjects not efpecially connected with the rural affairs of Norfolk, but equally relative to the rural economy of the Ifland at large.

Thus, feeing the neceffity of keeping the two regifters diftinct, in fome degree, I thought it right to let them remain (with a few exceptions) in the manner in which they were written: but, in order to connect them as intimately as the nature

of

of them would admit of, I digefted the
fubjects of the MINUTES, and fufpended
them to their correfponding fubjects in the
SYSTEM; through which means the two
regifters may be read together, or feparately, at the option of the reader.

I was induced to adopt this method,
with lefs hefitation, as I am ftill more
and more convinced that PRACTICAL
KNOWLEDGE is never conveyed more forcibly than in MINUTES, made while the
MINUTIÆ of practice are frefh in the
memory, and the attendant CIRCUM-
STANCES are ftill prefent to the imagina-
tion. Nor am I fingular in this opinion.
A mafterly writer conveys the fame fen-
timent, in more elegant language. " It
muft," fays he, " be acknowledged, that
the methods of difquifition and teaching
may be fometimes different, and on very
good reafon undoubtedly; but, for my
part, I am convinced that the method of
teaching which approaches moft nearly to
the method of inveftigation, is incompa-

rably

rably the beft; fince, not content with ferving up a few barren and lifelefs truths, it leads to the ftock on which they grew; it tends to fet the reader himfelf in the track of invention, and to direct him into thofe paths in which the author has made his own difcovery, if he fhould be fo happy as to have made any that are valuable."

I will place this fubject in a light comparative with two of the learned profeffions. MINUTES, in rural economy, are as CASES in phyfic and furgery, and as REPORTS in law. They are all, and equally, if equally authentic, PRACTICE IN ITS BEST FORM. For an agricultor cannot regifter an incident,—a furgeon, a cafe,—nor a lawyer, the proceedings and decifion of a court, with any degree of accuracy and perfpicuoufnefs, until he has afcertained, and fet before him, the facts and attendant circumftances refpecting it;—and has revolved in his mind the caufe, the operation, and the effect.

In

In doing this, he not only finds it neceffary to afcertain minutial facts and circumftances, which, otherwife, he would have overlooked; but is led on, by reflection, to inferences which, otherwife, would not have occurred to him : and, if he regifter fully and faithfully, he knows no more of the given fubject, when he has finifhed his regifter, than the perfon who may, afterwards, have read it. Confequently, he not only thereby renders his practice more valuable to himfelf; but, by reading his report, his minute, or his cafe, the ftudent gains full poffeffion of the practice of a practitioner.—Hence, principally, a barrifter is enabled to ftep into court, and a phyfician into a fick room, without the affiftance of felf-practice.

I will place thefe fubjects in another point of view. The attorney, the apothecary, and the common farmer, are enabled to carry on their refpective profeffions, or callings, without thofe fcientific helps.

The former depend upon the practice of their-masters, and their own practice, during their clerkship, or apprenticeship; as the farmer does upon that of his father, and the country he happens to be bred in. But why do we, in difficulties, fly from the apothecary to the physician, and from the attorney to the counsellor? Because they have studied their professions scienti-fically, have obtained a general know-ledge, and taken comprehensive views, of their respective subjects;—as well as of the sciences and subjects which are allied to them; and, added to these scientific aids, have made themselves masters of the practice, and the opinions, of the able prac-titioners who have gone before them; as well as of COTEMPORARY PRACTITIONERS.

With respect to the following MINUTES, it only remains necessary to say, that they were written in an active scene, and that more attention was paid to circumstances than to language. Those on husbandry were written, as I conceive all minutes on
the

the fubject ought to be written, in the
FAMILIAR LANGUAGE OF FARMING;
and, many of them, in the provincial
phrafeology of the Diftrict they were
written in. I confefs, however, that, in
revifing them for publication, I thought
it prudent to do away fome of the
FAMILIARISMS of the original Minutes.
If, in the prefent form, they furnifh fuch
PRACTICAL DATA and NATURAL FACTS
as may, in the end, be ferviceable to the
main defign, and, in the inftant, be acceptable to PRACTITIONERS, and ufeful to
the STUDENT, the intention of publifhing
them will be fully obtained.

London, Feb. 1, 1787.

CONTENTS

OF THE

SECOND VOLUME.

MINUTES.

1780.

CONTENTS.

DE-

CONTENTS.

CONTENTS.

CONTENTS.

CONTENTS.

MINUTES.

MINUTES

IN

NORFOLK.

1.

1780. SEPTEM- THIS morning, meafured
BER 22d. a fheepfold, fet out for
600 fheep, confifting of ewes, wedders, and
grown lambs.

It meafures eight by five-and-a-half rods,
or forty-four fquare ftatute rods; which is
fomewhat more than feven rods to a hundred,
or two yards to a fheep.

2.

OCTOBER 27th. A few weeks ago a tenant
afked for fome top-wood to under-drain
part of a clofe of arable land; which part
being cold and fpringy, fcarcely ever produced a crop; and, this morning, I have been
to fee the procefs of *under-draining* in this country.

Having from feveral years obfervation marked the fpringy parts, he began by circumfcrib-
VOL. II. B ing

ing them with a drain, made as hereafter defcribed, and then drew others within it in fuch
directions as he knew from obfervation (not
methodically) would convey the fuperfluous
moifture from the wet parts to a main drain
and outlet.

The drains were formed by two men, each
of them having a tapering fpade, and a hooked fcoop. The firft man took out a fpit, with a
fquare-pointed fpade ten inches long, feven
inches wide at the tread, and five inches at the
point; and, to make a fmooth footing for the
next man to ftand upon, drew out the crumbs
with a five-inch fcoop.

The other man funk it about eight inches
deeper with a round-pointed fpade, eight inches
long, five inches wide at the tread, and three
inches near the point; clearing out the bottom
with a narrow-mouthed fcoop; namely, two
inches and a half to three inches wide: the
drain, when finifhed, being a foot to fourteen
inches wide at the top; from eighteen to twenty
inches deep; and about three inches wide at
the bottom.

Thefe drains were filled with oak and alder
boughs in this manner :—

The fpray being ftript off, the woody parts
(from an inch and a half to three inches diameter)

meter) were laid in the bottom of the drain. If crooked, they had a chop given them in the elbow, and then preffed down to the bottom with the foot. If large, one, if fmall, two or three of thefe fticks were laid at the bottom; upon thefe the fpray, with the leaves on; and upon this a covering of heath. The whole, when trodden down, appeared to fill the drain within a few inches of the top.

The mould was then laid on and ridged up over the drain.

A roller paffed along and finifhed the operation.

The land was immediately plowed for wheat.

The quantity of land drained is about three acres:

The expence about five pounds, or one pound thirteen fhillings and four pence an acre, viz.

Opening and filling in 184 rods at 3d. - - - £. 2 6 0

Three loads of boughs (given him by his landlord) fuppofe - — — 1 10 0

Two loads of heath 14s. carriage 10s. 1 4 0
——————
£. 5 0 0

He

2.
DRAINING.

He has repeatedly experienced this method of draining, and has found it anfwer his expectations. He is a cautious judicious hufbandman, and would not lay out 3*l.* 10*s.* without a moral certainty of gain.

3.

TURNEPS.

NOVEMBER 8. An experienced farmer in this neighbourhood fays he has frequently found that fteeping old turnep-feed in water, and letting it lie a few hours in the fun before fowing, has brought it up much fooner than fowing it dry.

He adds, that this year, having neglected to fteep it, he had turnep-feed lay three weeks in the ground before it came up. He was advifed to plow in the few ftraggling plants which appeared foon after fowing, under an idea that the fly had eaten off the remainder : but he judged from experience that the principal part of the feed was ftill in the ground; he accordingly waited until rain fell, and has now, I fee, a very fine crop of turneps.

This is a valuable incident ; for it is highly probable, that in the beginning of the feafon, when old feed is obliged to be fown, many crops of turneps have been prevented by plowing the ground prematurely.

No-

4.   4.

NOVEMBER 11. *A.* and *B.* having feveral fmall pieces of land lying intermixed
with each other's eftates, agreed upon an exchange by arbitration.

The particular lands to be exchanged, and
the general outline of the agreement having
been previoufly determined upon ; and each
party having made choice of a referee; articles of agreement for exchange were figned.

The matters left to reference were thefe :

1ft. The rental value of the refpective lands in
exchange.

2d. To determine which of the timber-trees
growing on the premifes fhould be taken down
by the then prefent owners (and removed off the
premifes before July next enfuing) and which
fhould be left ftanding.

3d. The value of the timber, ftands, pollards,
and ftub-wood, which the arbitrators fhould
judge proper to be left ftanding on the premifes.

4th. A principal part of *B.*'s land lying at a
diftance from any of *A.*'s farms, except one
which is let on a leafe that has fix years to
run, during which time it remains at the
option of the tenant whether or not he will

rent

4.

EXCHANGE
OF LANDS.

rent thefe lands ; it was agreed that each party fhall, if required, hold his own land (or find a proper tenant) during the faid term of fix years, at fuch rent, and under fuch covenants, as the arbitrators fhould fix on.

On Monday the 6th inftant, the arbitrators met ; and having *previoufly* named an umpire, or third perfon, in cafe they fhould difagree in their award, entered upon the bufinefs ; which was thus conducted.

Having firft taken a curfory view of the feveral pieces to be exchanged ; and having fettled between themfelves the mode and rate of valuing the wood ; they took the whole before them in this manner :

The arbitrators, both of them men of fuperior abilities in the bufinefs they had undertaken, went firft ; pointing out which of the trees fhould ftand, and which be taken down : the latter were marked by chopping off a piece of the bark with an adze. The pollards and ftub-wood deemed fit to ftand were valued and minuted by the arbitrators themfelves ; and the timber-trees meafured by two carpenters (one chofen by each party), an account being minuted by an affiftant ; by whom likewife the number of ftands were taken.

The

The arbitrators, as they paffed along, caft their eyes upon the land, and feparately put their private valuations upon it.

The lands having been previoufly furveyed by two furveyors (one for each party) and the *rate* of valuation of the timber and other woods to be left ftanding on the premifes having been previoufly fixed upon by the referees, —it now remained to afcertain the value of the feveral parcels of land ; for which purpofe a fpecial meeting was appointed and held, yefterday.

To fimplify this important part of the bufinefs, and to render it as little liable to unneceffary cavil as poffible, it was agreed that the difference of rental value, whatever it might happen to be, fhould be calculated at twenty-five years purchafe.

The rental value of the refpective pieces therefore now remained the almoft only thing in fufpence. But in this they had differed widely in their valuations : in fome pieces fo much as four fhillings an acre.

Argument having been tried without effect to reconcile the differences, it was propofed by one of the referees to leave the matter to the umpire.

Finding

4.

EXCHANGE OF LANDS.

Finding things in this ſtate, I ventured to propoſe a mode of ſettlement which appeared to me not only brief but equitable. This was, to lay aſide intirely the particularized eſtimates; and, after ſetting a part which was tythe-free againſt a part of an inferiour quality, to exchange acre for acre.—It was agreed to by all parties.

There being a balance in the quantity of land under exchange of about four acres and a half, the buſineſs was now to fix a fair rental value upon this ſurplus. After ſome converſation it was fixed at fifteen ſhillings an acre.

RENT.

The rent of the land for the next ſix years was alſo fixed at the ſame rate; and the principal covenants entered into were, that the ſeveral pieces ſhould be left, as to crops, &c. in the ſame ſtate in which they now are.

Laſtly, the value of the wood to be left upon the premiſes being aſcertained by calculation, the buſineſs was ended.

The referees had put down in their eſtimates the *rent of the land* at twelve to ſixteen ſhillings an acre *.

* The quality of the lands in exchange are, conſidered collectively, ſomewhat above the par of lands in this diſtrict.

The

The *oak timber* they valued at eighteen pence, and the *aſh timber* at one ſhilling a foot, meaſuring all above ſix inches timber-girt *.

5. TIMBER.

The *ſtands*, one with another, at a ſhilling a piece (leſs than ſix inches a ſtand, more than ſix a timber tree).

The *pollards* principally from one to three ſhillings a-piece—ſome few at four ſhillings.

FIREWOOD.

The *ſtub-wood* in proportion to the pollards.

5.

1781. MAY 8. It is imprudent to truſt, in any degree, to tenants, in the pruning of timber-trees.

HEDGEROW TIMBER.

This ſeaſon I took unuſual pains to inſtruct a young man, whoſe farm is unmercifully loaded with wood, in what manner he ſhould *ſet up* ſome trees which were particularly injurious to his crops (namely, to take off the ſmall boughs cloſe to the ſtem, and to leave live growing twigs upon the large ones, to draw the ſap, and thereby keep the ſtumps alive); neverthelefs the havock committed on his farm is ſhameful.

* The timber in general coarſe.

It

5.

HEDGEROW TIMBER.

It is true, he blames his men; but this is no excuse: he promised to attend minutely to the business himself. I pointed out the boughs which were proper to be taken off: but for one I pointed out, he has taken off three.

Nor is he the only one who has made the same wilful mistake; and it is a want of common prudence to leave to a tenant a business of so much importance to an estate as the pruning of timber-trees; for he has a double interest in abusing his trust:---he disencumbers his farm, and fills his wood-yard.

In future, when I see it necessary that timber-trees should be lightened of their low-hanging boughs, whether for the preservation of the hedge, or the relief of the crops, I will send a wood-man to do it in a proper manner; and charge the faggots at a fair price to the farmer *.

6.

BURNING ANT-HILLS.

MAY 10. Some time ago, gave a tenant leave to cut and burn ant-hills off a dole belonging to his farm, upon a common.

* This rule I afterwards observed; and found it not only beneficial to the estate, but agreeable to the tenant; for under this regulation he found more of this necessary work take place upon his farm, than he had theretofore been able to get done.

His

His motive is the improvement of his farm by the aſhes ; and his pretext the improvement of the common : both of which good purpoſes will probably be obtained. He is to level the ground, and rake in graſs-ſeeds.

His proceſs is to cut them up with a heart-ſhaped ſharp ſpade or ſhovel, in irregular lumps of ten to fifteen inches diameter, and two to five or ſix inches thick. Theſe are turned graſs-downward, until the mould-ſide be thoroughly dry, and then ſet up graſs-out-ward until they are dry enough to burn.

The fire is kindled with bruſh-wood, and kept ſmothering, by laying the ſods or lumps on gradually as the fire breaks out, until ten to fifteen or twenty loads of aſhes are raiſed in one heap. The workmen have agreed to com-plete the proceſs for a ſhilling each load of aſhes.

This is a cheap way of raiſing manure ; be-ſides, at the ſame time, removing a nuiſance : and no man having ſuch an opportunity in his power ought to negleĉt making at leaſt an ex-periment. On ſome ſoils aſhes are found in themſelves an excellent manure ; and, perhaps generally, aſhes raiſed in this way would be found highly advantageous as bottoming for farm-yards and dunghills.

JUNE

6.
MANURE.

GRASSLAND.

GRASSLAND.

7.

June 28. The herbage of the dairy paftures (fee GRASSLAND, vol. I. alfo MIN. 107.)
confifting of rye-grafs, white clover, and a
few of the taller graffes, having run up in
patches to feed, I had it fwept over with the
fithe; partly to improve the feed, which would
foon have been much incumbered by the dry
ftrawlike bents; and partly for the fodder, this
year of fcarcity of grafs for hay.

Shut them up for a few days to frefhen:
gave one fhilling an acre for mowing; and to-
day have finifhed carrying fourteen jags (about
nine or ten tons) of hay off forty-feven acres.

The hay is more than tolerable; for the
paftures not having been too hard ftocked, there
was a fine bottom of white clover; which mixed
with the frefh ftalks of the blade-graffes, likewife cut in the fulnefs of fap, and the whole
made flowly in fmall cocks, the hay is green and
fweet to a great degree; and will next winter
no doubt be worth from fifty fhillings to three
pounds a ton.

Nine tons of hay at 55s. - - £. 24 15 0
Mowing 47 acres   £. 2   7
Making and carrying,
   about   - - -   2   7   4 14 0

Neat profit £. 20   0   0
befides

befides the fightlinefs; the improvement of
the feed; and the prevention of thiftles and
other weeds from feeding on the ground, and
being blown about the neighbourhood.

8.

JULY 10. Perhaps cattle and fheep fhould
be kept feparate.

While the dairy paftures were fwept (fee
laft MIN.) the cows were fhifted into a grazing
ground; but, notwithftanding there was a good
bite, and the grafs apparently of a defirable
quality, they did not fill themfelves, nor milk
fo well as they did before they were put in,
and after they were taken out; though their
pafture afterwards was apparently of a worfe
quality. But in the grazing ground were a
flock of fheep; whilft the dairy paftures had
nothing in them except the cows and a few
horfes.

Mr. Thomas Baldwin, of North Walfham,
fays, that having fheepfolded a piece of ground,
which, a drought fetting in, he could not, as
intended, break up; a good bite of grafs came
up where the fheep-fold had ftood. He put
his

9.

SHEEP.

his cows in to feed it off : they would not touch it : he turned his horses to it, and they eat it into the very ground.

9.

FENCE.
WALLS.

, July 21. Perhaps plant *ivy* againſt *ſea ſtone walls* to prevent their burſting.

Part of a wall before a cottage at Thorp is overgrown with ivy, part of it naked : the former is firm and upright—the latter burſt in many places; ſo as not to be made ſtrong again without a conſiderable part of it being taken down and rebuilt.

I O.

MANURE.

GRASSLAND.

July 21. In December laſt, ſome ſhovellings of a ſheepfold were ſet experimentally upon a piece of grafsland :—this hay-time I obſerve the ſwath there is nearly double to that in any other part of the piece.— The ſoil a good ſandy loam.

I I.

SHEEPFOLD.

July 29. Mr. Samuel Barber has, upon his Staninghall farm, a piece of olland * barley,

* *Olland*-barley ; that is, barley ſown after *Olland* ; a con-

a fmall part of which was fheepfolded once 12.
in a place; the reft undreffed.

Where the fold ftood the barley is, I ap- BARLEY.
prehend, double the crop. The veftiges of
the fold are difcriminable to an inch. The
crop is thicker upon the ground, the
ftraw ftronger and taller, and the ears fuller
and much larger. There cannot be lefs than
three coombs an acre gained to the firft crop,
by one night's fheepfold; befides an advantage to enfuing crops. The foil a light fcorch-
ing loam.

I 2.

AUGUST 3. The turnep crops of this TURNEP
neighbourhood have fuffered confiderably this CATERP.
year from a fpecies of caterpillars—provincially "black cankers"—which prey upon the
plants after they are in rough leaf; eating
them down to the ground; and totally deftroying the crop wherever it happens to be attacked by thefe voracious reptiles.

It is obfervable, however, that the deftruction is partial; many pieces being left un-

traction of *old land*,—and is now applied univerfally to
lays, or fward, produced by CULTIVATED GRASSES.

touched,

touched ; and those which are affected are only partially eaten, in irregular plots; which perhaps are entirely eaten off, while the rest of the piece remains uninjured.

It is still more remarkable that the sea-coast has suffered most ; the mischief decreasing with the increased distance from the sea. Perhaps the parent-insects were brought by the north-east winds which have prevailed this year.

That insects attempt, at least, to cross the ocean, seems evident from the observation of Mr. Arthur Bayfield, of Antingham, who says; that being on the sea-shore some years ago, he saw myriads of flies, *resembling* the cantharides, left dead upon the beach by the tide. These, probably, being becalmed, or meeting with contrary winds in their passage, became spent, dropt into the sea, and were drowned.

Mr. Thomas Shepherd, of Northreps, says, that this year a piece of early-sown turneps was seen to be almost covered with a species of fly resembling the grey horse-fly ; with this difference, that the head is black and the body yellow. From former observations of this kind he foretold the destruction of that piece of turneps by the " cankers :"— and his apprehensions were too well grounded ; for it was

totally

totally eaten up by them. What he adds is remarkable; he fays that thefe flies were brought by a long-continued north-eaft wind, and that the wind getting round to the fouth, there was not, in a few hours, a fingle fly to be found in the piece.

It is highly probable that thefe infects travel in flights, and that they are led about from place to place by the winds, or by other circumftances.

To prevent or check the devaftation committed by the caterpillars, various devices have been practifed by farmers whofe crops were affailed by them. Some rolled with a heavy roller. Some fowed lime over the plants. Others employed ducks; and others women and children to pick them off the plants.

Mr. Arthur Bayfield found ducks the moft efficacious; he collected feventy or eighty, and faved feveral acres of turneps through their means. He fed them twice a-day with corn, under an idea that "cankers," alone, would kill them.

Mr. William Barnard found hand-picking anfwer his purpofe. Five women and boys picked over ten or eleven acres of hoed plants in one week; about eighteen pence an acre.

Mr. James Carter, having one fide of a clofe entirely eaten up, and the other fide, which had been fown later, entirely free from caterpillars, dug a trench between the two parts, and put fome lime in the bottom of it, by which artful expedient he faved his turneps: for the caterpillars, in attempting to crofs the trench in fearch of frefh pafturage, fell among the lime, and were fmothered. Mr. Bayfield fays, that if the weather be dry, digging a trench without the lime will ftop them: for the fide of the trench being dufty they cannot crawl up, but roll back to the bottom; and by repeated attempts become exhaufted.

The farmers who hoed their plants while the caterpillars were upon them, and without ufing any precaution, inevitably loft their crops, befides lofing the expence of hoeing; for after the operation the whole of the caterpillars fell of courfe upon the comparatively few plants which then remained, and prefently eat them down to the clods.

In this cafe, the only remedy is to plow up the ground and fow a-frefh; an expedient which has been obliged to be practifed on, perhaps, fome hundred acres of turnep-ground this year.

About

About twenty years ago, it feems, the whole country was ftripped by this means ; the firft fowings being deftroyed throughout the county.

13.

AUGUST 3. It has long been confidered as one of the firft of vulgar errors among hufbandmen, that the berbery-plant has a pernicious quality (or rather a myfterious power) of blighting the wheat which grows near it.

This idea, whether it be erroneous or founded on fact, is no where more ftrongly rooted than among the Norfolk farmers ; one of whom mentioning with a ferious countenance an inftance of this malady, I very fafhionably laughed at him. He, however, ftood firm, and perfifted in his being in the right ;—intimating, that fo far from being led from the caufe to the effect, he was, in the reverfe, led from the effect to the caufe : for obferving a ftripe of blafted wheat acrofs his clofe, he traced it back to the hedge, thinking there to have found the enemy; but being difappointed, he croffed the lane into a garden on the oppofite fide of it, where he found a large berbery-bufh in the direction in which he had looked for it. The mifchief, according to his

de-

description, stretched away from this point acrofs the field of wheat, growing broader and fainter (like the tail of a comet) the farther it proceeded from its fource. The effect was carried to a greater diftance than he had ever obferved it before; owing, as he believed, to an opening in the orchard behind it to the fouth-weft, forming a gut or channel for the wind.

Hearing him thus particular in his defcrip-tion, and knowing him to be accurate in every circumftance as to fituation, I afked him how he accounted for the mifchief. He anfwered to this effect: the berbery and wheat blow at the fame time, and the duft, or farina, of the ber-bery being blown over the wheat when in bloom, is poifonous to it, and caufes the blight.

This, I confefs, ftaggered my incredulity; for if the farina of vegetables be carried to a confiderable diftance, and at that diftance have a quality of fructuofity towards their own fpecies;—and if fome vegetables are falubri-ous, others poifonous, to the animal creation, why may not the farina of one vegetable be carried to a confiderable diftance, and there be-come poifonous to the fruitfulnefs of another of a diffimilar genus * ?

* This, however, is evidently not the caufe ; for I have
fince

Being defirous of afcertaining the fact, be it
what it may, I have enquired further among
intelligent farmers concerning this fubject.—
They are, to a man, decided in their opinion as
to the fact; which appears to have been fo
long eftablifhed in the minds of principal
farmers, that it is now difficult to afcertain it
from obfervations; berbery plants having (of
late years more particularly) been extirpated
from farm-hedges with the utmoft care and
affiduity: one inftance, however, of mifchief,
this year, I had related to me, and another I was
myfelf eye-witnefs to.   Mr. William Barnard,
of Bradfield, fays, that this year feeing a patch
of his wheat very much blighted, he looked
round for a berbery-bufh; but feeing none
confpicuous in the hedge, which was thick,
he with fome difficulty got into it, and there
found the enemy.   He is clearly decided as to
the fact.   Mr. William Gibbs, of Rowton,
telling me that a patch of his wheat was blighted in the fame manner, and that he believed it
to proceed from fome fprigs of berbery which
remained in the neighbouring hedge (which a
few years ago was weeded from it) I went to

fince obferved, that the berbery blows feveral weeks before
wheat fhoots into ear.

C 3   infpect

infpect the place; and true it is, that near it we found three fmall plants of berbery ; one of which was particularly full of berries. The ftraw of the wheat is black ; and the grain, if it may be fo called, a mere hufk of bran; while the reft of the piece is of a much fuperior quality.

Thefe circumftances are undoubtedly ftrong evidence ; but do not by any means amount to proof.

14.

HARVESTING
WHEAT.

Augusт 9. Laft night in riding from Norwich, I faw a farmer, at Hainford, *mowing* fome wheat, which was dead ripe, and free from weeds. The gatherers immediately followed the fithe, and the waggon the gatherers; fo that it was harvefted at a trifling expence (at a time when all the corn in the country is ripe, and hands of courfe unufually fcarce) and was fecured in the barn, without any rifque from the weather. This, at a pinch, may be worth imitation.

15.

HAY-CHAM-
BER FLOOR

Augusт 22. An excellent and cheap hay-chamber floor is made in this country with *clay,* and rods.

Finifhed

Finifhed one to-day upon a farm at Suffield.

It meafures fix yards by eight, or forty-
eight fquare yards,

It took three hundred fplints (alder and
willow rods, about the thicknefs of a man's
wrift down to that of his thumb) at
1s. 6d.   —   —   £. 0 4 6

Three loads of clay (cafting and carriage near) —		0	4	6
A waggon-body-full of ftraw		0	2	0
Five days of a bricklayer and la-bourer, at 2s. 6d. —		0	12	6
One ditto to plaifter it when it is dry on the under-fide,		0	2	6
		£. 1	6	0

or fixpence half-penny a yard fquare.

N. B. The price, by meafurement, for labour
alone, is four pence half-penny a yard ; which
is a great deal too much.

This floor was made in the following manner :

The rods being trimmed (namely, the twigs
and tops taken off), they were laid acrofs the
joifts as clofe to each other as poffible. If
crooked they were " crippled" (had a chop in the
crooked part with a hook or hatchet) fo as to

C 4   make

make them touch every joiſt, as well as each other. No nails or other confinement.

The clay being well ſoaked with water, the principal part of it was mixed with long wheat-ſtraw; which was well worked into it by the means of a horſe, or man, treading it, and by raking it about with a turnep-hook; the reſt made mortar-wiſe, with a ſmall quantity of ſhort ſtraw.

The rods being bedded, and the clay pre-pared, the " dauber" laid a plank acroſs the rods to prevent his miſplacing them with his feet; and, ſtanding on this, laid on a thick coat of the ſtrawy clay, ſo as to cover the thickeſt of the ſplints about an inch thick, with a dung-fork; working it well in be-tween the crevices of the rods, and making it as level on the top as that rough tool would make it. This done, he went over it again with the mortar-clay, (ſtill ſtanding on his plank) and gave it a thin finiſhing coat with a trowel. The thickneſs of the rods and the two coats of clay is about three inches :—the thinner they are the ſooner they dry, and the lighter they are for the joiſts and timbers.

Where, from the uncouthneſs of the rods, the clay forced through between them, the dauber

with

with a hoe cut it off level with the rods on the under-fide, and for this purpofe drew his hoe over every part of it—a job prefently done.

In the fpring, when the floor is thoroughly dry, it is intended to be plaiftered on the under-fide, to cover the rods, and give it a parlourable appearance. This will take about a day's work.

A clay floor is preferable in two refpects to a boarded one : it is cheaper and *tighter*. Boards, except they be well feafoned, and without they be plowed-and-tongued, and laid down at a greater expence than can be beftowed on a farmer's hay-chamber, will let the duft and feeds through upon the horfes and harnefs ; whereas clay renders it as tight as lead.

Mentioning my doubts to the workman as to its duration, obferving that the rods, I was afraid, would foon rot ;—he anfwered, that did not fignify, for if the ftraw be well worked into the clay, the floor will remain firm, though the rods be rotten.

Mr. John Baker, of Southreps, whofe opinion in this cafe is decifive, corroborates the idea of clay floors being preferable to boarded ones ; and of their lafting a great number of years.

AUGUST

16.

WELD.

August 29. Laſt year, to try whether weld (*Reſeda luteola*—dyer's weed) be an object of the Norfolk culture, I ſowed one acre and three-eighths with two pints of tur-nep-ſeed, and two pints and a half of weld-ſeed, the 16th of Auguſt.

The ſoil, a lightiſh ſandy loam, had been plowed three times as a fallow for wheat ; gave a fourth plowing ; harrowed ;—ſowed the turnep-ſeed ; harrowed ;—ſowed the weld-ſeed ; re-harrowed, the horſes trotting.

It was hoed at a conſiderable expence with ſmall carrot hoes ; it neverthcleſs got full of poppies and other weeds.

On one end of the piece, where the turneps were a bad crop, the weld was very good ; but, upon the whole, only indifferent.

I am certain that in this experiment the turneps were extremely prejudicial to the weld; and there was no feed from them worth turning the ſheep to, until the plants began to run, in the ſpring; and then, in a few days, they ſtarted up, and drew the weld up with them, ſlender and ſickly. I am very clear in that, had the weld been ſown alone, and been twice hoed, the

the crop would have been much better, and the   16.
foil left cleaner.   WELD.

I apprehend there is no occafion to leave the
plants fo thick upon the ground as is ufually
done. I am perfuaded that fix or eight inch hoes
might be ufed with propriety in fetting out the
plants. If fo, the expence of hoeing would be
little more than that of hoeing turneps.

I am of opinion, from this experiment, as
well as from others that I find have been tried
in the county, that weld may be raifed with
confiderable profit in Norfolk; efpecially at
prefent (during the war), when weld is dear;
but I am at the fame time clearly of opinion,
that it is not the intereft of landlords to encourage the culture of it, without fome rigid reftrictions in their leafes to prevent their tenants
from carrying off their eftates fuch a quantity
of vegetable matter, without replacing it with
an equivalency of manure, agreeably to the ufual
covenant relative to hay and ftraw: for it is
not the *corn* only, but the *ftraw* likewife, that
is carried off the premifes in the fhape of weld:
perhaps to the amount of a ton or upwards an
acre.

17.

AUGUST 29. Laft autumn, in order to afcer-   SHEEP.
tain the proper *time of putting ewes to the ram*, I
made the following experiment:

17.
SHEEP.

The 20th September put a score of long-wooled ewes of different ages to a Leicestershire ram, and a score of Norfolk ewes to a Norfolk ram. Being in rather low condition, few of them took the ram till the beginning of October.

The 19th of October put twenty-three long-wooled and forty Norfolk ewes to the same rams, keeping the two breeds separate.

The 20th of November put the same rams to a score of each sort reserved for the purpose.

The early lambs were much the stoutest and best for stores ; and grass lamb was out of season before the late ones were fit for the knife.

But the crones * which took the ram early were not able to support their lambs in winter : for grass was scarce, and they could not break turneps.

Therefore, this year, all the young ewes have been put to the rams a week ago, and all the old ones are intended for the butcher before this year's grass be gone : for in a country where turneps are the principal spring food, crones appear to be unprofitable stock.

---

* Crones—old ewes which have lost their fore teeth.

AUGUST

18.   18.

August 29. Laſt autumn, made an accurate experiment on a large ſcale, with different manures for wheat, on a ſandy loam, ſummer fallowed.

Part of an eighteen acre piece was manured with fifteen or ſixteen loads of tolerably good farm-yard dung an acre; part with three chaldrons of lime an acre; the reſt folded upon with ſheep, twice; the firſt time at the rate of ſix hundred ſheep to a quarter of an acre (ſee Min. 1.); the ſecond time thinner.

In winter and ſpring the dung kept the lead; and now, at harveſt, it has produced the greateſt burden of ſtraw.

The ſheepfold kept a ſteady pace from ſeed-time to harveſt, and is now evidently the beſt corned, and the cleaneſt crop.

The lime, in winter and ſpring, made a poor appearance, but after ſome ſhowers in ſummer it flouriſhed much, and is now a tolerable crop; not leſs, I apprehend, than three quarters an acre: and in this country, where dung is ſo ſingularly valuable for the turnep crop, it is a ſatisfaction to know that ſummer fallowing and lime alone will inſure a tolerable crop of wheat.

From

18.

SHEEPFOLD.

From thefe data, the value of fheepfold, *in this cafe,* may be calculated.

By MIN. 1. it appears that one hundred fheep manured feven fquare rods daily. But the fecond folding was thinner ; fuppofe nine rods, this is, on a par of the two foldings, eight rods a day each folding.

The dung could not be worth lefs than half a crown a load ; and the carriage and fpreading ten fhillings an acre ; together, fifty fhillings an acre ; which quantity of land the hundred fheep teathed twice over in forty days.

Suppofing them to be folded the year round, they would, at this rate, fold nine acres annually ; which, at fifty fhillings an acre, is twenty two pounds ten fhillings a hundred—or four fhillings and fix pence a head.

In fome parts of the ifland the fame quantity of dung would be worth five pounds an acre; which would raife the value of the teathe to nine fhillings a head ; which, at two pence a head a week, is more than the whole year's keep of the fheep.

It does not follow, however, that all lands would have received equal benefit with the piece in confideration ; which, perhaps, had not been folded upon for many years ; perhaps

never

never before ; and fheepfold, like other ma-   18.
nures, may become lefs efficacious the longer   SHEEPFOLD.
it is ufed on a given piece of land.

19.

AUGUST 29. In the above-mentioned piece   SOWING
of wheat, I made a comparative *experiment*   WHEAT.
on the mode of fowing.

Part was plowed-in, agreeably to the common practice of the Diftrict, laying up the foil
in narrow ridges : part fown on the laft plowing, and harrowed in : part put in with Mr.
Duckett's drill-plow ; which, from fome
practical knowledge of it, I had confidered to
be well adapted to the Norfolk foil.

The fowings being made acrofs the manur-
ings, the two experiments became diftinct ; and
the refults clear and decifive. The time of
fowing the 31ft of October.

The refult of this experiment was not fo
ftriking as that of the laft. The part fown
over the furrow of the plow, and harrowed
in, is however, very perceptibly, the worft ;
but on comparing the part plowed in with
the part drilled, no obvious difference is to be
perceived. Had the drills been nine inches
inftead of twelve inches apart, I am of opinion
they

18.

SOWING
WHEAT.

they would have gained a preference ; but, from this experiment, there does not appear to me to be any advantage to be expected from the drill worth changing the custom of the country for.

SEED-
PROCESS.

Last spring I made similar experiments on the use of this implement with peas and barley. During the summer the drills seemed to gain a preference ; but, at harvest, it is a moot point whether the drill or the common plow has the preference : and although these several experiments were seen and attended to by some good farmers of the neighbourhood, I do not find that any of them are so much struck with the result as to be inclined to give up their present practice : neverthelefs I am of opinion

IMPLEMENT.

that this ingenious implement merits further trial.   Barley appears to be the crop for which it is most especially adapted in this country.

N. B.   In November last, I attempted to try the six-rowed, or winter-barley, against the common barley, as a winter crop; sowing some of each sort above; some under; and some in drills : but the pheasants, rooks, hares, and other vermin, subverted the experiment, and nearly destroyed the crop : therefore, to save it from disgrace, the scattered remains were plowed up in the spring, and the land sown with common barley.   AUGUST

20.

AUGUST 31. What a variety of enemies have turneps in this country! The " fly," the " canker," the " maggot" (at the root) and the " anbury," have this year already deftroyed myriads.

The *fly* took them in their infant ftate ;— the *grub* and *caterpillar* whilft their tops were yet fmall ; and, now, when their tops have almoft got their full fize, they are hourly dwindling with the *anbury*.

The *grub* in itfelf would not perhaps be fatal ; but the rooks, in order to come at it, pull up not only the plants which are attacked, but thofe alfo which are free from it ; and by this means clear them as they go.

The *anbury* is a large excrefcence, which forms itfelf below the apple. It grows, it feems, to the fize of both the hands ; and, as foon as the hard weather fets in, or it is, by its own nature, brought to maturity, it becomes putrid, and fmells very offenfively.

At prefent, the ftate of three fpecimens which I have taken up, and examined attentively, is this : —The apples of the turneps are juft forming (about the fize of walnuts in the hufk) while the anburies are already as big as the egg of a

VOL. II,   D   goofe.

goofe.—They are irregular and uncouth in their form, with inferior excrefcences (refembling the races of ginger) hanging to them. On cutting them, their general appearance is that of a hard turnep; but on examining them through a magnifier, there are veins, or ftring-like veffels, difperfed among the pulp. The fmell and tafte fomewhat refemble thofe of turneps; but without their mildnefs; having an auftere and fomewhat difagreeable flavour, refembling that of an old ftringy turnep. The tops of thofe which are much affected turn yellow, and flag with the heat of the fun; fo that, in the day-time, they are obvioufly diftinguifhable from thofe which are healthy.

It feems to be an idea among farmers, that the caufe of the anbury is the foil's being tired of turneps; owing to their having been too often fown on the fame land. This, however, is pofitively erroneous; for the piece from which I drew thefe fpecimens was an old orchard, and never before bore turneps in the memory of man.

Quere—Is it not caufed by the above-mentioned or fome other grub, that, wounding the veffels of the tap-root, diverts the courfe of the fap; which, inftead of forming the apple, forms this excrefcence?

AUGUST

21.

AUGUST 31. One fide of an eighteen acre piece of turneps was folded upon ; the reft of the piece manured with dung.

TURNEPS:

The part fheepfolded efcaped the devaftation of the " fly" *obvioufly* better than the part dunged.—

SHEEPFOLD.

Quere—Were the flies increafed by the dung, or were they trodden to death, or fhut up and fuffocated in their burrows, by the feet of thè fheep ?

22.

SEPTEMBER 8. Mr. Thomas Drurey, of Erpingham, a man whofe opinion is valuable in matters of hufbandry, fays, that marl is a certain preventative of the *anbury*.—He is alfo of opinion, with other judicious hufbandmen, that teathing the barley-ftubble which is intended for turneps, will caufe the anbury : his land, he fays, although it be old-marled land, is by this precaution in general free from anburied turneps.

TURNEPS.

23.

SEPTEMBER 12. Mr. William Barnard, of Bradfield, who was born (and refided until

DIBBLING
WHEAT.

about

about three years ago) at Great Ellingham, near Attleborough, gives the following account of the rife and practice of the *dibbling of wheat.*

The dibbling of peas, he fays, has been a cuftom of that part of Norfolk time immemorial; but the practice has not been extended to wheat above eighteen or twenty years; nor has it been in any degree general for more than ten years.

The practice of dibbling wheat probably arofe in this manner.—At Deepham, an adjoining parifh to Ellingham, lived one James Stone, a labouring man, who was, in that neighbourhood, a noted dibbler of peas, and who cultivated for himfelf a few acres which he rented with his cottage.—He had three children, who were as expert at "dropping" as the father was at "dabbing;" and having fome acre or two of clover-lay, which came in courfe for wheat, he conceived the idea of dibbling in the feed; probably thinking that he fhould thereby keep his children from idlenefs, and fave them, at the fame time, an unexpected fupply of bread.

He accordingly fet about putting *his fcheme* in execution, and prefently brought his neighbours

bours about him. Some of them fmiled, and others laughed at his experiment; he neverthelefs proceeded with his little corps, and finifhed his patch.

The land being in good condition, and the work being done in a mafterly manner, the plants came up fo ftrong and beautiful as to draw the eyes not only of his fellow-parifhioners, but of the whole neighbourhood.

Mr. Barnard well recollects the circumftance; for he paffed the clofe (which lay by the fide of a public road) every day in his way to and from fchool : and fays, that he has frequently feen the neighbouring farmers, in their way to market, light at the gate, and go into the piece, to view the crop, which was now become popular.

At harveft the crop proved extraordinarily good ; and the dibbling of wheat has, from that time, been more or lefs practifed in this circle of the county : the only one in which the practice is, even yet, become general among farmers.

Enquiring of Mr. B. the proportion which dibbled wheat in that country bears to the wheat fown broad-caft; he fays, there is as much dibbled as there can be hands got to put it in ; and apprehends that one-half of the wheat about Wyndham and Attleborough is dibbled in; adding, that when wheat is dear the work-people are engaged fome months before-hand; and frequently, when they are paid off for dib-bling peas in March, they are engaged for the wheat-feed-time.

Succeſſion. A clover-lay once plowed is what is generally made ufe of for dibbling; it has however been tried, with a confiderable fhare of fuccefs, on fallow ground.

Manure. The common practice is to fpread the dung, or. other manure, prefently before the ground be plowed. Some lay it on after the feed is in by way of top dreſſing. But Mr. B. is of opinion, that fetting on the manure in July, and letting it wafh into the foil before plowing, is the moft eligible way of manuring for dibbled wheat.

Soil procefs. If the foil be light and the wea-ther dry, the plowman keeps pace with the dib-blers :—the holes will not otherwife ftand; the fand running in and filling them up. The furrow—provincially " flags"—fhould be cut about ten inches wide, and be turned over flat and even; and, to make them lay ftill fmoother and firmer, they are rolled pretty hard before dibbling.

The

The dibbles made ufe of in this operation are of iron. The acting part is an egg-fhaped knob of iron or fteel fomewhat larger than a pigeon's egg. The fmaller end forms the point of the dibble; whilft from the larger rifes a ftring of iron, about half an inch fquare, and two feet and a half long. The head of it is received into a crofs piece of wood (refembling the crutch of a fpade or fhovel) which forms the handle.

The dibbler makes ufe of two of thefe tools; one in each hand; and, bending over them, walks backward upon the flags; making two rows of holes in each. The rows are ufually made about four inches apart, and the diftance in the rows from two and a half to three inches; namely, four holes in each length of the foot of the dibbler.

The great art in making the holes lies in leaving them fmooth and firm on the fides; fo that the loofe mould do not run in to fill them up before the feeds are depofited. This is done by a circular motion of the hand and wrift; which make a femi-revolution every ftroke: the circular motion beginning as the bit enters, and continues until it is clearly dif-engaged from the mould. The dibbles muft

D 4

come

come out clean, and wear bright, or the operation is not perfect.

Another difficulty in dibbling is to make the holes at equal diftances; more efpecially to keep the two rows ftraight and parallel with each other: for the dibbles being two diftinct inftruments, it requires fome practice to guide them with precifion; fo as to pierce the flag in the exact point required. To remedy this, couples have been invented to keep the dibbles at a given diftance; but this renders the implement complex, and prevents the learner from ever being able to ufe them fingly. A man muft be aukward indeed if he does not in a few days without this incumbrance make himfelf a tolerable mafter of dibbling.

A middling workman will make two motions, or four holes, in a fecond.

One dibbler employs three droppers; therefore one man and three children are called a fet. Each dibbler takes three flags, which he performs upon by ftages thus: He firft takes an outfide flag, and having gone fome yards upon that, he returns; not upon the next flag, but upon the other outfide flag of the three; and then finifhes his ftage by taking the middle one. This is done to keep his three droppers

fully

fully employed, and at the fame time to prevent his filling up the holes with his feet before the feeds are depofited. Were he to carry
but one flag with him, the droppers would have
to pafs each other repeatedly, and have three
times the ground to walk over; whereas by the
above contrivance they are always uniformly
progreffive, and each child finifhes its own flag.

The droppers keep up with their dibbler,
putting two or three grains of wheat in each
hole (but of peas only one); the girls carry the
feed in their aprons, the boys in their hats or
other contrivance. Out of thofe they take
about half a handful, and deliver the feed into the holes through an aperture made between the firft and fecond fingers. Much
time and patience is neceffary to teach a child
to perform this petty bufinefs with propriety
and difpatch.

The prefent price of dibbling a free light
foil is nine fhillings an acre and beer. It formerly was half a guinea. If the foil be ftiff or
ftony, it is now worth more than that money.
The dibbler is a fort of mafter of his fet; for if
he has not children of his own, he hires his
droppers, giving them fixpence a day each if
expert

23.

DIBBLING WHEAT.

expert hands, or threepence a day if learners; two of them being employed on one flag, each taking one row of holes: so that he pays for dropping, threepence a day for each row of holes. An expert dibbler will " hole" half an acre a day, which at nine shillings is four and sixpence, out of which he pays one shilling and sixpence to his droppers: but one-third of an acre is reckoned a fair day's work; which at nine shillings an acre is three shillings; out of which paying one shilling and sixpence, he has one shilling and sixpence left for his own day's work.

Quantity of feed. One bushel to fix pecks an acre; and, if the flags crack much in plowing, some throw on half a peck or a peck an acre, broad-cast, before rolling.

Covering the feed. This is usually done by going twice in a place with a bush-harrow, made by drawing thorns into a gate or a large hurdle. Either of these however Mr. B. says, and with reason, makes too large an Implement; for in so large a space as this covers at once, there will be protuberances which it will lay hold of too much, and probably pull up, and hollows which it will wholly miss.—He has

usually

ufually preferred a waggon ladder, which does
not cover more than four or five flags at once;
and to finifh this bufinefs more completely, he
always carries a fort of broom in his own hand,
when overlooking the work-people; in order
to cover more effectually any part which may
be partially miffed.

The advantages held out. There is a faving
of about a bufhel and a half of feed; which,
when wheat is fix fhillings or upwards, is alone
an equivalent to the extra expence of dibbling.

The rolling and treading is efteemed highly
ferviceable to the light lands of this country.

The edges of the flags being intimately united
by the rolling and the trampling, and the remaining fiffures being filled up by the harrow,
the graffes are thereby thought to be kept under; and fhould feed-weeds appear in the fpring,
the hoe has free admiffion between double row
and double row, to extirpate them; an operation, however, which I underftand feldom takes
place.

The feed being wholly buried in the body of
the flag, there is no " under-corn"; the plants
are uniformly vigorous; the ftraw, collectively,
is confequently ftouter, and the grain more
even, than that which is ufually produced from.

fowing

23.

DIBBLING
WHEAT.

sowing the seed broad-cast over the rough flag. For in this case, part of the seed falls through between the flags, and being there too deeply buried by the harrows, the young plants are longer in reaching the surface than are those from the seed which happens to fall in a more favourable situation; and which thereby gain an ascendancy they never lose : hence a number of underling plants, and hence the small shrivelled grains, which render the sample unsightly and unsaleable.

Another good effect remains to be noticed, the employment of the poor; and whether we view this in a moral, a political, or a private point of view, it is equally desirable. For the poor's rates of a country village fall principally on the farmer; and if he does not employ the poor, he must support them in idleness; more especially children.—Mr. B. says, that in the circle above-mentioned wheat seed-time is considered, by the poor man, as a second harvest.

Mr. —— Smith, of Heavingham, gives a somewhat different account respecting the advantages of dibbling wheat. He says, that he has frequently had eight or ten acres of dibbled wheat in a year; that he has usually made the holes as thick as they could stand,

so

fo as not to disfigure or interfere with one another; and has dropped two bufhels, at the expence of twelve or fourteen fhillings an acre.

He is clearly of opinion, that dibbling wheat makes the land foul; efpecially if it is not dibbled thick; and gives a very good reafon for this opinion; namely, where corn is thin weeds will be thick. He is pofitive that the grafs gets up more among wheat which is dibbled than among that which is fown broad-caft over the rough flag of one plowing: adding, that after dibbled wheat he has ufually been obliged to fow turneps the next year, inftead of firft taking a crop of barley; the common practice of this part of the country. He however acknowledges fully, that the ftraw of dibbled wheat is ftouter, and the grain evenner, and of a better quality, than that from wheat fown broad-caft after any procefs whatever.

Mr. John Baker, of Southreps, fpirited and judicious as he is in matters of hufbandry, has never had a fufficiently good opinion of dibbling wheat to give it a trial; not even by way of experiment. His chief objection to it is, that in *this* country, where the foil is fhallow, and the lays generally graffy, wheat cannot be fown in any manner with propriety on one plowing.

—— —— —— has tried it two or three different times : the firſt trial was on a piece of good land, with about three pecks of feed an acre : the crop good, and ſtood when moſt of the wheats in the county were lodged.—— The laſt was on a light ſhallow foil : it proved greatly too thin : not half a crop.

From the ſum of this information the dib‑ bling of wheat appears to be peculiarly adapted to rich deep foils; on which three or four pecks an acre dibbled early, may ſpread ſufficiently for a full crop : whereas light, weak, ſhal‑ low foils, which have lain two or three years, and have become graſſy, require an additional quantity of feed, and confequently an addition of labour, otherwiſe the plants are not able to reach each other; and the graſſes of courſe find their way up between them; by which means the crop is injured, and the foil rendered foul.

Dropping being the moſt difficult part of the bufinefs, it ſeems to be incligible to begin with wheat ; the grains of which being ſmall and ir‑ regular, are, to a learner, difficult and diſ‑ agreeable to feparate; whereas thoſe of peas, being larger round and ſlippery, are more agrecable to the touch, and more eaſily parted in the hand ; fo as to drop one or any other given number into each hole.

It

It further feems ineligible to fend children into the field, in any cafe, until they have prac-tifed, at home, in the art of feparating the feeds; by which precaution a wafte of feed, and a disfigurement at leaft of the crop, may be prevented. For the fame reafon it feems pro-per, that a young dibbler fhould be exercifed on fallow or other frefh-plowed ground not in-tended to be dibbled, before he be admitted in-to the field of practice.

24.

OCTOBER 10. Laft year Mr. John Joy, of Northwalfham, having a piece of turnep-ground which miffed, he fowed it with wheat; and, to keep his land in courfe, laid it down with clo-ver, the feed of which he *fowed in autumn*, pre-fently after fowing the wheat.

I faw the feedling plants early in winter; when they looked remarkably healthy. To-wards fpring I faw them again; but fome fevere frofts had cut them entirely down, fo as to make it doubtful whether they would recover or not.

I defired Mr. Joy to acquaint me with the re-fult; and yefterday we walked over one of the fineft fets of clover that ever grew: not having been

24.
SOWING
CLOVER.

been yet fed, the heads of the plants now ftand above the ftubble; but for which a fine fwath of clover-hay might be mown.

This is the firft inftance I have met with of fowing clover-feed over wheat in autumn.

25.

BUILDINGS.

OCTOBER 10. Formerly, a ridiculous prac-tice has prevailed in this country of running up the *peaks of gables* above the roof of the houfe. In many old houfes the coping of the gable ftands eighteen inches, perhaps two feet above the thatch or tiling, The effect of it is, the water of driving rains is collected by this un-neceffary elevation of the wall, and either drains through between the gable and the roof, or, if an offset be made to prevent this, foaks into the wall itfelf.

An old-fafhioned " flue" rotted by this means, was the other day, upon this eftate, thrown down by a guft of wind.

I mention the circumftance the rather, as this abfurd cuftom is not yet altogether laid afide; though the flues are now made much lower than formerly. In ftrict propriety, the coping of the gable ought to be level with the cover-ing.

For

For common buildings, when the covering is of tile or flate; more especially for a lean-to liable to the drip of the main roof; the best way is to continue the covering over the gable or end-wall; which is thereby effectually preserved at an easy expence.

26.

October 18. This morning rode to Witton to see some labourers from the Attleborough side of the county dibble wheat. They had finished.

Mr. Elmer shewed me what they had done for him :—the plants come up very strong, and look healthy. The quantity of feed, six pecks an acre; dropping four or five grains in a hole.

Mr. E. mentioned one advantage which did not occur to me before : the feedage of the lays from July to October.

27.

October 25. On Wednesday 17th instant went to the first day of the *Fair of St. Faith's*; a village near Norwich, where one of the largest fairs in the kingdom is held annually on that day for cheese, butter, and a variety of wares; but most especially the first; which is brought in great quantities out of Suffolk to supply this

Vol. II.   E   country

27.

CHEESE.

country during the winter months; when a Norfolk cheefe is not to be purchafed in this part of the county.

CATTLE.

The firft day of this fair alfo draws together a good fhow of cattle; principally " home-breds;" either for ftore, or for fatting on turneps the enfuing winter : for which purpofe, a fhow of Scotch bullocks are alfo exhibited upon a rifing ground at a fmall diftance from the Fair-field.

The fale of Scotch cattle continues for a fortnight, or longer time, until this quarter of the county be fupplied with that fpecies of ftock. (See BULLOCKS, Vol. I)

FATTING CATTLE.

Yefterday, attended the bullock fair.

There are fewer cattle this year than has been known for fome years paft (about four hundred upon the Hill yefterday), owing chiefly to a great many having been killed by contract for the Navy; a thing not practifed before in Scotland; and there were yefterday a greater number of buyers in the market than ufual (about fifty of the principal farmers in the county); fo that the Scotchmen had the game in their own hands.

The principal drovers are Tate, Wigglef-worth (Lord Galloway's fteward), Moffatt, Campbell, Stewart.

It

It is aftonifhing to fee the ftate and condition of the cattle: they look as frefh and as fleck as if they had not travelled a mile from home: fome of them tolerable beef. Even fo high as eleven pounds a piece was afked for fome bullocks; it was however to choofe four out of a large drove: but ten pounds was afked to draw fifteen or twenty.

Mr. John Baker bought fix fpayed heifers, which he drew out of a lot of thirty, at 7*l*. 15*s*. a head; and another neighbour drew twentyone of the remainder of the lot at 7*l*. a-piece: he afterwards bought feven of an inferior quality at 6*l*.

There were half a fcore in the fair fo low as 4*l*. but the price in general ran from 6*l*. to 9*l*. a head; for cattle which will fat to from forty to fixty ftone; but high as thefe prices are, Mr. Tate (the oldeft drover) fays; he has known them fome years ago twenty or thirty fhillings a head dearer than they are even this year.

Each drover hires meadows or grazinggrounds in proportion to his quantity of cattle; —the farmers in the neighbourhood preferving for the purpofe a full bite of grafs; for which the Scotchmen pay very amply. The charges on fale muft run high. The number of

at-

attendants, the high price of grass, and treating the farmers, " to the amount perhaps of a couple of guineas a day," must lower the neat proceeds very considerably, even of each bullock taken separately *.

The drovers do not bring their whole stock on to the " Bullock Hill" at once; but let them remain in the pastures until they are wanted; nor do they bring very large droves at once into the country; but keep them back in Lincolnshire, or perhaps in Scotland, until they see how the demand is likely to prove.

I did not learn the annual demand on a par of years; but was told that Tate alone brings some thousands every year into this country.

The larger bullocks are principally of the Galloway polled breed, and most of them very handsome; in general four or five years old; mostly black, some brindled, some dun, and some few red. (See article BULLOCKS, Vol. I.)

28.

OCTOBER 27. This morning rode again to Witton to see some work-people dibble wheat; and fortunately found them at work.

---

* The charges of drift from Scotland to Norfolk are, I have been told, from five shillings to fifteen shillings a head, according to the size of the bullock.

One

One man and one young woman dibbled, while three women and three girls dropped.

They proceeded thus : the man carried three flags, the women two. The man was followed by one woman, taking the firſt flag, and three girls taking among them the remaining two. The woman was followed by the other two women, each of them taking one flag. When the weather holds fair, the ſet do about three quarters of an acre a day, at ten ſhillings and ſixpence an acre.

. The man, the woman dibbler, and the two women " head-droppers," come from the Suffolk ſide of the county : the other woman and the girls are of this country; this being their firſt ſeaſon. One of them drops very badly; ſometimes putting ſix or ſeven " kernels" in a hole; beſides ſcattering a great many upon the ſurface. This ſhews the impropriety of ſuffering children to come untutored into the field. The head-droppers do it very quick and very neatly; dropping two, three or four kernels in each hole; and about five pecks an acre.

The diſtance of the holes, and the method of dibbling and dropping (except the arrangement of the droppers), exactly the ſame as de-

E 3   ſcribed

28.

DIBBLING
WHEAT.

fcribed by Mr. Barnard; whofe account is, I am now fully convinced, a very faithful one.

The feed was brined and limed.

The droppers carried their feeds in boys hats fewed up about half way acrofs, leaving an opening fufficient for the hand, with a ftring by way of a bow or handle. A bufhel with the feed ftood in the middle of the clofe; out of this they replenifhed their hats, every time they paffed it.

The foil lightifh loam (too light I am afraid to be dibbled with wheat), but had been marled laft year. It is a fecond year's lay, and was paftured this fummer.

It is plowed fleet, and very badly, the flags being much broken, and very uneven: were it plowed a little deeper, which I apprehend it might be with fafety, the flags would not break fo much, and there would be a better bed for the feed. The dibblers are obliged to keep a light hand, and make their holes fhallow, left otherwife they fhould ftrike their dibbles quite through the flags.

The flags are rolled before and " bufhed" after dibbling; the latter with a harrow made of a ftrong large hurdle, covering better than half a rod at once.

The

The plow and roller keep time with the dib-
bles; for if much rain fall upon the flags they
daub, and are difficult to dibble; if the wea-
ther prove dry, the sand runs in and fills up the
holes as fast as they are made.

28.

DIBBLING
WHEAT.

29.

OCTOBER 28. In May last I made an ex-
periment with *lime for turneps*, by spreading a
chaldron of lime (at the rate of three chaldrons
an acre) across each of two pieces of turnep
fallow, and marked the stripes with stumps.

No apparent benefit arose from the lime un-
til the late heavy rains fell; since which the
plants have flourished, and the good effect of
the lime is become evident.

In March last I also made a similar experi-
ment with *lime for barley*; but the crop did
not, in any stage, receive apparent benefit from
it. The summer, until after the barley had
finished its growth, was dry.

In the experiment with *lime for wheat* (see
MIN. 18.) the crop received no apparent benefit
from the lime until the soil had been moistened
with *summer* rains.

From these and other observations I am of
opinion, that lime does not act as a manure un-

MANURE.

TURNEPS.

BARLEY.

WHEAT.

LIME.

E 4   til

29.

LIME.

til it has been thoroughly flaked in the foil; and, from the laft mentioned incident, it feems as if the rains of *fummer* were neceffary to promote its operation.

30.

FURZE-
FOOD.

NOVEMBER 6. In a furze-ground, in which a large plot was cut down laft winter, there is now a crop of young fhoots from two to two and a half feet high : if thefe were now mown (which if the ftubs be cut tolerably level they might be with great cafe) there would be I apprehend two load of tender fucculent herbage an acre.

If furze-tops be that hearty and wholefome food they are reprefented to be, how eafily and with what advantage they might be in this manner collected : Cut the ftubs low and level; mow; and bruife the herbage with a broad wooden wheel in the cyder-mill manner.

Lands which will afford no other crop will produce furze; and although poor lands would not throw up fhoots like thofe alluded to, the crop might, no doubt, be mown, and the fhoots, if very fhort, be collected in a receptacle at the heel of the fithe.

men-

I mention this incident, and communicate
my reflections upon it, the rather, as I have
not met, either in theory or practice, with the
idea of collecting furze-food with the fithe;
the only thing wanted, perhaps, to bring it
into common ufe.

31.

November 10. The *Bullock Hill* at St. Faith's
is faid to receive no benefit from the *teathe* of
the bullocks which every year are fhewn upon
it daily, during a fortnight or three weeks.

This year it was wheat; and if one may
judge from the ftubble (notwithftanding the
wheat was dunged for), the crop was a very in-
different one.—The foil a lightifh fandy loam.

This is an interefting fact. It is faid to be
owing to the worthlefsnefs of the teathe of
" drove bullocks." This I much doubt, how-
ever; for the bullocks being many of them in
high cafe, and kept in grazing-grounds about
St. Faith's, fome of them perhaps within a
quarter of a mile of the Hill, the driving is
little more than the driving of fheep to a fold.
Some of them may, no doubt, come on to the
Hill immediately from Scotland; and they are
all of them of courfe driven more or lefs; and
there may be *fome* truth in this opinion.

That

31.

FAIRSTEAD.
TEATHE.

That the teathe of lean ſtock, and more particularly of cows, is much inferior to that of fatting bullocks, is a fact univerſally acknowledged throughout this county; and this may in ſome meaſure be accounted for from the oleaginous matter carried off by the milk of cows, and imbibed by the vaſcular carcaſes of lean ſtock in general. On the ſame principle, if ſtock be hard driven, and much exhauſted by perſpiration, and want of regular nouriſhment, their teathe may become inſipid and of little uſe to land; conſequently this reaſoning may in part be applicable to the Bullock Hill at St. Faith's: but, as before has been obſerved, there are numbers that come in good condition, and from good paſtures, at a very ſmall diſtance from the Fair-hill, and there is no obvious reaſon why the teathe of thoſe ſhould not be nearly equal to that of other fatting cattle: therefore, upon the whole, it ſeems probable that driving alone does not produce this intereſting fact.

MANURE.

May we not venture to think it poſſible that land may be ſatiated, or tired, even of the dung of cattle? The Hill in queſtion has been the ſite of a large fair for cattle during time immemorial: perhaps, were the fair removed and the ſoil manured with lime, marl, or ſuch

other

other *new* manure as experience would point out, it might continue to throw out great crops for many years.

This is a fubject worth inveftigating; for upon old grazing grounds, which have been fed and teathed with cattle during a length of time, the dung which falls from them cannot, on this hypothefis, be of any ufe to the land; confequently the ftock may, without injury to the pafture, be driven off in the night-time to teathe fome arable land; or the dung may, with advantage, be collected and carried off; whilft by mould, afhes, foot, &c. the grafsland may receive improvement.

32.

NOVEMBER 17. To-day compleated the "roofing" of a reeded barn.

I have attended particularly to the method, of laying the reed, and of fetting on the "roofing" of this building.

The method of laying reed is this:

No laths being made ufe of, a little of the longeft and ftouteft of the reed is fcattered irregularly acrofs the naked fpars, as a foundation to lay the main coat upon: this partial gauzelike covering is called the "fleaking."

On

On this fleaking the main covering is laid, and faftened down to the fpars by means of long rods — provincially, " fways"—laid acrofs the middle of the reed, and tied to the fpars with rope yarn; or with " bramble bonds ;" which, formerly, were much in ufe ; but which are now pretty much laid afide, efpecially for new roofs.

Reed is not laid on in longitudinal courfes, in the manner that ftraw-thatch is ufually put on, nor is the whole eaves fet at once. The workman begins at the lower corner of the roof, on his right hand for inftance, and keeps an irregular diagonal line, or face, until he reach the upper corner to his left.

A narrow eaves-board being nailed acrofs the feet of the fpars, and fome fleaking fcattered on, the thatcher begins to " fet his eaves," by laying a coat of reed; eight or ten inches thick, with the heads refting upon the fleaking, and the butts upon the eaves-board. He then lays on his fway (a rod about the fize of a fmall edder) about fix or eight inches from the lower points of the reed ; whilft his affiftant, on the infide, runs a needle, threaded with rope yarn, clofe to the fpar; and, in this cafe, clofe to the upper edge of the eaves-board. The
thatcher

thatcher draws it through on one side of the sway, and enters it again on the contrary side, both of the sway and of the spar: the affistant draws it through; unthreads it; and, with the two ends of the yarn, makes a knot round the spar; thereby drawing the sway, and consequently the reed, tight down to the roof: whilst the thatcher above, beating the sway and pressing it down, affists in making the work the firmer. The affistant having made good the knot below, he proceeds with another length of thread to the next spar; and so on till the sway be bound down the whole length; namely, eight or ten feet.

Another stratum of reed is now laid on upon the first, so as to make the entire coat eighteen or twenty inches thick at the butts; and another sway laid along, and bound down, about twelve inches above the first.

The eaves being thus completely set, they are adjusted and formed; not square with the spars, but nearly horizontal: nor are they formed by cutting; but by " driving" them with a " legget;" a tool made of a board eight or nine inches square, with a handle two feet long, fixed upon the back of it, obliquely, in the manner of the tool used by gardeners

deners in beating turf. The face of the leg-get is set with large-headed nails to render it rough, and make it lay hold of the butts of the reed.

Another layer of reed is laid on, and bound down by another sway, somewhat shorter than the last; and placed eighteen or twenty inches above it; and above this another and another, continuing to shorten the sways until they be brought off to nothing, and a triangular corner of thatching formed.

After this the sways are used their whole length, whatever it happens to be, until the workman arrives at the finishing corner.

By proceeding in this irregular manner seams between the courses are prevented; and unnecessary shifting of ladders avoided.

The face of the roof is formed and adjusted, like the eaves, by driving the reed with the legget; which operation, if performed by a good workman, not only gives the roof a beautiful polished surface; but at the same time fastens the reed; which, being thickest towards the butts, becomes, like a tapering pin, the tighter the farther it is driven.

Reed running from four to six or eight feet long, the heads meet at the ridge of the roof, whilst whilft the butts are ftill at a diftance from each other. For this reafon, as well as for that of the wear being lefs toward the ridge, the fhorteft (which is generally the worft) reed is faved for the upper part of the roof. But even fuppofing the uppermoft courfes to be only four feet long, and that the heads (belonging to the two fides) be interwoven in fome degree with each other, the butts will ftill remain fix or feven feet afunder; and the ridge of the roof confequently be left in a great meafure expofed to the weather.

32.
LAYING
REED.

To remedy this inconveniency, and to give a finifh to the ridge, a cap—provincially, a "roof"—of ftraw is fet on in a mafterly, but in an expenfive manner.

SETTING ON
ROOFLETS.

In this operation, the workman begins by bringing the roof to an angle with ftraw laid long-way upon the ridge, in the fame manner a rick is topt up; and to render it firm, to keep it in its place, and to prevent the wind from blowing it off, or ruffling it, he pegs it down flightly with "double broaches"; namely, cleft twigs, two feet long, and as thick as the finger, fharpened at both ends, bent double; perhaps with a twift in the crown; and perhaps barbed, by partial chops on the fides, to make them hold in the better.

This

This done, the workman lays a coat of straight straw, six or eight inches thick, across the ridge; beginning, on either side, at the uppermost butts of the reed, and finishing with straight handfuls laid evenly across the top of the ridge.

Having laid a length of about four feet in this manner, he proceeds to fasten it firmly down, so as to render it proof against wind and rain. This is done by laying a " broachen ligger" (a quarter-cleft rod as thick as the finger, and four feet in length) along the middle of the ridge, pegging it down at every four inches with a double broach, which is first thrust down with the hands, and afterwards driven with the legget, or with a mallet used for this purpose. The middle ligger being firmly laid, the thatcher smooths down the straw with a rake and his hands, about eight or nine inches on one side, and, at six inches from the first, lays another ligger, and pegs it down with a similar number of double broaches : thus proceeding to smooth the straw, and to fasten on liggers at every six inches, until he reach the bottom of the cap. One side finished, the other is treated in the same manner ; and the first length being completed, another and another length is laid, and finished as the

first ;

firſt; until the other end of the ridge be
reached.

He then cuts off the tails of the ſtraw, ſquare
and neatly with a pair of ſhears, level with the
uppermoſt butts of the reed; above which the
cap (or moſt properly the ROOFLET) ſhews an
eaves, of about fix inches thick.

Laſtly, he ſweeps the ſides of the main roof
with a bough of holly; and the work is completed.—(For the expence, ſee BUILDINGS and
REPAIRS, Vol. I.)

33.

NOVEMBER 17. A very ſecure way of *laying
pan-tiles* is ſometimes practiſed in this country.

- Having nailed on the pan-tile laths, the ti-
ler diſtributes reeds, ſo as juſt to touch each
other, between the pantile-laths; and, to keep
them in their place, inſerts one end of a piece of
old plaſtering lath or other ſplinter, under the
tyling-lath; preſſes it down upon the reed;
and inſerts the other end under the next lath;
weaving, as it were, theſe ſplinters between the
pan-tile laths and the reed.

Upon the reed he ſpreads a coat of mortar,
and on this lays the tiles.

For dairy or other lean-to's, and for common
garrets, the reed is covered on the inſide with

a coat of plaftering; which, with the fpars, &c. being white-wafhed, gives a neat appearance at a very trifling expence; and keeps the room as free from duft as if it were lathed and ceiled.

This is not a common practice; but it is a very good one; and is much cheaper than the ordinary practice of " interlathing" with plaftering laths.

34.

NOVEMBER 19. It is not the earlieft-done hedging which makes the ftrongeft fhoots from the ftubs. A piece of hedging was done on the lands late Mr. ——'s in the month of April. The face of the ditch ftands remarkably well; and the fhoots of white-thorn, cut down clofe to the face, are uncommonly numerous, and large; fome of them being near five feet high.

Perhaps there is an advantage in cutting thorns at that time of the year. When they have been cut off in winter, the fpring air has no furface to act upon; except the ftump, which barely fhews its head above ground: whereas thofe which ftand till the fap begins to ftir, have, by their quantity of furface, roufed

the

the fap in the root, without having yet exhaufted any of it; confequently when the top is taken off, the ftub throws out many and ftrong fhoots.

Therefore, if this reafoning be good, there is a judicious moment for cutting hedges and underwoods : namely, when the fap has begun to rife, but before any part of it has been exhaufted : and perhaps this time is when the tree or fhrub is beginning to bud : the young quick againft Suffield Common was cut in this ftate, and the fhoots are remarkably ftrong *.

35.

NOVEMBER 23. Having frequently feen the mifchiefs done to the lean-to porches of barns ; by loads of corn being drawn furioufly againft them in harveft; I have long wifhed to try fome method of prevention.

In building a new barn at Antingham, I threw the ends of an old beam into the jambs of the fide-walls; fo as to reach acrofs the floor, at the entrance of the porch ; low enough

---

* There is however a difadvantage in cutting thorns intended for hedging materials in this ftate ; as they are lefs durable than when they are cut in winter, when the fap is down.

to take the top of the load, and high enough to be out of the way of the flail; setting a man with his flail to give the workmen the proper height.

I find, however, that either the thrasher, or the bricklayer, has made a mistake; for yesterday the thrasher told me, that he frequently hits his flail against the beam.

The height from the floor, I find, is nine feet; fix inches more, he says, would be high enough; however, he being a middle-sized man, a foot may be necessary: and ten feet may perhaps be taken as a general height.

The mischief is usually done by large loads; to draw in which (especially if the barn-floor lies much higher than the yard) the horses are obliged to exert their utmost strength; but the load being once landed upon the floor, no farther exertion is necessary; nevertheless the horses being roused and spirited, or not under command, rush furiously on till they come to a check; which is generally the roof of the porch. A small load requires no extraordinary exertion, but is drawn in deliberately, and the horses of course are stopped at pleasure. The height of a pair of full-sized barn-doors is fourteen feet, and a high load will nearly touch the plate. Twelve feet high is but a small load. Therefore,

fore, in every refpect, ten feet high is a proper height for a CHECK-BEÀM.

36.

NOVEMBER 25. Oaks are obferved to grow
beft, and make the fineft plants and the moft
beautiful trees, when they are raifed undifturbed
from the acorn. The oak having naturally a
ftrong tap-root, it is almoft certain death to re-
move a large plant which has not been tranf-
planted or tapped whilft young: neverthelefs
if the tap-root has been properly taken off
from the feedling plant, it may afterwards be
removed at pleafure, with fafety.

Oaks may be tapped by taking up the plants
and taking off the tap-root with a knife, or it
may be done as they ftand, with a tapping
iron, or even a common fpade ground to an
edge. This, being introduced at a proper
depth beneath the furface of the ground, cuts
off the tap-root; leaving the principal part of
the lateral horizontal fibres undifturbed. When
the plants have got large (four or five years old
for inftance), this is perhaps the fafeft way of
treating them; for the lateral fhoots in this cafe
receive no check whatever, but continue to
throw up a regular fupply of fap to the plant;

whereas

36.

TAPPING OAKLINGS.

whereas by taking them up and removing them into a frefh fituation, they are feveral days before they begin to work; in which time the plant may receive irrecoverable injury.

A feed-bed of oaklings, five years old, I treated in this manner: In March-April tapped them all with common fpades, ground fharp; pruned fuch as were in any degree ftraight; and headed down the reft near the ground, to throw out ftraight fhoots to be trained.

Not a plant I fee is dead.

Had there been more of them cut down, the effect would have been ftill better.

37.

PLANTING.

November 25. A ftriking inftance of fuccefs in *tranfplanting large oaks* for ftandards occurs on Gunton Common. Scarcely a plant, of fome thoufands, has mifcarried, and very few which do not flourifh.

A perfon who had fome fhare in the bufinefs of this plantation tells me, that it was the employment of two men and a couple of horfes, almoft all the firft fummer after they were planted, to water them; not by a pailfull, but by a hogfhead, at once; which ferved for the fummer.

This

This was a rational method; a pailfull only
tantalizes and balks the plant; whereas a hogfhead depofited at its root affords a natural and
regular fupply, to be drawn up leifurely by
the fun during the courfe of the fummer.

38.

NOVEMBER 25. The afh delights in a moift
fituation, and will thrive even in an undrained
moory foil. How healthy and luxuriant are
thofe on Gunton Common, which grow upon a
low moory fwampy part; almoft upon a level
with the water: and even thofe on the ozier-
beds vie with the aquatics.

The afh is a thirfty plant. The road under
an afh is obferved to be always comparatively
dry; and it is probably from this abforbent
nature, that it is fo great an enemy to the her-
baceous tribe. Turneps, a fucculent plant,
ftarves under the afh; and corn never thrives
in its neighbourhood.—Clover, however, *feems*
to be an exception to this theory.

It is neverthelefs an undoubted fact, that the
afh is a deftructive enemy on arable land; and
it is highly improper to plant it in hedges.
It ought to be planted in wafte nooks and
corners; or, perhaps, for two reafons, on un-

F 4   im-

38.

THE ASH.

improvable fwamps, and on the fpringy fides of hills : it would be rendering them ufeful as fites of plantations ; and, perhaps, by its abforbent nature, would render them firm.

THE ALDER.

The alder, on the contrary, is obferved to make the ground it grows on ftill more rotten and boggy : it ought therefore, for two reafons, never to be planted ; namely, the injury to the land, and its own worthleffnefs.

39.

MARKETS.

NOVEMBER 26. This morning took a ride to fee *Holt Fair*.

This is a fair for " homebreds," or Norfolk ftock only ; no Scotch drovers frequenting it.

A neighbour bought nine three-year-olds (coming), five of them fteers, four fpayed heifers, forward in flefh, at 4*l*. 7*s*. 6*d*. a piece.

A farmer in the neighbourhood bought two of the fame age, but lean, though larger, and not out of condition, for 7*l*.

Some kind-growing two-year-olds (coming) were afked fifty-five fhillings a piece for.

Cows and calves fell very low in Norfolk. They were fold to-day from about fifty-five fhillings to three pounds ten fhillings a couple.

It is alfo obfervable, that lean ftock—" ftraw-jacks"—fell very low in this country, at this time

time of the year; while such as are forward enough to be finished with turneps, or with the addition of a little spring-grass, so as to be got early to market, fetch astonishing prices. Witness the forward cattle to-day, and the bullocks at St, Faith's.

The reason is this :—A farmer has so many more acres of turneps than he wants for his present stock ;—he must therefore either run the risque of selling his turneps, or buy stock which he can finish in the spring, otherwise he will be overstocked the next year.

It is observable that the heifers (of the nine above-mentioned) are forwarder than the steers; insomuch that the purchaser hopes to finish them with turneps ; but the steers he expects will require some grass at the spring of the year. It was an observation made, and agreed to, that the grazing-grounds about Foulsham (where these came from) fatten heifers faster than they do steers. In corroboration, a by-stander said, that he this year sent a parcel of young-stock to these grounds ; the heifers came home almost meat, the steers little better than when they went.

This, if a fact, is highly interesting.

NOVEMBER

40.

40.

FATTING CATTLE.

NOVEMBER 28. How profitable are the little *Iſle-of-Sky Scots* to the Norfolk farmer, who has rough meadows for them to run in?

— — — had eleven bought laſt Hempton-green fair (juſt twelve months ago) for three guineas a piece. They were kept entirely on ſtraw and ruſhy graſs, which nothing elſe would have eaten, until the month of May; when they were turned into ſome Norfolk meadows, (worth about ten ſhillings an acre) where they remained until September: ſince when they have been at good lattermath. They are now ſome of them quite fat, and the reſt nearly ſo; one with another, they are worth about ſix pounds a piece.

Suppoſing each occupied an acre of meadow, which (with town charges) reckon at - - 0　12　0

Straw over and above the dung - - 0　　5　0

Ten weeks lattermath, at 10 ſhillings

　　(the price for ſuch cattle) -　-　0　10　0
　　　　　　　　　　　　　　　　　　　　—————
　　　　　　　　　　　　　　　　　　£ 1　7　0

A neighbouring farmer bought a parcel at the ſame time, and at the ſame price; alſo ſome refuſe ones ſo low as five-and-twenty ſhillings

shillings a piece; two of which he sold a few days ago for eleven pounds four shillings.

These, however, were followers at turneps the first winter. In summer they were sent to a grazing-ground : since harvest they have been in the stubble and " rowens," at good keep.

His other bullocks had nothing but straw in winter; were shifted about in the meadows during summer; since harvest they have been in the stubbles; and are now at turneps. They have grown very much, and are now getting on very fast.

It is observable, however, that all these Scots were bought in very cheap.

41.

DECEMBER 1. A prudent farmer in this District makes a very proper distinction between laying up "wheat-riggs" where there are pheasants, and where there are none. In a part of his farm tolerably free from game, he lays it up in six-furrow work ; but towards the covers, in wide flat beds; having found by experience that pheasants always begin to scrape on the sides of the furrows, where they can easily come at the grain ; the mould being there loose, and easily falls back into the furrows : therefore, the

WHEAT.

GAME.

41.

FLOWING
for
PHEASANTS.

the fewer inter-furrows the lefs mifchief they are capable of doing: for while they fcrape upon a flat furface, "they bury two grains by fcraping up one;" befides its being a work of much greater labour to come at them.

He fays he always "lays" to lofe the two outfide furrows or drills: if therefore he laid his land in fix-furrow ridges, one-third of his crop muft be inevitably loft, at feed-time; befides the depredations he is liable to, during the winter, and at the approach of harveft.

42.

HEDGES.

December 6. The mal-treatment of hedges in this country is painful to look upon; and there appears to be only one way of preventing a Norfolk farmer from deftroying them.

Unneceffary reftrictions I confefs are hateful; but to fuffer unneceffary deftruction of things fo effential to an inclofed eftate as are live hedges, would be equally unpardonable; and I am determined henceforward to ftem, *if poffible*, the vile practices, fo prevalent in this country, of "outholling" and "cutting kid*:"

* "Outholling"—fcouring out the ditch—provincially, the "holl'—for manure, without returning any part of the mould to the roots of the quick. — "Cutting kid"— knocking off the lower boughs of tall hedges; leaving

wide-

A regulation of this kind will not be taking from the farmers the privilege of cutting kids for their " par-yards," nor of collecting mould for their yards and dunghills; but it will be obliging them, while they furnish themselves with these two necessary articles, to do justice to their fences.

Under this regulation the farmer will not calculate how few rods of ditching he can make shift with; but how many loads of mould and hundreds of kid he shall be in want of. Thus the interest of the tenant and that of the land-lord will become intimately connected.

43.

DECEMBER 14. This autumn I met with a singular instance of *sowing wheat after turneps by two furrowing*. (See SOIL PROCESS.)

The first plow skimmed the surface, and threw it into the last-made trench; on this furrow the seed was sown, and covered with the bottom furrow brought up by the second plow; the

wide-spreading tops, to over-hang the young shoots, and smother the underling plants; rendering, of course, the bottom open and fenceless; whilst the roots of the surviving tree-like plants being left naked of mould, these in length of time dwindled away for want of a proper supply of nourishment. See art. HEDGES, vol. I.

feedsman

feedfman always keeping between the plows, and fowing the feed by hand between the furrows.

. The plits being taken off very thin, the two reached only a mean depth; fo that no frefh foil was brought up.

Two plows and one feedfman finifhed from an acre to five roods a day. The harrow was juft run over to break the furface, and let the feedling plants freely out. The land is laid into warps, not into ridges.

This method is fomewhat tedious; but the plants come up beautifully even, and the furface, of courfe, is free from rubbifh.

The plants do not come up in drills, but promifcuoufly; occupying the whole furface. This the Norfolk farmers feem to think preferable to their ftanding in rows: and, no doubt, the foil in this cafe is the moft uniformly occupied by the plants.

44.

DECEMBER 17. The "water-workers" in Norfolk have a very expeditious way of fcouring-out old drains which are grown up with grafs and filt.

They firft mark out the edges of the drain with a fharp fpade, or other inftrument, cutting

ting through the depth of the mud. If the
drain be wide, they make another cut along
the middle, and then crofs it, fo as to feparate
the whole into large fquare pieces of three or
four fpits each.

The workman then takes a large hook, with
three flat prongs, and a ftout long wooden handle—provincially, a " mud-croom,"—and,
ftanding by the fide of the drain, draws out the
"tuffucks;" placing them regularly on either
fide ; and, laftly, with a fharp fhovel, forms the
bottom of the drain, and fhovels out the
loofe mould.

45.

DECEMBER 18. In my ride this morning I
obferved two or three inftances of young hedges
which are ruined through the bank being fet
injudicioufly on the upper fide of the ditch.

Ditches on hill fides fhould be made
to face up-hill; efpecially where the fubfoil is fpringy. For if the fprings work
through, under the bank, they foon undermine
and let down the face, together with the layer,
into the ditch. The outfide of the ditch fhooting in is of much lefs confequence.

'46.

46.

REARING
CATTLE.

1782. JANUARY 9. Obferving, to a good hufbandman, that his three-year-olds were rather
fmall; he faid, Yes, they are; adding, that his
turneps were but indifferent laft year; and that
he was too eager after bullocks; but he now
wifhed he had done better by his ftore beafts:
for he always found that they paid beft for
" grazing :"—that is, for good keeping.

This was the obfervation of a fenfible, el-
derly, judicious, capital farmer; and came immediately from experience.

47.

RENT-DAYS.

JANUARY 9. The times of the year for the
receiving of rents fhould be regulated by the
produce of the country, and the objects of the
farmer's culture.—He ought not to be obliged
to difpofe of his produce to a difadvantage, nor
fell it under the market-price. Nor ought he,
after his money is received or due, to have too
great indulgence; left he may be tempted to
fpeculations; which, in the end, might hurt
both himfelf and his landlord.

In a corn-country, Chriftmas is of all others
the moft improper time for the farmer to pay
his

his rent at : he has juſt time enough to do himſelf all the injury poſſible. Stimulated by an honeſt pride of carrying the whole balance ; or fearful of the frowns of his landlord ; he hurries out his corn, unmindful of the lowneſs of the price, or the waſte he is committing on his " ſtover."

Were he called upon at Michaelmas, he could not commit this unpardonable waſte : if at Lady-day, he could have no temptation to do it. Beſides, at Chriſtmas, tithe, tradeſmen's bills, the land-tax, and other quarterly rates come upon him ; and it is not the loſs of the ſtover only, but the mealmen and maltſters, knowing his ſituation, take their advantages.

This year furniſhes a ſtriking inſtance of the impropriety of receiving at Chriſtmas in Norfolk.

We have not yet had ſcarcely ſo much as a hoar froſt, nor one flake of ſnow ; cattle in many places are even yet abroad, at graſs ; yet the major part of the tenants of this neighbourhood have already thraſhed out three-fourths of their corn. Many of their yards are ſeveral feet thick with ſtraw, with ſcarcely any intermixture of teathe ; and ſome of them without being ſo much as trodden.

There

47.
RENT-DAYS.

There is another evil confequence, in Norfolk, of receiving rents at Chriftmas : it is full as much as the *poor* farmer can do, with all his mifchief, to raife money for his landlord : he dare not lay out a fhilling on bullocks to feed off his turneps ; which he is of courfe obliged to fell at fuch a price as he can get, and have them eaten off when and in what manner beft fuits the purchafer; whereas, had he time to thrafh out his corn deliberately, he would find money to buy bullocks, and to pay his landlord.

Suppofing the farmer to have paid his laft fhilling to his harveft-men (which God knows is at prefent the cafe with farmers in general) his only refource is confequently his crop. He firft begins upon his wheat, in order to raife money for his fervants wages, and the parifh-rates, at Michaelmas. His feed-wheat muft next be thrafhed out, or purchafed : a few bullocks is probably wanted; and the next quarter's rates, tithe, and tradefmen's bills muft be paid at Chriftmas. Thus without opening one fheaf for his landlord, he muft do confiderable injury to his ftover. What then muft be the confequence, if, in the fame time, he thrafh out in addition thereto more than his half-year's rent ?

How

How differently this matter would ſtand, were tenants indulged until the latter end of February or the beginning of March.

The buſineſs of the barn would then take its natural and regular courſe : the ſervants wages and Michaelmas rates being diſcharged, and the ſeed-wheat and ſome bullocks being provided, the farmer would, about the beginning or middle of December, get his ſtock into his yards, and begin in earneſt upon his barley.

By Chriſtmas he would find no difficulty in diſcharging his tithe, tradeſmen's bills and pariſh-rates; and would have the two principal months for thraſhing before him (beſides perhaps a ſurplus in hand) to raiſe money for his landlord.

His rent being cleared up to Michaelmas, and his flails ſtill being of courſe kept going, his Eaſter and Lady-day rates would be regularly paid; beſides a ſufficient overplus for the purchaſe of ſuch clover or other ſeeds as might be wanted during the ſpring ſeed-time.

In April and May his bullocks travel to market; and, by the beginning of June, his purſe begins again to overflow; but after this his receipts are trifling.

The beginning of June, therefore, is the time when he ought to pay to his landlord as

much

47.
RENT-DAYS·

much money on account of the current year's rent as would leave him a fufficiency (with his dairy and other fmall receipts) to pay his Mid-fummer rates and get in his harveft.

The firft of March and the firft of June have one peculiar advantage as rent-days; not only in Norfolk, but in every other country; they do not interfere with quarter-days; and, in Norfolk particularly, they are leifure-times of the year.

48.

BUILDING.

JANUARY 10. It is economical to *lay tiles on mortar*, or ceil the room they cover; they are otherwife fubject to every guft of wind; not from its action upon the outfide, but from finding, when pent up on the infide, an eafy paffage through the covering.

An inftance occurred the other day : a farm-houfe had two or three yards fquare of tiling blown off by the late winds; not on the wind-ward, but on the leeward fide of the houfe; and from over the only room about it which is not ceiled.

49.

JANUARY 10. How ftrong and lafting is the current of cuftom! The Norfolk farmers, while

while corn fold high, were affiduous to culti-
vate every inch the plow could reach : old
marl-pits were levelled : nooks and corners
grubbed, and broken up : and even bogs were
converted into arable land. Grafsland, of
courfe, became wholly out of fafhion, and totally neglected : and now, when corn is low,
the fame practice ftill prevails : fcraps of
arable land are ftill purchafed at more labour
than they are fometimes worth; while the
meadows are fuffered to remain a difgrace to
the country; notwithftanding they would pay
trebly for improvement.

50.

JANUARY 11. The other day, I obferved
in the practice of a fuperior hufbandman the
following method of *deftroying ant hills*. With
a common fpade, ground fomewhat fharp, he
divided the hill into four quarters. With the
fame inftrument he then pared off the fward of
the quarters, an inch to two inches thick ;
leaving the triangular turves pared off faft at
their bafes, folding them back upon the
adjoining fward. This done, he dug out the
core of the hill; chopping and fpreading the
mould abroad; and leaving a hollow bafon where

G 3   the

the hill ftood, in order to collect the winter's rains, and thereby effect a radical cure. Laftly, the folds of fward were returned as a cover to the excavation, leaving the furface graffy, nearly level, and fcarcely difcernible from the furrounding fward.

This operation is aptly called " gelding;" and, though not univerfal, is a moft excellent practice.

Between Michaelmas and Chriftmas is the proper time for performing it; for then the excavated mould becomes tempered by the winter's rains and frofts; and the folds of fward have time to unite with the foil before the fummer's drought fet in.

51.

JANUARY 13. What a difgrace, and what a field for improvement, are the meadows of this county ! The farmers hire marfhes and grazing-

grounds at the diftance of twenty or thirty miles, and give high prices, when at the fame time many farmers might, with a common fhare of attention and management, have them at a much cheaper rate within the limits of their own farms,

But

But cuftom and prejudice are doughty champions to deal with : whilft a Norfolk farmer is beftowing more " coft" upon his arable land than, at the prefent prices of corn, he can ever regain from it, he is " doing rarely well by his land ;" but the moment the foot of improvement fteps on to his grafs-lands, be it even to open a few gripes to let off the furface-water, the eyes of the country are upon him ; for he is " buying his mea-dows." Were he to carry a load of muck from his par-yard on to his meadow-land, a ftatute of lunacy would be the probable con-fequence.

51.

GEN. MAN. OF FARMS.

· Prejudice, however, is not the only thing againft the improvement of the Norfolk mea-dows. A want of knowledge in the art of draining is a fifter-caufe ; for of the few who attempt to drain their meadows, fcarcely any are acquainted with the method of performing it properly. They make their drains much too fmall, too numerous, and cut them in improper directions ; nor do they ever go to a proper depth to do the work effectually ; for fhould they chance to dip to a bed of gravel they have done won-ders, and there they ftop ; for their fpades and " mud-crooms" can go no farther.

MEADOWS.

Nor

Nor is the method of *draining* the only part of the mifmanagement of the Norfolk farmers in regard to their meadows,—they do not feem to be aware that *preffure* is a main improvement of boggy moory land. I have never feen nor heard of a roller being drawn over a meadow fince I came into Norfolk!

There are, however, fome few exceptions to this general mal-treatment of meadows to be met with.

The Rev. Mr. Horfley of Swayfield has drained his meadows in a capital ftyle, and Mr. Samuel Barber of Stanninghall is manuring his with foot, &c. and clearing them from ant-hills, furze, alders, and other incumbrances.

This laft is a great nuifance in meadows; an alder not only encumbers the fpot it ftands on, but is allowed on all hands to render moory foil ftill more rotten. It is a vile inhabitant of or in the neighbourhood of a meadow; for the feeds being blown about by the wind, they are trodden by cattle into the foil over the area of the meadow; where, fpringing up among the herbage, the young plants embitter the grafs, and render it altogether impalatable to ftock.

In improving meadows, the main objeft is to difengage the mould from collefted moifture:

for

for while any part of the black moory peat-
bog foil lies in contact with water, the whole
will, like a fponge, be filled with moifture:
and it is in vain to attempt to render the furface dry, while the bottom remains in water.
Therefore, drains deeper than the bed of
moor are effentially neceffary.

Meadows have generally a rivulet running
through them: this, although it may have worn
itfelf down to the gravel, fhould neverthelefs
(as it in general may) be confiderably deepened;
enough to lower the *furface* of the water *below
the moor*; and ftill enough more to allow for a
defcent in the drains to be laid into it.

The rivulet fhould be deepened (as fhould all
" water-work" be performed) in autumn;
when the foil is in its firmeft ftate: not in the
fpring (as is the almoft univerfal practice), when
the moor is fopped with water, and the quick-
fands all alive.

The rivulet, or other common fhore, being
lowered; and the fand or gravel (if any) fpread
over the adjoining moor (or, if a bad mould,
ufed to level the inequality), and the furface-
water (if any) let off into the fhore; the meadows ought to remain in this ftate until the
enfuing autumn; by which time the lower mar-
gins,

gins, towards the main drain, will have acquired a degree of firmnefs, perhaps, fufficient to admit of the lateral drains being cut to their full depth.

Very rotten meadows, lying on a blowing oozy quick-fand, cannot however, with any propriety, be finifhed the next year : therefore, in thefe, the upper moory ftratum alone fhould be raifed; laying it as far from the edge off the drains as the arm and fpade can reach.

In the courfe of the enfuing fummer the mould ought to be turned over to forward its digeftion; and to bury the weeds, which never fail to grow upon it in great abundance; and which being turned under in the fulnefs of fap, are very beneficial in promoting the digeftion of the whole mafs.

In autumn the drains ought to be finifhed— the inequalities done away, and the manure fpread over the furface; *provided* this can be yet done with fafety.

But fhould the quick-fand be ftill fo ftrong as to endanger the fides of the drains, go no deeper the third year than can be done with fafety; deferring the finifhing fpit until another, or even another, fummer has rendered the fubfoil firm, and the fprings are effectually killed.

This

This is dividing the expence; doing the bufinefs effectually; and treading fure ground.

The drains fhould not be cut, as is generally the cafe, perpendicular to the rivulet; but either parallel with it, or, if their mouths be laid into it, in an oblique direction; in order that they may act more effectually upon the fub-foil; as well as to clear their mouths the better at the rivulet.

Nor fhould the open drains be too numerous: for by that means the roller and carriages are prevented from being turned between them.

Above all, the drains ought to be made of a fufficient fize: their depth fhould be regulated by the depth of the moor and its fubftratum of quick fand, and confequently by the rivulet, which ought to follow the workman a confider-able way up the new-made drains. Their width ought to be fufficient to deter ftock from at-tempting to crofs them; otherwife the fides are foon trodden in, and the ftock endangered.

Nothing is more common than to hear of ftock being fmothered in the meadow-drains: laft fummer, a horfe was fmothered in a fuite of meadows, which for a trifling expence might be made firm enough to bear any ftock, and lay feveral weeks before he was found.

The

The utility of large wide drains is obvious in a meadow adjoining to the suite abovementioned; a drain six or eight feet wide, and five or six deep, lays dry a meadow of eight or ten acres: a carriage might, even now, pass with safety by the side of it.

If the beds be made less than twenty yards wide there is not, as has been observed, room to turn a roller or waggon with safety upon them; if, therefore, the open drains, at that distance, be not sufficient to make beds of that width sufficiently dry and firm, under-drains should be laid into them.

If the beds be made wider than thirty yards, a carriage will be wanted to set about the mould, which rises out of the new-made drains, and which will afterwards arise from the parings of the sides, and the shovellings of the bottoms. But if they be made within that width, a man will be able to manure the whole without that additional expence; for if the mould be cast, in the first instance, as far as may be from the drains, and be afterwards, in turning it over, removed still farther from them, the farthest shovel-full will not require to be cast more than ten yards.

It is obvious that, in draining a meadow in this manner, the paltry gripes and water-

furrow

furrow with which meadows in general abound, would become ufelefs; and would require to be filled up with alders, other rubbifh, and dead mould, dug out of the new drains. The furface mould however ought, as above-intimated, to be referved for a better purpofe; namely, to be fpread over the finifhed beds **as** a manure. Its effects on a meadow which laft year I had frequent opportunities of obferving, was ftriking; it appeared to kill the rufhes and other aquatics; and brought up a thick matt of white clover, and other luxuriant graffes.

51.

MEADOWS.

52.

JANUARY 19. A fingular inftance of fatting fwine now occurs in this neighbourhood.

SWINE.

The other day, Mr. S. of C. had thirty or forty bacon-hogs at peas; put into long open troughs, in the middle of the yard. Now, he has fifty or fixty porkers at barley and oats.

The pigs look healthy and well, and, Mr. S. fays, fat apace. He keeps the yard well-littered, and they have water to go to.

He fold fifty laft week at the Hill at Norwich at nineteen fhillings and fixpence, and fifty more this week at home at feventeen fhillings.

lings. He bought them a few weeks ago at about half a guinea a head,

He shewed me one which he had killed for Walsham market: the meat was peculiarly delicate, and quite fat enough; it weighed four stone, valued at four shillings to four shillings and sixpence a stone.

Mr. S. says, he not only finds that they fat very fast; but that the drovers are particularly fond of pigs fatted in this manner; they travel better than sty-fed hogs; and do not shrink so much with their journey.

They are making him a valuable yard of dung, with very little attendance, and without the expence of house-room. There is a cart-shed in the yard, under which they may run in bad weather.

Mr. S. argues in favour of his plan, that pigs never do better than when they help themselves, as in stubbles, or at a barley-rick: give a pig acorns, he says, in a sty, and they are wasted upon him; but let him pick them up himself under the oak, and he will get fat.

Mr. S. mixes one bushel of oats to a coomb of barley; in order that the pigs may grind the barley, and thereby prevent its passing through

them

them whole. It has the defired and, indeed, a ftriking effect.—Mr. S. broke feveral parcels of dung, but not the trace of a whole grain of barley in the yard. The oats not being a favourite food, prevent the pigs from eating the barley too greedily; as well as being hufky, they require a longer time to be chewed. Mr. S. treats buck in the fame manner, with the fame effect: peas I find are not unfrequently put among buck for the fame purpofe.

This is to me a new idea. Mixing chaff with oats for horfes, to promote the maftication of the latter, is an old, and now almoft univerfal, cuftom; and mixing different forts of food for hogs, in order to obtain the fame valuable effect, is felf-evidently judicious.

53.

JANUARY 24. Mr. S. of W. a fteady money-getting farmer, rears his calves in this manner. (See REARING CATTLE, Vol. I.)

He begins about Michaelmas, and continues till about Candlemas.

Their food is fkim-milk with a little wheat-flour. They have alfo chopped turneps in a trough and hay in a rack.

As foon as they learn to eat turneps freely, the pail is entirely left off; the turneps affording

ing them both meat and drink; thefe with a little hay. being their, only fuftenance. Some farmers give them oats and bran ; but Mr. S. efteems them dear feeding.

The time of their taking to turneps is un-certain : where there are older calves that have learnt to eat turneps plentifully, the young ones readily learn, by picking up the crumbs made by the old ones *.

About March, the firft-reared are turned out among the fatting bullocks, in the day-time, and in a few days, if the weather permit, are turned out altogether.

During fummer they are kept in the clo-vers, or at other high keep; and by next au-tumn are ftout enough to ftand the par-yard. This is efteemed a main advantage of rearing calves early in the feafon ; for thofe reared late in the fpring want two years nurfing.

The price of calves, about ten days old, is eight or ten fhillings ; and of buds or yearlings, from twenty to thirty fhillings ; fo that twenty fhillings is an out-fide produce of a reared calf; fifteen fhillings, perhaps, is nearer the par.

---

* Breaking the turneps with a mallet has been found to induce calves to take to them fooner than when they are cut with a fharp-edged tool. Perhaps, pounding them, and mixing the pulp with milk, would be ftill better.

This

This cannot be adequate to twelve months extraordinary care, expence, and hazard; especially to a large farmer, who has, *at present*, more material objects to attend to.

Mr. B. of the same place, convinced of this, rears no calves: he finds that he can *at present* buy young home-breds and Scots cheaper than he can rear his own stock. But Mr. B. is a good judge of stock. For a small farmer, or for any one not thoroughly conversant in the business of buying and selling, it may be more prudent, and certain, to bring up his own calves: for, having learned from experience, how much stock his farm will carry, he goes on mechanically; so many cows—so many three-year-olds —an equal number of two-year-olds—and the same number of buds—with every year nearly the same quantity of turneps and clover to feed and fat them on. If his turneps prove under par, he sells part of his three-year-olds; if above, sells part of his turneps; and this seems to be the *natural basis* of the Norfolk husbandry.

54.

54.

JANUARY 24. The following is an accurate account of the *peat-grounds* of the fens.

	£.		
The " turf-man" pays for rent	0	4	0
For cutting from 1s. 6d. to 2s.	0	1	9
For " chimneying" (that is, piling them lattice-wife to dry)	0	0	6
For boating to the ftaith 6d. to 1s.	0	0	9
	£. 0	7	0
Profit and hazard (great quantities are fometimes fwept away by the floods)	0	1	6
The felling price per thoufand	£. 0	8	6

The peats, when cut, are about four inches fquare (but dry to about three inches and a quarter) ; and from two to three feet long, or of a length equal to the depth of the moor ;— every foot of which, therefore, affords nine peats : each yard 81 : each rod 2,450½ : and each acre 392,040 : which, at 4s. per thoufand amounts to the fum of £.78 8s. 2d. an acre : befides the additional advantage of having uncovered a ftratum of earth, which, in many parts, produces reed, fpontaneoufly ; and on which, it is highly probable, that valuable aquatic might on every part be propagated.

55.

JANUARY 25. The farmers of Woodbaſt-   MARL.
wick, in the ſouthern part of this Diſtrict, have
their marl chiefly from Norwich in boats
round by Yarmouth, forty or fifty miles. Sometimes they bring it by way of back-carriage
from Thorp-next-Norwich, about ſix miles;
at other times from Horſtead, and other neighbouring pits, convenient for back-carriage :
none within five or ſix miles.

The uſual quantity ſet on is eight or ten
middling loads an acre. At Norwich they pay
one ſhilling—at Horſtead eighteen pence a
load, uncallowed.

The carriage (as back-carriage) is reckoned
worth about three ſhillings or three ſhillings
and ſixpence; ſo that it coſts them about four
to five ſhillings a load; or fifty ſhillings to
three pound an acre.

The marl brought by the wherries is worth
at the ſtaith about four ſhillings the middling
load.

56.

JANUARY 25. Mr ——, of Woodbaſtwick   FATTING
has eleven large Scotch bullocks (from fifty to   CATTLE.

ſeventy

56.

BULLOCKS
IN YARDS.

feventy ftone) at *turneps in the yard*. They eat nearly two load a day—fix would eat about a load.—They are given to them whole (except the tails, which are cut off in the field) with their tops on; in double bins; with ftraw fcattered about the yard; ferving them both as fodder and litter.

Thefe bullocks coft the latter end of October one with another about 7*l*. 10*s*. ahead. Suppofe they weigh by the latter end of April fixty ftone on a par, and fell for four fhillings a ftone; the produce, deducting the expence of fale, will be about 4*l*.—at 4*s*. 6*d*. a ftone, 3*l*. 10*s*.—at 5*s*. a ftone, 7*l*.

If fix bullocks eat a load of turneps a day, one bullock would eat thirty loads in fix months. Twenty loads an acre is efteemed a fair crop. Therefore, at four fhillings a ftone, thefe bullocks will pay 2*l*. 13*s*. 4*d*. an acre; at 4*s*. 6*d*. a ftone, 3*l*. 13*s*. 4*d*.; and at 5*s*. a ftone, 4*l*. 13*s*. 4*d*. an acre for the turneps, ftraw, and attendance: — fuppofing them to take fix months at turneps to bring them to fixty ftone a head; which, I apprehend, is near the truth.

57.

FATTING
CATTLE
ABROAD.

JANUARY 25.—Mr. Samuel Barber, whofe accuracy may be depended on, fays, that twelve acres

acres of turneps upon his Stanninghall farm, have carried thirty-five fatting bullocks, followed by forty-five cows, highlanders, and other lean stock, together with fourscore fatting sheep, five weeks and three days; that is, reckoning eight sheep to one bullock, forty-five fatting, and forty-five lean bullocks; from forty to fifty stone each.

57.
BULLOCKS.
ABROAD.

In six months these bullocks would not eat, at this rate, quite sixty acres: but the turneps are very "thight" and very good.

Mr. Barber attributes the good proof of his turneps this year on his Stanninghall farm chiefly to their " thightness," He says he never minds how close the hoers leave the plants, so that they draw their hoes between them. He says he has suffered some pounds this year, on his Baſtwick farm, through the hoers, in his absence, being suffered to hack them out too thin *.

TURNEPS.

The same judicious husbandman says, he treats his Stanninghall farm (a light dry soil) for turneps, and for olland barley, in this manner: the firſt plowings, whether they be two or three,

SOIL-
PROCESS.

---

* Mr. Baker of Southreps, whose opinion in this case is equally valuable, holds out the same ideas; saying, that he is always attentive to his hoers, to see that they do not set out the plants too thin.

he

he gives very fleet, and fetches the foil up the laft plowing a full pitch; by which means he fows his feed amongſt a mould which has never been expofed to the drought; and, confequently, contains a degree of moiſture very favourable to the feedling plants.

To this management he attributes, in fome meafure, his great fuccefs in turneps this year, They are indeed the beſt in the country, and on a foil whereon turneps have not grown, with any degree of fuccefs, for many years,

For olland barley, he endeavours to break the flag as little as poffible, fo that the grafs be killed: he therefore would chufe not to break up his olland till after Chriſtmas. With this procefs he fows the barley above-furrow.

58.

JANUARY 29. In a converfation, to-day, with two of the firſt farmers in the county, a comparifon between the prefent times and thofe of fifteen to twenty years ago, became the fub-ject.

The price of barley was, then, from five fhillings to feven fhillings a coomb; of wheat, from ten fhillings to fourteen fhillings; and beef three fhillings and fixpence a ſtone. Now, barley

barley is eight fhillings, wheat twenty-two fhillings, and beef four fhillings to four fhillings and fixpence; yet, in thofe days, farmers had plenty of money, and actually increafed in riches; whereas, now, they are moneylefs, and are every year finking in poverty.

To explain this paradox feemed difficult: the price of day-labour is fomewhat decreafed; fervants wages the fame, now, as then; houfe-keeping fomewhat more expenfive, as to the price of its particular articles; but, upon the whole, it is not more fo; for farmers, principal farmers, now keep lefs company than they did in thofe times. One of them obferved, that he pays the fame price for a coat, and the fame for a fhirt, he did formerly; and as to market and other perfonal expences, he is clear that among capital farmers they are lefs now than they were then. The poor's rate, it is true, falls heavy at prefent; but he fays that he pays only fourteen pounds now for what he then paid ten pounds: this therefore is not of material confequence; and this excellent hufbandman, fenfible and well-informed as he is, feemed willing to affign the caufe to fome inexplicable hidden myftery.

H 4   At

At length, however, he produced an idea which goes a great way towards explaining the *apparent riches* of former, and the *apparent poverty* of the prefent, times.

In every corner there are moneyed men : formerly they diffufed their riches through the neighbourhood they lived in :—it was no uncommon circumftance for a farmer even to be afked to take money; whereas, now, through a want of private credit and moneyed faith between man and man, and ftill more through the prefent high rate of intereft to be made on government fecurity, the monies which were difperfed in the country among farmers and tradefmen are now all called in,

This explains very fully the *apparent riches* of former times and the *apparent poverty* of the prefent : but it does not explain why farmers formerly grew rich, but now grow poor.

The late rife of rents at once fully developed the whole myftery. For although the ufurer's money might affift the farmer in purchafing ftock, &c. to an advantage; yet this advantage was in great meafure cancelled by the intereft which he had annually to pay for it ; whereas the money arifing from the comparative lownefs of rent required neither intereft nor even principal to be repaid.

Thus,

Thus, fuppofing farms to be raifed thirty per cent. within the laft fifteen or twenty years; and fuppofing that, among middling farmers, the rife in the poor's rates, and the extra expence of houfe-keeping, is adequate to the advance of produce; the farmer who now juft makes ends meet on a farm of one hundred and thirty pounds a year, had formerly a furplus of thirty pounds left in his pocket to buy ftock, &c. at the beft market *.

This, even the fecond year of his leafe, he found of great advantage; but the third year, the thirty became fixty; the fourth, ninety, or perhaps one hundred pounds; for the intereft, or a proper management of the money, had increafed his ftock; fo that by intereft upon intereft, or by other advantages made of the money, a careful, induftrious, *fortunate* man found himfelf, at the end of his twenty-one years leafe, to be worth eight hundred or one thoufand pounds; and confequently got, very defervedly, the name of being a rich farmer.

* A ftriking inftance of the lofs arifing from a want of loofe money to buy ftock when the markets are low, occurs this year: at Kipping and Kenninghall fheep-fhows (a few months ago) the fame lambs might have been bought for five fhillings and fixpence, which are now worth half-a-guinea a head.

But

But the cafe of the man who now takes a farm of a hundred and thirty pounds a year, is very different.

Let us fuppofe him to have a capital juft fufficient to ftock it, and help him through the extra expences of the firft year.

His crops turn out tolerably, and having common good luck with live ftock, the neat produce of his farm juft clears its expences, buys him a new coat, and pays his landlord: but this done, he finds himfelf without a fixpence left in his pocket for manure, or to go to a cheap market with.

This however is not all. In the courfe of the year, he lofes a cow, perhaps a horfe. What is to be done? He is pennylefs, and cannot borrow a fhilling in the whole country. Why, he muft either do without, to the great prejudice of his farm, or fell fome other part of his ftock to replace them with.

The next year his wheat or his turnep-crop fails him. He has not a fhilling before-hand to carry him over the difficulty; he confequently becomes in arrear with his landlord; his fpirits are broken; his land not only wants manure, but even labour and teathe; for he is glad to fell his bullocks before Chriftmas to

keep

keep his landlord in temper :—the confequence 58.
need not be traced,

Thus it appears that the poverty of prefent   FARMERS.
farmers, more particularly of middling and
fmall farmers, refults in fome meafure from an
advance in the expences of houfe-keeping and
an advance in the parifh-rates; but principally
from the prefent fcarcity of money, and from
the late rife of rents.

59.

FEBRUARY 5. In finking a well near Gun-   THE OAK.
ton-Houfe, the workmen it feems traced the
tap-root of an oak, through an uniformly
white fand, to the depth, I think, of twenty
feet. The tree was neverthelefs uncommonly
healthy and beautiful.

This fhews that a ftrong foil is not neceffary
to the production of fine oaks.

There might, however, be one circumftance   SUBSOIL.
favourable to this oak. The ftratum which it
grew in might be impregnated with the drain-
age of the houfe and offices; for of fo abforbent a nature is this bottomlefs bed of fand,
that it drinks up the whole drip of the houfe,
together with the overflowings, and wafte water, and filt of every denomination.

Nor

59.

SUBSOIL.

Nor is this a fingular inftance of the ab-forbency of the Norfolk foil; for of a fimilar nature is the moft frequent fubfoil of the county: dig a marl-pit through to the fand, the water immediately vanifhes.

60.

REPAIRS.

FEBRUARY 5. *Buttreffes*, to ftay-up old buildings, are very aukward, very expenfive, and very fubject to decay, if not well fecured from the drip of the building they fupport: yet, if walls lofe their upright, fomething is neceffary.

Buttreffes, however, may frequently be avoided, by thickening the foundation, and forming an arch-like foot or underpinning to the whole part affected.—Witnefs a tall fence-wall at Northreps; and a dwelling-houfe at Bradfield; where a buttrefs, in the front of a good houfe, would have been very unfightly.

The *fpring* or width at the bafe, as alfo the height, fhould be in proportion to the degree and height of the bulge to be fecured.

Where the whole wall has given way and overhangs much, a tall buttrefs may be ne-ceffary; though even in this cafe, fupporting the beams and rebuilding the wall from the

foundation

foundation is generally more prudent :—a large buttrefs fwallows up a great quantity of brick and mortar ; and, when raifed, is but a temporary relief.

A large blue flate forms an admirable *roof* for a buttrefs :—an inftance occurs upon Antingham-hall farm.

61.

FEBRUARY 5. A neighbouring farmer having one fide of a clofe of turneps which he could not get off faft enough to be fown with wheat, he cut off their tops with a fpade, gave the tops to his cows, carted the bottoms into a new-made adjoining ditch, (backing the cart and tipping them in) and covered them over with a little ftraw ; and, over this, with bramble-kids, to keep the ftock from them.

Here they lay until wanted in a froft, when the cart was again backed to the ditch, and the turneps loaded with a fork.

He fays, that his beafts eat them as well or better than frefh-drawn turneps ; and that in general they came out as found as when they went in. Had the tops been depofited with the roots, they would probably have

brought

61.
PRESERVING
TURNEPS.

brought on a fermentation, and have spoiled the whole depofit.

Might not this practice be extended to the prefervation of turneps in the fpring?

Turneps, this year, began to run the beginning of January: they have now, in general, got fpring fhoots five or fix inches long; and, if the prefent open weather continue, the roots muft be confiderably exhaufted; and the land very much drawn, long before bullocks in general are finifhed, or grafs begins to grow. But if they were now (when labour is cheap and plentiful) topped and carted into dry ditches, or formed into ftacks with ftraw *, their goodnefs might be preferved, and the land be got into forwardnefs for barley.

If they were ftacked in or near the yard, there would not, for fhed or ftraw-yard bullocks, be any labour loft.

Whether, after this remarkably mild winter, the fpring prove very mild, or very fevere, they would, by this means, be removed out of harm's way.

62.

THE ASH.

FEBRUARY 7. There is, in a grove at Gunton, a large afh, (at leaft a load of timber in

---

* Perhaps hurdles, fet chequer-wife, would be found convenient receptacles.

it)

it) which is *disbarked* entirely round the stem, about a foot from the ground. On one side the upper and lower barks are separated about a foot from each other; on the other side not more than three or four inches: they seem to be drawing towards each other, and may in a few years unite.

This tree was probably disbarked by deer, from five to ten years ago; yet it is not only alive, but apparently as growing and healthy as any tree in the grove.

63.

FEBRUARY 7. I have frequently observed that the face of a ditch over which *ivy* has spread itself, stands invariably.

Perhaps, on a sandy soil, where the face of the bank is perpetually running down like an hour-glass, plant or sow a drill of ivy near the feet of new-made ditches.

64.

FEBRUARY 7. The roof out of repair, the whole fabric is in danger.— Not only the spars, but the " plansher," nay, even the ground-

64.

REPAIRS.

ground-floor, I have feen rotten through a bad roof.

Perhaps fend a thatcher and bricklayer round to each farm annually : if nothing be wanted upon it, there may no doubt be half a day's-labour loft ; but if there is, a few fhillings laid out in time may, in a courfe of years, produce a confiderable faving.

If the landlord take care of the roofs and foundations—the tenants will, for their own conveniency, be ready enough to remind him of the repairs wanted on the infide.

65.

MEADOWS.

FEBRUARY 7. A ftriking inftance of the fhameful management of meadowland in Norfolk occurs upon the church-farm at —— ——.

The late tenant was afraid to truft his ftock in one of his meadows : he has loft feveral cattle and horfes in it—the fkeleton of a horfe now lies there.

The prefent tenant could not get his ftock into it, until, at a confiderable expence of heath and fand, he made a gangway.—To him (who has taken it for only one year certain) I could not value it at more than five fhillings an acre : yet I will venture to fay, that for the

trifling

trifling expence of twenty shillings an acre, properly laid out in the course of next summer, it would, in two or three years time, be worth from twelve to fifteen shillings an acre.

I will give an estimate of the expence, to shew the *real* improvement which the meadow-lands of Norfolk are capable of.

This meadow is a parallelogram lying on a flat, and contains five acres, two roods, seven perches.

A rivulet runs on one side of it, upon a bed of gravel, and five or six feet below the surface of the meadow. Across the meadow, perpendicular to the rivulet, are two drains, grown up with hassocks, and trod in by cattle; and round it is a watery ditch, also full of grass and mud.

There are about eighty statute rods of ditching, and about forty statute rods of draining.—The ditches might be scoured for a shilling, the drains be opened for sixpence, the long rod.

80 statute is about sixty-three long
   rods, at 1s. - - - 3 3 0
40 ditto, about thirty-one, at 6d. 0 15 6
                         ————
                      £ 3 18 6

But the drains could not be opened level with the rivulet for that money; nor could

65.

MEADOWS.

they, for that, be made fences : for one shilling a rod they might, I apprehend, be done
effectually, which is an addition of -   0 15 6
                                        _____
                                         £ 4 14 0

Nor could the ditches, perhaps, be
carried round level with the rivulet
(which they ought to be, the workmen
leading a dead water all round) for one
shilling a rod: for fourteen-pence I believe they might: this is a further addition of   -   -   -   -   -   0 10 6
                                    _____
                                     £ 5   4 6

Besides this three trunks, or arches, would
be wanted as an entrance, and for communications between the beds; the stuff, too, would
require to be set about : these, however, come
under the idea of annual and ordinary expences;
we may therefore say, that for the inconsider-
able purchase of five guineas an improvement
worth fifty or sixty pounds might be obtained.

Perhaps when a meadow is so situated that
the rivulet cannot be sunk below the moor, lay
the main drains into wells, dug at a convenient
distance from the rivulet, and pump the *remaining* water into it. One length of tree would
do, and a man would pump out a great quantity of water in a day; and what are a few days
                                     works

works compared with the difference between a
drained and an undrained meadow?

Perhaps a ftubborn quickfand might be
overcome by digging a well near it.

66.

FEBRUARY 8. It is an excellent cuftom of
the Norfolk farmer to erect *rubbing-pofts* in the
different parts of the inclofure he is feeding or
teathing; they keep the ftock from the fences,
and furnifh them no doubt with an agreeable,
and perhaps a falutary, amufement.

Some I fee draw the crown of a tree, with
the lower part of the boughs left on, into the
middle of the clofe: this is lefs trouble than
putting down a poft, is eafily rolled out of
the way of the plow, and feems to be ftill
more agreeable to the cattle.

67.

FEBRUARY 9. Mr. Arthur Bayfield (whofe
good fenfe and judicious management have repeatedly engaged my attention) fows the principal part of his wheat in four-furrow work,
with this peculiarity :—He fows only half the
feed before the plows. (See WHEAT, Vol. I.)

The firft plowman fets out a very wide
" back"; fo that the tops of the firft two fuc-

row

67.

SOWING
WHEAT.

rows do but barely touch each other. The feedſman follows, and ſows the remaining half of the ſeed in the trenches made by the firſt plow.—Another plowman follows, and, with a neat narrow furrow, covers the ſeed and makes up the ridges.

It was on my obſerving to him, the other day, the evenneſs with which his wheat comes up, that he told me his method of putting in the ſeed.

Farmers in general he thinks ſow too much of their ſeed on the warps, by which means the tops of the ridges have more than their proportion of ſeed; unleſs the ridges be made very narrow, which occaſions a loſs of labour.

Mr. B.'s four-furrow work is nearly as wide as the ſix-furrow ridges of ſome farmers; and it is impoſſible for wheat to come up more beautifully than his does this year.

68.

TURNEPS.

FEBRUARY 9. Laſt year, there were turneps ſold as high as 5*l.* an acre; a price ſeldom, if ever, before known in Norfolk. At the beginning of this ſeaſon, four pounds ten ſhillings, ſome ſay four guineas and a half, an acre was

re-

refufed for turneps—The fame turneps are now worth about three pounds.—Good turneps are fold for fifty fhillings, tolerable ones for forty fhillings.

The reafon for this rapid fall of turneps is twofold : the opennefs of the winter, and the fcarcity of bullocks, this year; owing to their high price at Michaelmas, and to the poverty of the farmers.

A. gives forty fhillings for tolerable ones, and is allowed to bring fome home; but he pulls and tends the reft himfelf (*A.* fays pulling and ftraw is worth twenty fhillings).

B. took in lean three-year-olds at two fhillings a week, but their owner would not continue : *B.* therefore fold him the turneps at fifty fhillings an acre (middling) ; *B.* to pull and tend ; but the purchafer to find ftraw (*B.* reckons pulling, &c. worth ten fhillings an acre.)

C. agreed (early in the feafon) with *P.* at three pounds; *P.* to pull, tend, and find ftraw ; which *C.* reckons at fifteen fhillings, viz. five fhillings the ftraw, and ten fhillings the attendance.

69.

**BULLOCKS
AT
TURNEPS.**

69.

FEBRUARY 9. It is a general obfervation, that in this remarkably warm open winter, fhed-bullocks have done very badly ; while bullocks abroad have done extremely well.—A perfon who is a competent judge in this matter in-ftances fome bullocks, which he faw the other day, that have fcarcely got any thing during feveral weeks they have been at turneps :— his remark was, that they fweat out as much as they lay on ; that their coats are continually wet ; their backs being covered with drops of fweat.

In cold winters, bullocks are obferved to do beft in fheds ; but they do not travel fo well to market as bullocks fatted abroad or in the open yard.

This being an interefting fubject, and of great importance to this and every other light land Diftrict, I have collected the particular practice of fuch individuals as bufinefs, or other circumftance, has thrown in my way.

Mr. Barber, at Baftwick, (a fomewhat tender foil) gives his bullocks turneps in bins in the open yard. At Stanninghall, (a dry firm foil) he keeps them wholly abroad, fhifting them every day, or every two or three days, giving them ftraw in a moveable four-wheeled ftraw-rack.

Mr.

Mr. Thomas Seago, of Hanworth, throws
the beginning of the feafon, and afterwards
chops the turneps, and gives them in bins in
the ftraw-yard.

Mr. John Hylton, of Felmingham, fats them
abroad.

Mr. Arthur Bayfield, of Antingham—Abroad
in the day ; and, if near home, puts them into
the ftraw-yard at night ; but rather than drive
them any diftance, backward and forward,
keeps them abroad altogether, with very little
ftraw. Says, that his land being light requires
to be trodden. Thinks that bullocks kept wholly
in the yard fhould have their turneps in covered bins,—a kind of double narrow fhed acrofs
the yard ; for in cafe of froft and fnowy weather,
the turneps given them over-night, in open
bins, are frequently left untouched, and are
obliged to be taken out, and replaced with frefh
ones, the next morning.

Mr. Robins Cook, of Felmingham—Abroad
in the day; in the ftraw-yard at night; no
turneps in the yard, nor ftraw in the field.—
Says, they eat the ftraw greedily on their
coming into the yard in the evening :—ufed to
give them ftraw upon the headlands ; not fcat-

tered about thin, but all in one place, so as to be able to make a little manure; but this was only because he had not a spare yard to "stow" them in.

At Albro' (a more tender soil) he used generally to graze half a dozen bullocks in the house: he attended them himself, chopping all their turneps. They eat, he says, (contrary to common opinion) as many turneps in the house as they do abroad: six of them more than a load a day. Four o'clock in the afternoon, he says, is their principal hour of eating:—used to rack them up with the tops; the offal thrown to the buds.

Mrs. Swan, of Suffield, fats them abroad.

Mr. Forster, of Bradfield—Abroad; with straw scattered under the hedges.

Mr. Jonathan Bond, of Walsham—Fourteen abroad.

Mr. Henry Helsden, of Antingham, fats them at *two years old*:—has no meadows, and cannot keep them till three years old. Has them always at "high keep:" being from the time they are dropt either at turneps, clover, or in the stubbles:—fats them abroad.

Mr. James Helsden, of Suffield—Sixteen abroad.

Mr.

Mr. F. Le Neve, of Bradfield, has ten abroad, and two cows " by the head."—Why keep the cows in the house and the rest abroad ? " Be- " cause the cows are backwarder than the " other, and I shall be able to bring them " forward by good tending in the shed."

Mr. John Joy, of Walsham, has five Scots; one four-year-old home-bred; eight three-year-old ditto; one two-year-old ditto; and two cows with their calves by their sides.

The four-year-old home-bred is a beautiful bullock, and very forward : — the three-year-olds, being more given to growing, do not fat so fast. Mr. Joy is clearly of opinion, that a four-year-old home-bred will beat any Scot.

The cows and calves are quite new to me; though Mr. Joy says, that " running calves" are, and have been, very common things in this country. They are sent up to London with the cows, and have been known to fetch as high as six or seven pounds a piece *. The cows are very old; yet notwithstanding the calves draw

---

* I was afterwards told that a gentleman near Norwich sold a year-and-half-old calf for ten pounds! It was offered to the butcher at nine pounds, or at five shillings a stone : he accepted the latter. On weighing it, the four quarters weighed forty stone! But it seems to be well understood that " running calves weigh like lead."

them,

69.

RUNNING
CALVES.

them, the wonderful effect of turneps is such that they are getting fat apace: one of the calves (a heifer) is as sleek as a mole; and has already dropt a dug of confiderable fize: the other is not fo forward; its mother being very old, and gives little milk. The calves eat turneps as freely as the reft of the cattle. What an admirable end is this for old cows!

REARING
CATTLE.

Some of the three-year-olds, and the two-year-old, are fpayed heifers; but, through the negligence of the cutter, fome of them have not been clean fpayed, and are frequently running to bull; a circumftance which is of great hindrance to their fatting.

BULLOCKS
AT
TURNEPS.

Mr. Joy keeps his bullocks entirely abroad; giving them ftraw fcattered over the clofe; or, in hard weather, under the hedges: he never puts them into the yard at night; thinking that driving them backward and forward is prejudicial to their fatting.

FATTING
CATTLE.

Mr. Jonathan Bond, of South-Reps, has eight *two-year-olds* at turneps; generally grazing two-year-olds: this year they are rather backward; but expects they will reach about thirty ftone a piece with about fix weeks grafs. Two-year-olds he allows do not finifh fo early as the three-year-olds; but, if they be kept well from the

time

time they are dropt, they pay very well.   It is   69.
obfervable that the heifers are not only for-   FATTING
warder but larger than the fteers, though dropt   CATTLE.
at the fame time : they are open, and had the
bull about Chriftmas.

Mr. William Mann, of Bradfield, has fix *two-
year-olds* at turneps ; they are doing very well ;
and, with a little grafs, will be very good meat.
They were early calves (between Michaelmas
and Chriftmas) and have a mixture of the Suffolk breed in them.   One of them (*a dun, but*   BREED OF
horned) will weigh upwards of forty ftone : this   CATTLE.
is one inftance in favour of the Suffolk breed.

Mr. Baker of South-Reps keeps his beauti-   BULLOCKS
ful heifers bought at St. Faith's (See MIN. 27.)   AT
entirely abroad ; giving ftraw under the hedges ;   TURNEPS.
and fhifting them every day : they have thus
far done well indeed.

70.

FEBRUARY 9.   In riding over the eftate, I   REARING
have alfo made a point of collecting informa-   CALVES.
tion refpecting the rearing of calves, a fubject
of confiderable importance in every county.

Mr. Barber rears none : he fats his calves, and
kills them for the Pad-market at Norwich.
(See CATTLE, Vol. I.)

Mr. Thomas Shepherd, of North-Reps, rears
none : but fhrewdly obferves, that he cares not

how

70.
REARING
CALVES.

how many his neighbours rear. Mr. S. (as well as Mr. B.) is a judge of stock, and a frequenter of fairs and markets; and finds, no doubt, he can buy young stock cheaper than he can rear them.

Mr. —, of —, gives milk once a day (look but indifferently) with turnep-tops and oats and bran mixed together in a trough, and hay in a rack (the hay bad):—begins about Christmas.— Says, that one early calf is worth two backward ones; and instances it from last year's experience.

Mr. William Barnard—Milk twice a day with bran only (look well):—gives neither turneps nor tops, till they are a month or five weeks old.

Mr. John Hylton rears twelve to fifteen (he has a marsh)—reared three this season in August; they are now almost as large as yearlings. These had milk four months; in common he gives milk twice a day, with turnep-tops, for two months; and once a day for as much longer as he has milk: if milk be scarce, he makes milk-porridge.

Mr. William Sewell rears eight or nine.— Says, that he has had calves get quite fat on turneps and hay, when he has had bullocks in the yard; and the calves have been, of course, well tended;

tended : much, he fays, depends upon attendance.

Mr. Robins Cook rears about twelve ; keeps them at the teat twice a day, till three or four weeks old ; and once a day, till three or four weeks older : then offers them the pail ; but, if they refufe, or are difficult to learn to drink at that age, he leaves them to take their chance at turneps, hay, and water.

Generally lofes three or four a year in the gargut *.

Mr. Arthur Bayfield rears twelve to fifteen ; ufed to rear eighteen or twenty.—Takes them off the cow at a fortnight or three weeks old : finds no difficulty in learning them to drink at that age :—keeps them at milk twice a day, until ten or twelve weeks old ; with turneps, turnep-tops and hay ; but no bran, &c. Cuts the turnep-tops, to prevent their being littered about.

Mr. Jonathan Bond, of North-Walfham, keeps eight cows ; rears ten calves : buys them chiefly of the drovers :—drove calves very dear this year ; from twelve to fifteen

* " Gargut," or " murrain," taken fuddenly : a fort of mortification between the fkin and the flefh : the fkin upon the part is faid to be " as hard and harfh as the crackling of roaft pork."

fhillings

shillings at a fortnight old. Gives them turneps, hay, and about three pints of milk, once a
day. Says, that too much milk makes them
neglect the turneps; but keep them short of
milk, and they foon take to them: turns
them to grafs about the middle of April; by
which time he reckons they cost him about
twenty shillings a head; and fays, that a bud of
a year old may be bought for twenty-five shillings. But he adds, that bringing them up
within himfelf, he does not mifs the charge of
them.

Generally lofes two or three every year by
the gargut.

Mr. James Helfden, of Suffield—Eight cows:
rears about ten calves; fats fixteen to twenty
bullocks (his farm of the middle fize): gives
his calves hay, turneps, and milk twice a day,
while young; after ten weeks or three months,
once a day: begins about the middle of March
to put his oldeft out into a piece of turneps,
three or four hours in the middle of the day,
to play about and eat the turnep-tops.

Mr. ———— keeps eight cows; ufually rears
eight calves; but turneps being fcarce, he rears
none this year, meaning to buy eight or ten buds
at the fales.

Mr.

Mr. John Waller brings up fix: takes them off at two or three days or a week old: milk twice a day as long as he can give it; and then once a day as long as he has it; gives alfo hay, turneps, and bran; but no oats.

Mr. John Joy takes them off at about a fortnight old: milk twice a day for about a month, and once a day for a month or fix weeks longer; until they can be turned out in the fpring into a pightle of turneps: alfo gives them turneps, hay, and barley-ftraw, which, by way of a change, they eat as well as hay. Mr. Joy generally lofes fome every year in the gargut. He fays, as foon as they are dead there is a jelly formed between the fkin and the flefh: they are taken fuddenly, and die prefently after being taken: fome bleed and rowel them with " gargut-root" (*helleborus fœtidus*) in their tail or dewlap; feldom recover.

Mr.——, of South-Reps, begins between Michaelmas and Chriftmas.—Takes them from the cow about three weeks or a month old, and endeavours to make them " lufty;"—gives them about half a pint of milk once a day, with hay, oats, and bran; *but no turneps.* I afked him why? He gave me for anfwer, that his father, mother, himfelf, nor any of the family, had

70.

REARING CALVES.

GARGUT.

had ever given their calves turneps :—he added however, that oats and bran are heartier food; and that the milk is enough for them without turneps : his calves, no doubt, look well, and so do his buds and two-year-olds. Afked him if he did not find oats and bran expenfive. He faid, that the fix which he has now, have eaten about three bufhels of oats, and two bufhels of bran, in about fix weeks; which time they have been from the cows; they being now about ten weeks old. This is no great expence; not being above three-pence a head a week (*if he be accurate*). He fpeaks in raptures of oats for calves. He keeps them at milk until the tur-neps are gone; when he begins to make cheefe.

Mr. William Mann, of Bradfield, has already eleven this year : begins between Michaelmas and Chriftmas : lets them fuck ten days : milk twice a day for a month or five weeks after-wards; and once a day until they do well upon hay and turneps; or until he can turn them out a few hours in the day into a turnep-clofe: Thinks that the milk is of little ufe to them, after they begin to eat turneps well : gives them the turneps whole; only tailing them, and freeing them a little from dirt : gives no

oats

oats nor bran: he is remarkable for fine young stock: he is very affiduous in keeping his calves well-littered.

Mr. Henry Helfden, of Antingham, begins before Chriftmas: takes them off at a fortnight old; fometimes at three weeks; by which time they get "rarely ftrong", but do not take to the pail fo well: gives them new milk twice a day for about a fortnight; and fkimmed twice a day for a fortnight longer; and about three pints or two quarts once a day afterward; until the weather be warm enough to turn them out entirely to turneps: gives them the turneps in the houfe, whole, thrown upon the litter: learns them by cutting off the crown, breaking up the furface, and pouring milk into the inequalities. If hay be fcarce or bad, gives a few oats and bran: look very well.

71.

FEBRUARY 10. Young Swann, of Suffield, had, the winter before this, fome of the beft turneps in the country. Seeing him, laft fummer, fowing fome in what appeared to me a flovenly manner, the furface being covered with chick-weed, groundfel, charlock, and other rubbifh pulled up by the harrows, I afked him

71.

SOWING
TURNEPS.

why he did not give his land another earth before he fowed it. He anfwered, that the land
was not foul; and that he, purpofely, let the
feed-weeds get to a head : having found, from
the experience of two or three years back,
that his turneps fucceeded beft when the feed
was fown in that manner : faying, that he believed the " wreck" fhaded the young plants,
and kept the fly from them. I afked him if
the rubbifh was not in the way of the hoe : he
faid, not much; for being young, and tender, it withers away to little or nothing, before the plants be fit for the hoe.

Two or three days ago, I examined this clofe
of turneps; the plants are *thinner* than one
would wifh, (perhaps owing to their being badly hoed) but there is not a "*fqually patch*" in
the whole piece.

There may be two advantages arifing from
letting the foil lie fome time before the laft
plowing : it acquires a degree of texture, and
moiftnefs, favourable to the infant plants;
and is prevented, by the dead weeds, from
being, afterwards, run together by heavy rains.

72.

CATTLE AT
TURNEPS.

FEBRUARY 10. Afking Mr. A. Bayfield, if
his cattle were not fometimes *choaked* with
turneps;

turneps; he faid no; he never loft but one in his life. I afked him if he ufed a rope: he faid he had one; but never ufed it, except the time he loft his cow. If falt and water will not cure them, he pours down a hornful of *falt and melted greafe*; fuch as hog's-lard or any kind of common greafe. This he never (except the once) found fail.

This is an idea worth preferving: warm oil and falt would perhaps have the fame effect.

Mr. Bayfield, who may be called one of the moft orthodox farmers in Eaft Norfolk, is clear in that a *three-year-old* " homebred" will fat as kindly as a *four-year-old* " marfhlander" or " Scot."

He inftanced it, to-day, in a three-year-old of his own bringing up, which he bought, when a calf, of the calf-drovers; and which evidently difcovers a near relationfhip to the fhort-horned breed. He is now at turneps with the reft of the three-year-old Norfolk ftock; but, notwith-ftanding he was at head keep all laft fummer, he is neverthelefs ftill a rawboned grow-ing fteer; while the Norfolks are as foft as moles, and feveral of them begin to drop their points. The Norfolks will fat to from forty to forty-four ftone; the Lincolnfhire, if

he

72.

BREED OF
CATTLE.

he were to be kept another year, would reach at least seventy.

But this peculiar quality of the Norfolk stock does not depend on size; for Mr. B. says, that a three-year-old Scot (still smaller perhaps) is as difficult to fat as a three-year-old marsh-lander. He says, it is bad management to attempt it; but keep them on until they be four years old, and they will make famous " over-year" bullocks: adding, that at that age they will generally pay for keeping over-year.

73.

FARM-YARD
MANAGEM.

FEBRUARY 10. It seems to be a received idea among the Norfolk farmers, that the straw which is *eaten* by cattle is in a manner wasted as to manure. Mr. S. I remember, as an argument in favour of his plan of fatting pigs loose in the open yard, said what a rare parcel of muck they make, compared with what neat beasts would have made from the same straw. " A parcel of lean hungry stock, says he, come " into a yard and eat up all the straw : see there " lies a bundle of straw as big as a man can carry."

Mr. B. the other day, intimated the same idea : however, on putting the question, he ac-knowledged

knowledged that a little dung and a little trodden ſtraw do well together.

In the north of England the farmers make
their cattle eat almoſt every blade of their
ſtraw, ſo that they have ſcarcely any left to litter their ſtalls with. Give a Yorkſhire and a
Norfolk farmer equal quantities of ſtraw, the
Yorkſhireman would keep more cattle, and
carry out his dung at a leſs expence; whilſt
the Norfolkman would make more muck.
But quere, Whether is the manure better or
worſe? and quere, Which of the two, upon the
whole, is the better management?

Much perhaps may depend on the quality of
the ſoil to be manured. A large quantity of
long dung would, perhaps, for ſtiff cold land,
be better than a ſmaller quantity of ſhort. But
perhaps, for a *loamy* ſoil, ſhort dung is the beſt.

74.

FEBRUARY 12. In my rides, this winter, I
have endeavoured to inform myſelf reſpecting
the *winter-management of ſtore-cattle.*

Mr. A. Bayfield's yearlings and milch-cows
follow his bullocks, and lie in the par-yard at
night: his two-year-olds, and dry cows, go
abroad in the meadows, &c. in the day, and are

K 3   put

put into the par at night: they have not yet had a turnep. Mr. B. fays, however, he fhall now begin to give them fome; for if young ftock are ftarved in the fpring, they are ftinted for the whole year. Cows in calf, he alfo juftly obferves, will do with lefs keep than any other ftock, until within a few weeks of their calving.

Mr. John Hylton.—His turneps failing, he has few bullocks this year; and thefe he buys turneps for; and brings home fome for his cows. Neither his two-year-olds, nor even his buds, have yet broken a turnep this year; he having the principal part of the few turneps he grew ftill upon the ground; faying, that he fhould be diftracted if he had not a plenty of feed in the fpring; fo as to be able to favour his ollands, until they got a good bite, and the ground covered. A good farmer never ftarves his ftock.

Mr. Jonathan Bond, of Walfham, makes three divifions in his par-yard: his buds; his two-year-olds; and his cows. Says, that the gargut, fome people think, comes from the buds being "horned" by the larger cattle; but fays, he does not believe that there is any thing in it; for notwithftanding his precaution, he has loft three this year by the gargut.

Mr.

Mr. James Helfden, of Suffield, ftows his buds in a battoned ftack-yard, at the end of a barn. He always takes care to place fuch corn in this ftacking-place, as will require to be "barned" the beginning of the feafon; fo that he has it every year free in time enough for a "calves par" (a good plan).

Mr. John Joy, of Walfham, has now fix or eight cows, ten two-year-olds, and eleven buds follow his bullocks: his young ftock had no turneps till after Chriftmas.

Mr. Edward Bird, of Plumftead, has his two-year-olds out at keep as followers at one fhilling a week: they have plenty of turneps, and go into a par-yard at night.

Mr. William Mann, of Bradfield, has eight buds out at keep for ten-pence halfpenny a head a week. They have their fill of frefh turneps, every day; going "at head;" not as followers. He grazes his two-year-olds, this year: in general he fells them in the fpring to be kept over-year; but this year they being forward he fats them himfelf, and they are doing extremely well.

74.
WINTER MAN. OF CATTLE.

WINTER KEEP ON TURNEPS.

75.

75.

FEBRUARY 12. Every foil feems to have its own ftock.

In Lincolnſhire the foil is rich; the grafs long and foft; and the ſheep there are large and in-active: In Norfolk the foil is lefs productive; the grafs ſhort and hard; and the ſheep light and active.

A ſheep-walk, in this neighbourhood, ftocked jointly with thefe two *varieties* of ſheep, con-tains alfo a *variety* of foil: one part, lying low, is a rich, moiſt foil; bearing a foft rich grafs: another lies high, and is a drier lighter foil; bearing a hard benty grafs.

The prefent ftock were principally bred in this ground; and, whether Norfolk or Lincoln-ſhire, were many of them perhaps dropt near the fame ſpot on the fame day; neverthelefs turn them mifcellaneoufly into this ground and they will, in a ſhort time, feparate themfelves, even to a ſheep; the Lincolnſhires * drawing off to the Lincolnſhire foil; and the Norfolks to their own dry fandy loam: and, whilſt there continues a plenty of grafs in both parts, the two breeds will keep themfelves as diſtinct and feparate as rooks and pigeons.

* Including a mixture of the Huntingdon and Leiceſter-ſhire breeds.

76.

76.

FEBRUARY 12. The long-wooled ewes (fee laft MIN.) have lambed with great difficulty, this year. The fhepherd has been obliged to affift the major part of them.

Thefe ewes were *therefore* kept at grafs until after they had dropt their lambs; the fhepherd having been taught by experience that ewes at turneps are liable to mortify, upon receiving the fmalleft injury in lambing; much more liable than at grafs.

77.

FEBRUARY 12. There feems to be fomething peculiar either to the air or the foil of this county. The face of a ditch, though formed of a dead ill-coloured fubftratum of mould, becomes, in a few years, black and rich in a high degree; fo as to be coveted by the farmer almoft as much as dung. When he re-makes his fence he carefully faves this rich, or rather enriched, mould (for according to the cuftom of ditchers the face is always made of the worft mould): or, if he throw down a fence, he as affiduoufly preferves both the face and the back for the bottoms of his farm-yard or dung-hills.

Does not this incident afford us an idea applicable to the enrichment of the foil in general?

ral? Is it not highly probable, that by ridg-
ing up a fallow so as to resemble the banks of
ditches, or as nearly as could be done with im-
plements and horses, the soil would thereby
be meliorated?

It might certainly be done in this way:
with a common plow, gather up the soil into
four-furrow or six-furrow ridges, and afterwards, with a heavy double-mould-board plow
and a strong team, force up the whole, by degrees,
into high, sharp, angular ridges; which, in due
time, might be reversed in a similar manner *.

78.

FEBRUARY 16. Last night being uncommonly severe, by wind frost and snow, I rose
early this morning, to observe the effects of such
unusual severity upon the young lambs.

I expected to have found them shivering
and setting up their backs, pinched through with
cold: instead of which they were prancing
against the trees, and running races in a stack-
yard upon some hay which the ewes had pulled
out, as if the sun had shone out in the middle

---

* This would likewise give an opportunity of deepening
the soil; and of forming, if practicable, a fresh pan.
(See SOIL, Vol. I).

of

of April!—not one pitiful tone, nor a crooked back, among near a hundred and fifty.

The ewes have been well-kept all winter; and have now plenty of turneps, and a rough hay-ſtack to run to. This ſhews the effect of good keep: the ſhepherd very properly obſerved, that let lambs have plenty of milk, and they neither fear nor care for any weather.

What a pleaſure, and how profitable, to do well by ſtock! Had theſe ewes been ill-kept, numbers of lambs muſt have been loſt during the laſt fortnight of ſevere weather; whereas, with their preſent fluſh of milk, ſcarcely one of ſeven or eight ſcore has ſuffered by it.

79.

FEBRUARY 23. A conſiderable part of a farm which lies toward the coaſt, being hilly and very badly ſoiled—more eſpecially the tops and ſides of the hills, which have always been full of rabbits in ſpite of all endeavours to deſtroy them—the tenants laſt year applied for leave to convert this part, about ninety acres, into a rabbit-warren. Leave was given, and an allowance made them of half the eſtimated expence of raiſing a ſodwall fence round theſe ninety acres.

The

The fence is nearly finifhed, and the warren has this year turned out beyond expectation: it is valued, by one who ought to be the beft judge of its worth, at forty pounds a year; which is nine fhillings an acre.

As the part of a farm, thefe ninety acres are not worth five fhillings an acre: at the prefent price of barley, they are not worth more than four fhillings an acre.

Thus, for ten pound a *real* improvement of twenty pound a year has been made and fecured; for the warrener will, through neceffity, hereafter keep the fence in repair.

The fence is made about four feet high, and three feet thick; faced with green-fward; and capped with furze, fo as to project eight or ten inches over the face. Some of it was done for a fhilling a rod; but the fpring putting in, fourteen or fifteen pence a rod of feven yards was obliged to be given.

A neighbouring warrener, this winter, gives nine-pence for the wall, without the capping; which he does not mean to put on till the wall be thoroughly fettled. This is very judicious: feveral rods of that abovementioned fhot down in different places.

There are feveral patches in the vallies and fome on the tops of the hills which have ufually

been

been tilled. Some of thefe were laft year, and fome of them ought to be every year, culti-vated for the rabbits : thus, when the grafs gets foul or moffy, plow it up; fallow; fow turnep-feed for prefent feed (they will not let rape get up), and to prepare the foil for barley and grafs-feed the enfuing year. Thus a re-gular fucceffion of feed might be kept up.

The way the Norfolk warreners take to de-ftroy eagles, kites, and other birds of prey is natural and fimple. Thefe birds are fhy and fufpicious : they like to fettle where they can have a clear view round them for fome di-ftance : a naked ftump or a hillock is their fa-vourite refting-place. The warreners, therefore, raife mounds of earth of a conical form in dif-ferent parts of the warren, and place fteel traps upon the points of thofe artificial hil-locks.

80.

FEBRUARY 28. About two months ago I took a fample of wheat to North-Walfham market; with an intent to make myfelf ac-quainted with the bufinefs of the corn-markets in this country.

North-Walfham is an afternoon-market (fee MARKETS, Vol. I.) ; corn all fold by fample; fome some in the market-place; but chiefly at the Inns.

Having made my election of a miller, and finding that he " quartered" at the Bear, I went to his room (he was not in till near six) and shewed him my sample: namely, about two handfulls, put in a piece of brown paper; which, agreeable to the fashion of the country, was gathered up in the hand, and tied with a string, in the manner of a pounce-bag.

He asked the price; I told him the best he gave that day: he said a guinea was the highest: I had previously understood that a guinea was " the top of the market," and sold it him at that price. He asked how much there was of it; I told him about fifteen coombs. He marked the name, the quantity, and the price upon the bulge of the paper, and the business was done.

His room was set round with farmers, who, the conversation being audible, were witnesses to the bargain.

Another sample I took to his mill; wishing to see the construction and economy of a Norfolk mill;—and afterwards sold him the remainder of the quantity; namely, about thirty coombs.

Not

Not having received for the two former parcels, he defired I would give him a week's notice before I called upon him for the money. —Laft week I gave him notice, and this evening I have been to receive it.

His room was full of farmers, fmoaking their pipes, and drinking *punch*; excepting one, with whom he was doing bufinefs at a fide-table.

My turn prefently fucceeded; and we agreed the account thus:

1782.
Jan. 10. 15 Co. 3 Bs. " bare;" or 15
            Co. full meafure, at 21s. a
            coomb, or 21*l.* a laft of
            21 Co.   -   -   -   15 15   0
    26. 16 Co. 3. at 21*l.* 10*s.* - 17   2 11
Feb. 9. 15 Co. 3. at 22*l.* 10*s.* - 16 17   6
    16. 14 Co. 3. at ditto   -   15 16   1

        63 Coombs bare   £. 65 11   6
From which he deducted 1*s.* a laft (of
21 Co.) for what he called " carriage," being a perquifite to his fervants,   -   -   -   -   0   3   0

                    £. 65   8   6

Having received the amount, *figned a receipt*, and thrown down a fhilling towards the liquor, the bufinefs was finally concluded.

81.

81.

81.

PLANTING.

FEBRUARY 28. Mr. A. Bayfield aſking me
if I would not have ſome " wood-layer" put
into the places where the pollards (*oaken* pollards) were taking out againſt Suffield Common,
I told him yes, he might have a little oak-layer.
" Why," ſays he, with his uſual coolneſs and
good ſenſe, "would not a little aſhen-layer think
" you, Sir, be better? I have known aſhes thrive
" rarely well after oaks, but have ſeldom known
" oak-layer take where an oaken timber or
" pollard has been taken down."

This is a valuable obſervation. It has long
been obſerved, that an old orchard ſeldom
bears planting as an orchard a ſecond time :
nor is wheat after wheat, equal to pulſe or
graſs, after wheat; or wheat after pulſe or
graſs.

82.

BREEDING
SHEEP.

MARCH 1. In drawing off ſome mixt-breed
hoggards for ſale, it is obſervable, that thoſe
between long-wooled ewes and a Norfolk ram
are handſomer ſtock, and forwarder, than thoſe
which have been bred from Norfolk ewes by
a Leiceſterſhire ram; and that in *this* caſe the
ewes have always great difficulty in lambing.

83.

83.

MARCH 2. Afking a fenfible intelligent far-   TURNEPS.
mer, who rears a large proportion of calves to
the number of cows he keeps, how he gets
milk for his calves, he anfwered, "turneps give
the cows fuch a flufh of milk the calves feldom
want."

Turneps, he fays, are fine things for cows: COWS.
they fcour and cleanfe them, and fet them forward in the fpring, when they come to be
turned out to grafs; adding, that cows kept at
dry meat, not only lofe their milk in winter,
but the beft part of the fpring-grafs is gone
before they get to the full of their milk.

This may be one reafon why cows which
have no turneps do fo badly in this country;
whofe hay is dry and ftrawy; and the grafs far
from being of a fucculent quality.

84.

MARCH 3. This morning I ftood a confi-   BULLOCKS
derable time to fee fome fatting heifers "break"   BREAKING
their turneps. Being all at feed, they let me   TURNEPS.
ftand among them unnoticed; and having
been about four months at this employment,
they performed it with a dexterity, which af-
forded me confiderable entertainment.

VOL. II.   L   In

In theory, it feems difficult for an animal, deftitute of paws, and with teeth only in one jaw, to get to pieces a turnep, which he cannot contain in his mouth; more efpecially when it is thrown loofe upon hard ground: one is led to imagine, that it would roll or flide away from him, as he attempted to bite it; but no fuch thing happens. I faw feveral turneps begun and finifhed without being moved an inch from the place they fell in from the cart. Had the bullocks been furnifhed with paws, or even hands, to hold them with, they could not have done it more dexteroufly.

Having fmelled out a turnep they like, they prefs it hard againft the ground with the gums of the upper jaw, applied upon the top of the turnep, toward the fide which lies fartheft from them, fteadying it with the upper lip: then inferting their teeth on the oppofite fide and biting fomewhat upward, they take off a fmall piece, proportioned, in fome meafure, to the fize of the turnep. Having tafted the firft bite, and fmelt at the broken part, they take another flice; perhaps not thicker or larger than a crown-piece: and thus continue to take off, or rather fcoop out, flice after flice until nothing is left but the tail of the turnep, and a fhell a fhell of rind, in the fhape of a fleeting difh, and of a fimilar thicknefs ; carefully fmelling, between the bites, at the part they intend next to take off.

The crown and upper part of the rind they eat, but feem ftudioufly to leave the tail, and the under part of the rind, which had ftood in contact with the foil.

If a bullock break off a larger piece than he can gather up with his tongue as his head hangs downwards, he lifts up his head, and fhoots out his nofe and neck, horizontally, until he gets it between his grinders. Crowns, and very fmall turneps, he treats in the fame way.

This part of the bufinefs, however, he performs fomewhat clumfily ; and it is, probably, in this act that a fmall turnep, or a piece of a large one, glancing from between the teeth, gets into the throat and caufes fufflation, or " choaking".

The tongue of a bullock is lefs flexible, and worfe adapted to the purpofe of turning over and adjufting a morfel of folid aliment, than are the tongues of carnivorous animals, or thofe of the human fpecies. The natural food of graminivorous animals is foft, and no way liable to flip from between the teeth in grind-

L 2

84.

BULLOCKS BREAKING TURNEPS.

ing; their tongues being adapted to the purpofe of gathering up their aliment, rather
than to that of affifting them in chewing it.

85.

TIMBER.

MARCH 3. In thinning timber-trees, whether in hedges, or in open grounds, it is generally advifable, when two trees grow amicably
together, their branches intermixing, and their
tops of equal height, forming as it were one
top, to leave them both ftanding : for, if one of
them be taken away, the beauty of the other is
fpoilt, and its atmofphere changed : the evil
effect of this treatment I have frequently obferved.

But when one of them has got the fuperiority fo far as to overhang the other, it is generally right to take the underling away, and thereby add beauty and ftrength to the mafter-plant.

Twin timbers, however,—more particularly
double ftems growing from the fame ftub,—are
dangerous to horned cattle. I have lately
heard of more than one accident by trees growing fo near together that cattle could juft get
their horns through between them ; and having
got them there could not find the fame way to

ex-

extricate them; but falling down in the struggle, were strangled. I have since heard of a horse being lost in a similar manner *.

86.

MARCH 5. Mr. John Waller, of Antingham, shewed me, to-day, seven ewes with fourteen lambs by their sides: and a fifteenth, which he gave to his boy, is also alive.

Last year he had nine lambs from three ewes; eight of which he actually reared, and are now alive; namely, six with the ewes, and two "cotts" or "cotties" (a name for lambs reared by hand; a common practice here).

His sheep are, in appearance, of the true Norfolk breed. He says he has had the breed eight or nine years, and they have seldom had less than two lambs a piece. *He keeps them well.*

The Norfolk ewes, in general, bring but one lamb.

* A still more singular accident occurred to my own knowledge. A mare, probably in fighting with the flies, struck her hind-foot into a cleft between two stems of whitethorn, open at the bottom but narrowing upward; and being a high-bred, spirited mare, struggled until she tore her foot off; leaving it behind her in the cleft!

87.   87.

March 5. When the white-thorn is dead thro'
age or improper treatment, or from being over-
hung by trees or ftub-wood, it is difficult to get
young layer to " take" in the old bank.   There
are two things againft it ; the drynefs of the
bank ; and its having been already *cropped.*

Thefe two objections are in a great meafure
removed, with little inconveniency, or additional expence, by throwing the bank entirely
down, about Michaelmas ; letting it lie *fallow*
all winter ; tabling the new ditch the latter
end of February ; and putting in the layer,
and finifhing the fence, the beginning of
March : for, by this means, the mould gets
a thorough drenching, and receives the benefit
of a winter's expofure to the froft and fnow.

There are generally roots and ftubs in an
old ditch-bank fufficient to pay (in this county)
for the labour of throwing it down ; and the
difference between making a new ditch and
vamping up the old one, is not more than twopence a rod.

This Minute arifes from a tenant's being defirous
to remake a ditch, which is loaded with ftub-
wood of forty or fifty years growth ; and which
                                                        has

has fo totally deftroyed the quick, that frefh layer would be wanted from end to end.

On examining the bank I found that, from the cover of the pollards and ftub-wood, it is, even now, as dry as chalk; and entirely occupied by roots and fibres of various forts. I therefore advifed him to let it remain until Michaelmas, and treat it in the manner above defcribed.

He acceded to this the rather, as it is a plan which is far from being theoretical in Norfolk, being, I find, frequently practifed.

88.

MARCH 5. Riding acrofs Felmingham Heath, to-day, I obferved a piece of new ditch-bank, out of the face of which young furzes were fhooting, in the place where quick-fets are ufually put in; but without any being amongft them.

Looking round, I perceived that this was not a mere experiment; for the neighbouring hedges (of a fort of an encroachment) were of the fame fhrub; and many of them invulnerable fences; even againft the heath ftock. One which had been recently cut in the face (with a few left on the top as a blind) was as

L 4   thight

thight as a wall. In general, however, they were getting much too old; fome of them dying; and others thin at the bottom.

I am nevertheleſs fully convinced that a furze-hedge, *with proper treatment*, is, upon a light unproductive foil, a fufficient and eligible fence.

89.

MARCH 7. This morning, went to fee *the method of cutting reed*.

The time of cutting reed does not commence until Chriſtmas; and continues till the young ſhoots begin to appear: the fap is now beginning to rife; the ſtems, below the water, being already green.

The cutters have a boat to carry them from the banks to the " reed-rond"; which, in this cafe, lies at a ſmall diſtance from the ſhore.

Some they cut ſtanding in the boat; fome ſtanding on a plank, laid partially, or wholly, upon the mud and roots of reed, matted intimately together.

The workmen cut it upwards, gathering the reed in the left hand and arm under-handed, with fickles (reaping-hooks are too ſlippery for the reed) as much below the water, confe-quently

quently as near the root, as may be; it being
an idea, even unto a proverb, that one inch
below the water is worth two above it; for the
part which now appears green changes to a
blackifh-brown, and becomes as hard as horn;
whereas that which grows above the water is
brittle, and of a more perifhable nature.

Having encumbered their boat they pufh it
to the fhore, and make up the reed into
fheaves (with thumbands made of ftraw) of
fuch a fize that five of them will make a fathom of fix feet in circumference: (fometimes the fheaves are made fix to a fathom)
fixty of thofe fathoms are a load; and a hundred and twenty are termed a hundred of
reed; worth about three pounds.

The matts of roots frequently feparate in
cutting the reed, and float about the water,
ftill propagating reeds in fmall clumps; not
larger, perhaps, at firft than the top of a
bufhel.

This feems to be the fpeedieft way of propagating reed; namely, feparate the beds of roots;
drag them to different parts of the water; and
fatten them with ftakes, until the roots get
hold of the bottom.

The ftarlings have done confiderable damage to this patch of reed: the outfides look
fair;

89.

STARLINGS
ENEMIES
TO REED. .

fair; but the infides of the clumps are very much broken down, by their roofting among it; more particularly while it was green, before it had received a firmnefs of ftem to bear them. I have feen thoufands at once light among it. In the fens, the reed-men are great enemies to thefe birds; and (if one may judge from the proportional damage they have done in Suffield-pond) with great reafon.

90.

HEDGES.

MARCH 8. I have at length nearly finished fetting out this year's wood and ditching.

In the courfe of the feafon I have made the following obfervations, and have endeavoured to adhere to the following rules refpecting timber-trees and pollards in hedges.

HEDGE ROW
TIMBER.

In regard to TIMBER-TREES, however, I have not been able to purfue entirely the line of conduct I have laid down from this and laft year's experience: it may, neverthelefs, be right, while the fubject is full and frefh in my mind, to minute my prefent ideas on this important department of rural economy.

I am clearly of opinion, that all fuch timber-trees as are now decaying; *alfo* fuch as are full-grown, though not yet decaying, but are fo fituated as to overhang or otherwife

crowd

crowd the neighbouring ſtands or timberlings, or the young timber-trees which are in a more youthful and growing ſtate ; *alſo* ſuch part of the growing timbers themſelves, as, by ſtanding too cloſe, crowd and check each other, ſhould be marked and ſold at the preſent market-prices ; though theſe prices may be ſomewhat below par.

For if to the intereſt of the money, which would ariſe from ſuch ſale, be added the decreaſe of value, or the injury incurred by ſuffering timber of the above deſcription to remain ſtanding, the proprietor of ſuch timber is loſing annually from five to ten per cent. of its preſent value, by ſuch improper conduct. Thus ſuppoſe an eſtate has five thouſand pounds worth of timber upon it, bearing the above deſcription ; its proprietor is loſing from three to five hundred pounds a year by ſuffering it to remain ſtanding.

Whenever the price ſhall hereafter riſe to what may be eſteemed a fair ſelling price, then, but not till then, falls ought to be made of all *full-grown* timbers ; *alſo* of ſuch growing trees as, from their ſituation, are or may ſoon become injurious to each other. Much, no doubt, depends on embracing the lucky moment of ſale ; nevertheleſs, perhaps, more money

90.

HEDGE ROW
TIMBER.

money has been loſt than gained, by ſpecu-
lating nicely in this delicate matter.

The dead wood and hanging boughs of all
timber-trees left ſtanding ought to be removed;
and the younger timberlings trained in ſuch
manner as will induce them to take the de-
ſired outline, and riſe in the moſt profitable
form.   Oaks in hedges naturally grow low
and ſpreading, doing more injury to the hedge
and the adjoining incloſures than their own
value, in that form, can ever repay; whereas
tall well-headed oaks are at once ornamental
and valuable to an eſtate;—without being, in
any conſiderable degree, injurious to the occupier.

Being fully convinced of this, from almoſt
daily obſervation, I am clearly of opinion, that
every opportunity ought to be taken to propagate oaks in hedges; not by putting in young
plants where old trees have been taken down;
but by ſearching for, and preſerving, young
ſeedling plants (more eſpecially where a hedge
is cut down), and carefully training them up
wherever a vacancy will admit them:—Or, if
ſuch do not riſe naturally, by putting in tranſ-
planted plants in vacant hedge-banks and waſte
corners; at the ſame time dibbling acorns
round them, in order that, in the courſe of a

few

few years, the woodman may have his election of the propereft plant to be trained.

This however is not the bufinefs of a day, nor of one year, but requires an annual attention ; embracing convenient times, and favorable opportunities, as the bufinefs of the eftate is profecuted; confidering this as one of the moft material objects belonging to its management.

With refpect to the POLLARDS, I have followed thefe rules :—

Such as were not likely to throw out, in twenty or twenty-five years, a top equal to the prefent value of their ftems, I valued to the tenants as fire-wood.

Thus fuppofing the body of an old pollard to be worth, as fire-wood, two fhillings; but from the appearance of the prefent top, when compared with thofe of the neighbouring pollards, it was not likely to throw out, in twenty or twenty-five years time, another top of two fhillings value, I marked it to come down, and charged the tenant two fhillings for it, over and above the value of its prefent top : for the intereft of the money will, at the end of that time, be more than the top-wood would have been had it been left ftanding ; befide the mould-

90.
TIMBER.

HEDGE ROW
POLLARDS.

mouldering and wafte of its own body, and the incumbrance it would have been to the eftate.

Such, alfo, as ftood particularly in the tenant's way, or which crowded a young ftand or timber, or where they ftood too thick, I took down, valuing them to the tenant as fire-wood; but with this invariable provifo, that if, on cutting off their butts, they proved found, they were to be taken for the ufe of the landlord; the tenant having a deductory allowance made for the quantity of firing-blocks fo taken.

Alfo, if a pollard, of a proper fize, appeared to be at prefent found enough for a gate-poft (more particularly if gate-pofts were wanting upon the farm they ftood on), but which from its prefent appearance it would not be at the time the ditch would want to be made the next time, I marked it to come down :—for a good hanging-poft is worth five fhillings; whereas a firing-pollard of the fame fize is not worth more than one fhilling.

But fuch thriving pollards as did not ftand particularly in the way of the fence or the tenant, and fuch as were not wanted for any particular ufe; alfo fuch as were likely to throw

out

out another top, and ftood well upon the bank, fo as not to injure materially either the tenant or the fence, I invariably left ftanding: for, al-though coals may at prefent be plentiful, and coafling-veffels fufficiently numerous, and have an unobftructed paffage from Newcaftle to Cromer; yet who can foreknow the revolu-tions in nature and nations which may here-after take place? and who will be hardy enough to fay that Eaft-Norfolk cannot experience a want of materials for firing? The face of the country is no doubt at prefent too much encumbered with pollards, to the great inconveniency of its prefent occupiers: but it may be well to leffen their number with a prudent hand; left, by fweeping them away indifcriminately, we may entail on pofterity a ftill greater inconveniency.

90.

HEDGE ROW
POLLARDS.

91.

MARCH 14. On Monday evening laft, about eight o'clock, the wind rofe very high; blowed hard all night; continued blow-ing all day on Tuefday; and in the evening blew a violent gale.

REPAIRS.

There

91.

REPAIRS.

There has fcarcely one thatched roof upon this eftate efcaped, entirely, its fury. Many of them however are only ruffled; but great numbers (an hundred at leaft) are broken, more or lefs; fome of the breaches confiderable: whilft the tiled roofs have efcaped without any confiderable injury.

Had the practice propofed in MIN. 63. been adopted a few years ago, perhaps not a breach would have happened; for where the roofs have been overlooked in the courfe of the laft year, even the thatched ones are hardly ruffled; whereas, in the ftate in which feveral of them ftill remained, there is three or four months work of a thatcher to repair them.

THATCH.

Reed in particular ought to be driven or relaid whenever it begins to flip, or the bindings begin to decay :—it is the reed-roofs in general which have fuffered.

REED.

There is one advantage in reed, however; it may moft of it be gathered up and relaid.

92.

REPAIRS.

MARCH 14. The bricklayer and thatcher employed upon this eftate live at a diftance.—

This

This inconveniency I have frequently experienced, but never so much as now, when such a number of petty, but exigent, jobs have been created by the late high winds:—the tenants are solicitous to have their furniture and their corn secured from the wet, and I cannot give orders to the thatcher or bricklayer without riding or sending two or three miles to them, or their coming as far out of their way to me.

92.
REPAIRS.

Upon a large estate, a master or foreman carpenter, master bricklayer, thatcher, and blacksmith, ought to live in the immediate neighbourhood of the manager.

GEN. MAN.
OF ESTATES.

93.

MARCH 16. Since the late severe weather set in, it has been remarked that bullocks abroad have done unusually ill; whilst those in sheds have done well. (See MIN. 69.)

BULLOCKS
AT
TURNEPS.

Are not these a sufficient hints to farmers to keep their bullocks abroad in warm weather, and take them up, or at least par them, in severe weather? Whilst they are buds and two-year-olds, they are nursed in a warm well kidded par-yard; but, at a time when they are en-

VOL. II.   M   titled

titled to every indulgence the farmer can give
them, they are expofed to the weather, be it
ever fo inclement; with fcarcely a hedge to
fhelter them : their only fhelter being too
frequently nothing better than a row of naked
" buck-ftalled thornen bulls."—No wonder,
then, that after the remarkably mild weather
we had at the beginning of winter, the late
fudden change fhould give a check to fuch as
have been expofed abroad*; deftitute of fhelter,
and, confequently, deftitute of that temperature of *mind* as well as of body, which, *perhaps*,
is effential to their thriving.

Mr. Cook, of Felmingham, whofe opinion
in this cafe is valuable, corroborates thefe obfervations; fo far, at leaft, as they relate to
the temperature of the body. A good lodging,
he fays, is a great thing to a bullock:—his
expreffion was, " it keeps them warm within;
" and when they get up they ftretch them-
" felves, fhooting out their hind legs as if
" they meant to leave them behind in the par-
" yard."—Whereas after having lain upon
the cold ground, more efpecially if it be *wet*,
" they become cold on the infide; and, on
" rifing, ftick up their backs, with their four

* Homebreds are here fpoken of.

" feet

" feet drawn together, as if they were afraid to
" move them from the place they ftand in."
Cold weather, he fays, no doubt checks bullocks
which go abroad very much; more efpecially
if it be *wet*; adding, that " if their *backs be dry*
" they do not fo much mind the cold."

94.

MARCH 25. AYLSHAM FAIR. This feems
to be a fair appropriated to dealings between
farmer and farmer, rather than to drovers and
profeffional dealers. It is chiefly noted for
plow-horfes; which, at this feafon of the year,
become valuable to the Norfolk farmer; every
hand and hoof becoming bufily employed
againft barley feed-time. It is, however, upon
the whole, a fmall fair; and the fairftead uncommonly fmall and incommodious.

To-day the number of cattle were very few:
not more than one hundred head in the fair:
and thofe in general of a refufe kind.

It feems to be a fact, univerfally underftood,
that the quantity of ftock in this county, has
of late years very much declined. There have,
it is generally allowed, been fewer young cattle reared of late than there were formerly:
owing, it is thought, to the lownefs of price;

arifing

94.

FAIR OF
AYLSHAM.

arifing probably from a fcarcity of money, and from the failure of the turnep-crops for fome years back.

CATTLE.

·The few which were in the fair to-day feemed principally to confift of fuch as had been at turneps; and had got a little flefhy; but ftill required a confiderable time, and good keep, to finifh them. There were alfo a few cows and calves, and a little young ftock. The number

HORSES.

of horfes was confiderable (perhaps a hundred) fet up againft rails, placed on a rifing ground, to fhew their fore-hands to advantage. Ten to twelve pounds the higheft prices; even for young horfes.

95.

PLANTING.

MARCH 26. This morning marked out the weedling-plants of a plantation, made by the late Sir William Harbord twenty-five to thirty years ago *.

It confifts of the following fpecies of trees :—

Oaks,	Scotch Fir,
Afh,	Larch,
Beech,	Alder.
Chefnut,	Hornbeam.

* On counting the rings of different fpecies, I found the number to be thirty or thirty-one.

The

The *Scotch fir* has outgrown every other
fpecies; and the plants, though few, are be-
come a burden to the grove. The wood being
of quick growth, the plants have not only out-
topped the reft, but have, in general, had time
enough to furnifh themfelves with boughs on
every fide; fo as to cripple the beautiful oaks
and beeches which ftand near them. If therefore Scotch firs be planted in a grove, by
way of variegation, they ought to be kept trimmed below; which would check their growth,
and in fome meafure prevent their doing
mifchief: but, even with this reftriction, they
ought to be admitted into fociety with a fpar-
ing hand.

The *larches*, too, where they ftand free from
the Scotch firs, are of a confiderable fize; but
they are not equally mifchievous with thofe;
their boughs being lefs extenfive, and more
rotted off below: they are, neverthelefs, injurious to their deciduous neighbours. Where
they ftand thick, among the firs, they are
drawn up ftrikingly tall and flender, or are fo
much over-hung as to be crippled, or entirely
fmothered.—Marked great numbers that were
dead or dying.

The *oaks* are many of them beautiful plants;
but are either entirely crippled by the firs and

larches,

95.
PLANTING.

larches, or, where there is any head-room, are drawn up much too tall and flender.

The fame may be faid of the *beeches*; and it is curious, though painful, to fee how they ftruggle for the light, wherever they can *fee* a peep-hole.

The *afhes*, too, where they ftand among the firs and larches, are either fmothered outright, or are drawn up much too tall and flender. In a part where they ftand alone, without any ad-mixture except a few alders, there are fome moft beautiful plants.

The *chefnuts*, if one may judge from this in-ftance, is totally unfit for a mifcellaneous grove. There is fcarcely one of this fpecies enjoys the fmalleft portion of fun-fhine: the few which ftill exift are chiefly underlings; and fome of them not much larger than when they were planted.

It muft be obferved, however, that much may depend on the *foil.* This plantation di-vides a rank moory meadow from a good, found, upland foil; fome parts of it partaking of the former, fome of the latter quality.

The larches and the chefnuts, obvioufly, do beft on the dry foil. The Scotch firs, too, feem to have gone off upon the moory foil; there

there being fome, but very few, left upon it; and thofe coarfe and ftunted. The afhes do remarkably well on the moory parts. In one particular place; not the wetteft; there is a parcel of perhaps the moft beautiful plants that ever grew —their fkin as fmooth and clean as that of the beech; and, though not more than twenty-one inches in circumference, they are not lefs than forty feet in height; and as ftraight as gun-barrels. The oaks, beeches, and a few hornbeams, thrive wherever they have been planted, and can get their heads out. They do not, however, feem to have been planted on the very wet parts.

The largeft of the firs meafure in circumference, at five feet high, - 39 inches.

Larches,	- -	36
Chefnuts,	r -	28
Beeches,	- -	32
Alders,	- -	32
Afhes,	- -	21
Oaks,	- -	28
Hornbeams,	- •	—

The greateft collective height of the plantation is about forty feet.

This plantation furnifhes a ftriking inftance of the mifchiefs enfuing from the want of a proper attention to infant-groves.

In

In this cafe, judicious thinnings would, evidently, have been highly advantageous. Great numbers of plants have perifhed, and come entirely to wafte; and, of the two hundred and eighty which I have now marked, one hundred are dead, or nearly fo.

This, however, is the fmalleft fhare of the lofs; for thofe ftill remaining are drawn up too tall and flender; and with tops too fmall and infignificant, to make due progrefs towards large timber-trees.

In point of *profit*, the beft method now to proceed by would be, to take down all, or the greateft part, of the Scotch firs; trimming up the few, which perhaps might be left with propriety; and thinning very confiderably, *but by degrees*, the larches, and fuch of the other fpecies as might require it.

But, in point of *ornament*, this, for a few years, might be injurious: however, in the end, both ornament and utility would, beyond a doubt, be increafed by it; and the immediate acquifition of materials for repairs would be very confiderable.

How many entire roofs of cottages, lean-to's, and other out-buildings; and what a fupply of rails, common ladders, and rough fcantling might

might be drawn from this small plantation: enough to keep the common buildings of the estate in repair for some years: and this, too, with a trifling expence of sawing, compared with that which is neceffary to the reduction of grown timbers into small scantling *.

96.

April 3. Spent the afternoon with the Rev. Mr. Horseley, of Swayfield; and walked with him over his improved meadows.

They are the only meadows in the county (at leaft that have fallen under my obfervation) which have been managed with any degree of fpirit or judgment.

Mr. Horfeley fays, that when he purchafed them (fome eight or ten years ago) they were a mere morafs: fo very rotten that it was difficult even for a man to walk acrofs them; producing very little herbage fuperior to rufhes and mofs. They are, now, (even after this uncommonly wet feafon) firm enough to bear the largeft cattle; and are covered with a turf equal in appearance to the richeft grafsland.

* I flatter myfelf no apology is neceffary for the length of this Minute: planting is an important branch of rural affairs; and it is in tall plantations, rather than in the nurfery, we ought to ftudy the great principles of the art.

Mr.

Mr. H.'s plan of improvement was this: Having lowered a rivulet, which runs through them, fo as to fink the furface of the water about four feet below the furface of the meadow, he cut drains, feven feet wide, and four feet deep, *parallel to the rivulet* ; and, with the excavated mould, filled up the fmall drains which had formerly been cut; and levelled the other inequalities ; fo as to render the furface fmooth and even.

Thefe drains were at firft made at about twenty or thirty yards diftance from each other ; but Mr. H. is now filling the major part of them up; they having performed the office of laying the ground dry ; and he is of opinion, that the rivulet and the fence-drains, alone, will be fufficient to keep it fo.

Thefe meadows confift of eighteen acres; divided at prefent into four " fhifts," by the rivulet and two parallel main drains; which are barely feven feet wide ; but the cattle fometimes attempt them ; and eight feet—fay half a rod—is the leaft width that fence-drains ought to be made.

The rufhes were fubdued by the fithe, the mofs by manure, and the herbage improved by the fweeping of the hay-chamber fcattered on

in

in the fpring. Neither the harrow nor the
roller has yet been introduced.

Mr. H's method of treating his meadows,
now in their improved ftate, is, to feed them
every year, and to fhift his ftock repeatedly ;
beginning at one end, and proceeding regularly, fo as to make two or three revolutions
in the courfe of the fummer : and, whenever he
takes his ftock out of one of his pieces, he
makes a point of fweeping down the weeds
and rough grafs. An admirable practice ; by
which a frefh rowen-like bite is prepared
againft the return of the ftock; befides the
weeds being thereby effectually kept under.

Mr. H, fays, that he has fatted both fheep
and bullocks on this improved morafs ; and
that they fat very kindly. He further fays,
that it gives cows a great flow of milk ; and
Mrs. H, fays, that the butter from it is perfectly good.

Enquiring of Mr. Horfeley, if he had kept an
account of his expences fince his firft purchafe ;
he faid, no; but was clear in the main fact;
namely, that the improvement greatly exceeds
the expence of improving : adding, that he
could have fold the land in its improved ftate
for twice the amount of the purchafe-money.

It

96.

MEADOWS.

It has every appearance of being now worth from twenty to twenty-five shillings an acre.

97.

BULLOCKS
AT
TURNEPS.

April 14. I have given particular attention to the management and progress of the two lots of bullocks, which I was present at the buying of, at St. Faith's fair. (See Min. 27.)

It is a striking and interesting fact, that, notwithstanding there was only fifteen shillings a head difference in the purchase-money of these two lots, there is not less than forty shillings a piece difference in their present value.

A great advantage, no doubt, arises, to a judge of cattle, from having the choice of a drove; drawing out only a few of the head bullocks. But in this case the drove was small; and I remember Mr. B. was dubious in his choice of the last two or three of his lot: the disparity, therefore, at the time of purchase was not very great; being, in some individuals, scarcely perceptible to the eye of a judge.

From these and other circumstances, I am convinced that much depends upon the *management* of bullocks at turneps, as well as upon

upon judgment in purchafing them : for, of feveral parcels of fatting bullocks, which I have had an opportunity of making my obfervations upon this winter, none have done equally to Mr. B's lot of heifers.

His turneps, no doubt, are good ; and fo are thofe of many of his neighbours ; and the fuperiority of management appears to lie in letting them have plenty of frefh turneps; with plenty of followers ; and in their being regularly fhifted every day.

98.

APRIL 14. What a trifling expence of labour has been incurred by —— farm, from Michaelmas 1780, to Michaelmas 1781.

It contains near four hundred acres of arable land ; with about fifty acres of meadow.

The whole expence of workman's wages, the harveft month included, is no more than - - - - £. 186 2 7½

To which muft be added, the bailiff's falary - - - 35 0 0

£. 221 2 7½

Thus the whole expence of labour and houfekeeping (for the bailiff and all the men boarded themfelves and drank their own beer) is not

nearly

98.
LABOUR.

nearly equal to the rent of the land: for this farm, if freed from game, is worth from two hundred and fifty to three hundred pounds a year.

RENT.

A farm of the fame magnitude in Surrey or Kent could not have been managed for twice the money. And this accounts for the high price which land bears in Norfolk. Land which lets here for fifteen fhillings an acre, would not in Surrey or Kent (at twenty miles diftance from London) let for more than half the money.

LABOUR.

The lownefs of day-wages; the quick dif-patch of bufinefs; and, moft efpecially, the practice of plowing with two horfes, and going

SOIL-PROC.

two journies a day; account in a great meafure for the difparity.

99.

SHEEP.

APRIL 16. The fhepherd telling me that a cutter in the neighbourhood could extract the concealed tefticles of ridgil lambs; and he having laft year experienced the inconveniency of three or four of thefe troublefome and dangerous animals, I let him fend for him. This morning he has cut three; the whole number, it feems, this year. They are now from fix to eight weeks old.

Having

Having cut off the end of the bag, and drawn the tefticle contained in it, he proceeded to take the other out of the fide oppofite to that on which the palpable tefticle lay *.

The lamb was laid flat on its fide, upon the ground; one man holding it by its neck and fore legs; and another ftretching it out, by drawing its hind legs back; both of them at the fame time preffing their hands hard to the ground; fo that the lamb had no liberty to ftruggle.

The cutter then clipt off a patch of wool, about the fize and fhape of a duck's egg, clofe below the loin, and about half way between the huckle and the fhort ribs.

He then made an incifion wide enough to admit, freely, his fore finger; with which he fearched for the ftone, and prefently brought it out; and, difentangling it very dexteroufly from the film with his knife, drew out the ftring.

He immediately fowed up the orifice, and coated over the wound with cart-greafe.

It is remarkable that the concealed tefticles

---

* It increafes the difficulty in cutting ridgils, when the palpable tefticle has been priorly extracted; as the operator, then, knows not which fide to cut on; and is frequently obliged to cut both fides before he finds the concealed tefticle.

all

99.

CUTTING
RIDGIL
LAMBS.

all lay on the fame fide; namely, the right fide; the contrary fide to that on which females are cut. This made the operation rather awkward to his hand; he neverthelefs performed the bufinefs fo fkilfully, and with fo much dexterity; that he extracted the two firft in a few minutes. But the laft was a remarkably difficult cafe; the tefticle being very fmall, and braced up clofe to the vertebræ; and it is obfervable, he could fcarcely draw the palpable tefticle of this lamb out of its bag: the punifhment to the animal feemed full as much in one operation as the other.

The price of cutting, a fhilling a piece.

APRIL 22. The wind being cold, kept them in the houfe all night:—but the cutter, though the wind continued very pinching, thought it proper for them to go out in the day-time for the fake of exercife: they got very ftiff for fome days, but are now doing very well.

APRIL 30. One of them, neverthelefs, is fince dead:—owing, I apprehend, entirely to their being too much expofed to an unufually piercing eafterly wind.

100.

100.

APRIL 20. There is an alertnefs in the fer-vants and labourers of Norfolk, which I have not obferved in any other diftrict.

That "cuftom is fecond nature" is verified every hour. How quick and alert are the tradef-people and handicraftmen in London! They will difpatch as much bufinefs in a given time as the very fame people, had they been bred in fome parts of the country, would have done in twice that time. The cafe is fimilar with the Norfolk hufbandman. Whilft a boy, he is ac-cuftomed to run by the fide of the horfes while they trot with the harrows. When he becomes a plowman; he is accuftomed to ftep out at the rate of three or four miles an hour : and, if he drive an empty team, he either does it ftanding upright in his carriage, with a peculiarity of air, and with a feeming pride and fatisfaction, . or runs by the fide of his horfes, while they are bowling away at full t: ·.

Thus both his body and his mind become active : and if he go to mow, reap, or other employment, his habit of activity accompanies him ;—and is obvious even in his air, his man-ner and his gait.

VOL. II.   N   On

100.
WORKMEN.

On the contrary, a Kentifh plowman, accuftomed from his infancy to walk, whether at
harrow, plow, or cart, about a mile-and-a-
half or two miles an hour, preferves the fame
fluggifh ftep even in his holidays; and is the
fame flow, dull, heavy animal in every thing
he does.

That the Norfolk farm-labourers difpatch
more work than thofe of other countries is an
undoubted fact; and in this way, I think, it
may be fully accounted for.

101.

MARKETS.

MAY 4. Went this morning to fee the
clover-feed market at Norwich.

The feeds are brought chiefly from Suffolk,
and the Suffolk fide of Norfolk. Many of
them are in the hands of the growers themfelves; fome in thofe of jobbers, who collect
them of the farmers. They are principally
contained in coomb facks, containing four
bufhels, of fixty-fix pounds each, together with
two pound a bufhel for over-weight; fo that a
bufhel is only a term ufed for fixty-eight pound
of clover-feed, at Norwich market : or for fixty-
fix pound, in other parts of the county.

The feeds are principally brought into market in thefe coomb facks; in which feveral
hundred

hundred bufhels may be feen ftanding: and in the middle of the market are a pair of large fcales, adapted to the weighing of a whole fack, or a lefs quantity; the farmers paying fo much a draft for the ufe of them.

Befide what are thus brought into market, the dealers have quantities at their refpective warehoufes *; and great quantities are alfo fold by corn merchants, and even bankers, by fample. Indeed, at this feafon of the year, almoft every man of bufinefs, who has got a little loofe money, is a dealer in clover-feed.

The market, however, does not confift wholly of red clover-feed:—there are pro-portional quantities of " fuckling" (white clover); alfo of " hulled Nonfuch" (trefoil); alfo of " black Nonfuch" (trefoil in the hufk); alfo of " white Nonfuch" (darnel or rye-grafs); and of " black and white Non-fuch;" namely, a mixture of the two laft forts.

* One Cunningham is by much the largeft dealer: he lives near Harleftone; and buys up his feed in that neigh-bourhood, and in Suffolk. Enquiring as to the quantity fold, I was told (in the afternoon) that he had fold, in the courfe of this day, a hundred coomb of clover-feed!— thirty or forty coomb of it, however, were to country dealers.

N 2   The

101.

CLOVER-
SEED MARK.

The prices, more particularly of " clover," (that is, red clover) is very fluctuating : laft year prime feed was bought from eighteen to twenty fhillings a bufhel. It has been known fo low as fifteen fhillings; and three pounds ten fhillings a bufhel has been given in this market.

To-day the prices were as follow :

Clover, twenty fhillings to thirty fhillings a bufhel.

Suckling, fixpence to eight-pence a pound.

Darnel, twelve to fifteen fhillings a coomb.

102.

BULLOCKS
AT
TURNEPS.

MAY 4. A fortnight ago, Mr. ——— fent twelve of his Scotch heifers, bought at St. Faith's, (See MIN. 27. and 97.) to Smith-field.

To-day he fhewed me the falefman's account.

They fold from eight pounds five fhillings to eleven pounds a piece—the neat proceeds a hundred and ten pounds, or nine pounds five fhillings a head. They coft fix pounds fifteen fhillings; fo that they left a profit of about fifty fhillings a head.

They were at turneps about twenty-five weeks; and confequently paid no more than two fhillings a week for their keep, notwith-ftanding the prefent high markets.

They

They were not highly finifhed ; but turneps being almoft done, and grafs backward, the proprietor of them judged wifely in felling off the beft of them now, that he may be able to finifh the remainder the more highly with grafs.

103.

May 5. The late beating rains have wafhed down the face of many hundred rods of ditching.　New-raifed ditches have fuffered moft; but where the face looked to the north-eaft, ditches which have been made even two or three years, have fuffered confiderably.

Where new ditches have been raifed this fpring, in the Norfolk manner; namely, very upright, with the layer planted almoft at the top of the bank; much mifchief is done; for not only the face, but the layer alfo, lies by the heels in the " holl," for many rods in a place : and this, it feems, is a misfortune not uncommon in Norfolk; yet ftill the farmers perfift in raifing their live fences in this moft injudicious manner.

I have the fatisfaction to fee thofe ditches which I raifed laft year, with an offset, and with the layer planted on the firft fpit, all ftanding: indeed, ditches raifed in this manner, cannot readily take effential hurt by beating rains; for fhould either the foot or the upper part of the facing fhoot, the layer is ftill fafe.

It is the cuftom here to oblige the ditchers to make good the breaches of the firft year, gratis. This, however, if the work was properly done, is this year rather hard upon them. But be this as it may, there needs not a ftronger proof of the frequent *mifcarriages* of Norfolk ditches than this cuftom.

104.

MAY 5. It feems to be a growing practice, in this country, to fow furze-feed on the backs, or rather upon the tops, of ditch-banks.

There is, however, one great evil attends it, when fown upon the top; for, growing quicker than the white-thorn, the furze, in a few years, over-hangs, and fmothers the young hedgeling; efpecially if it be neglected to be cut down, or trimmed off, on the face fide: a work which is too often, and, indeed, almoft univerfally neglected.

But if the feeds be fown upon the *back* of the bank, this evil is in a great meafure prevented;

vented; and the furze being principally intended as a defence of the back of the bank
from cattle, it is extraordinary that the cuſtom
of ſowing it upon the top ſhould continue.

Laſt year I ſowed upwards of a hundred
rods, and this year about two hundred: my
method has been this.

Two men, with a ſpade, a broom, and a
common glaſs bottle, furniſhed with a perforated ſtopper *, proceeded thus: the firſt
man chops a drill with his ſpade, from two to
three inches deep, and at about two-thirds of
the height of the bank. In this fiſſure the
other man ſcatters the feed through the hole in
the cork, at the rate of thirty long rods to a
pound of feed. This done, one of them, in
order to repair the cracks and partial breaches
made on the bank by chopping the drill, pats
it with the back of his ſpade above and below
the mouth of the drill, which is purpoſely left
open; whilſt the other, with the broom, ſweep-
ing upwards over the mouth of the drill, covers
the feed with looſe mould; yet leaves the mouth

104.

RAISING
HEDGES.

SOWING
FURZE-
SEED.

* A wooden cork, pierced with a gimblet, about the ſize
of a ſwan's quill; the inſide burnt ſmooth with a wire, and
the outſide bound with thread to make it ſtick ſecurely in
the mouth of the bottle.

N 4 ſufficiently

104.

SOWING
FURZE
SEED.

sufficiently open to permit the young plants to make their way easily out of it; and to catch the rains which trickle down the upper part of the bank †.

Two men will sow 120 rods a day   0   2   4
Four pounds of seed at 15d.   0   5   0
$$\text{£. } 0 \quad 7 \quad 4$$
Somewhat more than one halfpenny each statute rod, for seed and sowing.

HEDGE
WOODS.

On light sandy soils, in which the furze generally thrives abundantly, but where white-thorn, if the soil be barren as well as light, is an age in coming to a hedge adequate as a fence, the furze is the most eligible shrub to be propagated singly; and in every soil in which the plants will thrive, it is an excellent guard to the back of the ditch, forming a much warmer shelter for cattle than white-thorn, or any other deciduous shrub, owing to its numerous branches and leaves; more espe-

† The shooting of the bank is the only thing to be feared in this case; it ought not therefore to be made too steep; and ought, at the time of making, to be sowed with grass-seeds. (See HEDGES, Vol. I.)

cially

cially if thefe be increafed by timely cutting; or, which is much preferable, by trimming off the ends of the branches.

The almoft only inconveniency of a furze hedge is its becoming liable to be killed by fevere froft. It is probable, however, that a hogged hedge would ftand the froft better than one which is fuffered to overgrow itfelf, and expofe its roots and ftems to the inclemency of the weather: even fhould a hogged hedge be killed to the root, it feems probable that thro' the numeroufnefs and compactnefs of its ftems and branches, it would remain a fufficient dead hedge, until another live one might be raifed from frefh feed.

Another inconveniency of a furze hedge is, in theory at leaft, its fhedding its feed, and over-fpreading the adjoining land. This inconveniency, however, I have not feen in Norfolk; and I believe is not to be apprehended, if French feed (which may be had of any feedfman in London) be fown,

105.

MAY 8. WALSHAM FAIR.—This fair, which is held the Wednesday se'nnight before Whitsunday, is a considerable fair for fat bullocks; also for cows and calves, and young stock.

The cattle begin to come in about seven, and continue coming until nine or ten; the fairs as well as the markets of Norfolk being held late in the day.

There were several hundred head of cattle at Walsham to-day, and had they been collected into *one* fair-stead, would have made a good show.

The principal buyers were the Norwich, the Wells, and the country butchers; also some dealers for the London and St. Ives's markets; and probably some under-finished bullocks were bought by those farmers who had grass and money of those who were in want of both.

I saw a steer and a heifer, good meat, and weighing about seventy stone the two, sold for sixteen pounds eight shillings, which is more than four shillings and eightpence a stone.

Also

Alſo two large, but not fat, ſteers, weighing together about one hundred ſtone, ſold for twenty pounds ten ſhillings, which is only four ſhillings and a penny a ſtone.

Alſo ſix two-year-olds, good meat, but not finiſhed, and weighing about thirty ſtone each, for ſix pounds twelve ſhillings a head; about four ſhillings and five-pence a ſtone.

Cows and calves, in good demand; ſold from three to ſix pound.

Lean two-year-olds worth from fifty ſhillings to four pound.

Yearlings (now near eighteen months old) from forty to forty-five ſhillings.

It is notorious, that there are very few *fat* bullocks in Norfolk this ſpring; owing, it is ſuppoſed, to the unkindlineſs of the weather, and to the bad quality of turneps, which, it is ſaid, are this year thicker-ſkinned, and of a weaker quality, than uſual.

There were not twenty " right fat " bullocks in the fair: the few that have been finiſhed this ſpring have been ſent to London; the markets there having been very good.

Bullocks ſold laſt Monday in Smithfield for upwards of five ſhillings a ſtone, and they have not fetched leſs than that price for ſeveral

105.

SMITHFIELD
MARKET.

ral market-days laſt paſt. But Smithfield market is a lottery; and, I apprehend, four ſhillings and ſixpence at Walſham is a better price (charges and riſque of road and market conſidered) than the *chance* of five ſhillings in London.

106.

DISTRICT.

MAY 12. On Friday morning ſet out in company with Mr. John Baker, of South-Reps, to ſee the country, and the celebrated huſbandry of the FLEG HUNDREDS.

We went by the ſea-coaſt, and returned by the " broads" and more inland parts of the country.

We paſſed through the following hundreds and pariſhes.

PARISH,

	PARISH.	SOIL.	HUSBANDRY.	
N. Erpingham.	Thorp Market	light	paſſable	106. DISTRICT.
	South-Reps	ditto	good	
	Gimmingham	ditto	paſſable	
	Trunch	deeper	good	
Erp. & Tunſtead.	Knapton	good	ditto	
	Paſton	ditto	ditto	
	Backton	ditto	ditto	
Happing.	Walcot	very good	ditto	
	Haſbro'	ditto	ditto	
	Leſſingham	ditto, with marſhes	ditto	
	Hempſtead	ditto	ditto	
	Palling	ditto	ditto	
	Waxham	ditto, and very flat	Mr. B———	
	Horſey	ditto	ditto	
W. Flegg.	Winterton	light, but rich	paſſable	
Eaſt Fleg.	Hemſby	a rich loam, with common fields	ditto	
	Ormeſby	ditto ditto	ditto	
	Kaiſter	ditto, with marſhes	ditto	
	Yarmouth	ſurrounded by low grounds and water	almoſt all common	
	Maltby	rich loam, with commons	nothing extraordinary	
	Filby	ditto, and broads	paſſable	
W. Fleg.	Burrow	rich loam	ditto	
	Rolleſby	ditto	ditto	
	Repps	ditto, with common fields	ditto	
Happing.	Potter Hayham	do. with marſhes & broads	ditto	
	Catfield	ditto, with low grounds	ditto	
	Sutton	ſtill flattiſh	ditto	
	Stalham	good ſtrong land	good	
	Brunſted	ſtill ſtrong	very good	
	Eaſt Ruſton	yet friable	excellent	
Tunſtead.	Redlington	ſtrong good loam	ditto	
	Witton	ditto, ſome lighter	good	
	Edenthorp	ditto	ditto	
	Backton	a charming ſoil	ditto	

Knapton to Thorp ſee above

From

106.
DISTRICT.

From a general view of this detail, the hundred of HAPPING (and not the hundreds of *Fleg*) ſtands higheſt on the ſcale of huſbandry: and, as I ſet out without prejudice, I could have no other bias to my opinion than that which I received from the objeſts which ſtruck me.

FLEG.

The *ſoil* of the FLEG HUNDREDS is rich; ſome parts of it being naturally fertile; in a very high degree; and the reſt rendered ſo by clay, marl, and " Yarmouth muck." The arable parts are here ſpoken of.

THE FLEG HUNDREDS.

But there are in theſe hundreds large traſts which are covered with water, or occupied by reed and other aquatics; and others which are frequently overflowed in winter, but afford in ſummer extenſive marſhes, or grazing-grounds, for lean Scots and young cattle.

Thoſe are another ſource of riches to the arable lands; on which the marſh-ſtock is kept, and generally fatted on turneps, during the winter months; beſides great quantities of manure being alſo raiſed from ſedge and other litter cut out of theſe fens and marſhes.

THE FLEG HUSBANDRY.

We called upon Mr. Ferrier, of Hemſby, who occupies his own eſtate, and is univerſally acknowledged as one of the beſt farmers in " Fleg."

" Fleg." He very obligingly fhewed me his farm, and favoured me with a recital of his practice.

The Fleg farmers, it is true, get amazing crops; they reckon from ten to twelve coomb of wheat, and fifteen to twenty coomb of oats, an acre, no very extraordinary produce: but when we learn that crops like thefe are produced from the fucceffion, or from any management nearly refembling the fucceffion, of wheat, barley, clover, wheat, oats, wheat; every perfon converfant in farming muft exclaim, that the foil which will bear fuch treatment is extraordinary indeed; more efpecially when he is told, that the crop of wheat which follows the oats is generally better than that which preceded them; the oat-crop being thrown in as a damper of the raging fertility of the foil.

Mr. Ferrier, who is a very fenfible, judicious, plain farmer (though formerly a failor) having obferved that wheat after clover, or a fummer fallow, became too rank to ftand, and ran too much to ftraw to yield a large produce of grain, ingenioufly contrived this intervening crop of oats, in order to correct the over-abundant fertility or ranknefs of the foil; and in this his

fupe-

106.

SUMMER
FALLOW.

superiority of management seems principally to consist. He seems to consider a summer fallow as the most dangerous process that can occur upon a farm; for the wheat crop which succeeds it he has found invariably spoilt through an over-rankness; and what appears much more extraordinary, the barley crop which follows the wheat is in this case generally too small; owing, as Mr. F. supposes, to the wheat having too much impoverished the soil: this however does not accord with the practice of wheat, oats, wheat. I have no doubt of Mr. F.'s veracity, or of the fact, but apprehend it is produced by some other cause than the poverty or exhaustion of the soil.

FLEG SOIL.

Mr. Ferrier's soil is principally a rich dark-coloured loam, except one piece or two, which are of a more sandy nature. A piece near his house is pecularly fertile: he never knew it to fail producing a valuable crop. A recently-made ditch gave me an opportunity of examining it. It is one uniform mass of rich black loam, for more than two feet deep; and under this lies a brick earth; a soil, this, capable of producing madder, woad, hemp, or any other vegetable of our climate which requires a rich deep soil. The principal part of his estate, how-

however, is of a much fhallower foil, not deeper than the plow goes; and its prefent very amazing fertility he afcribes in a great meafure, to his having *clayed* it. Indeed to this fpecies of improvement the fertility of the Fleg Hundred is allowed to be principally owing.

Mr. F. gave me an opportunity of examining his clay-pit; which is very commodious; the uncallow is trifling, and the depth of the bed or jam he has not been able to afcertain. It is worked, at prefent, about ten or twelve feet deep.

The colour of the foffil, when moift, is a dark-brown, interfperfed with fpecks of white; and dries to a colour lighter than that of fuller's earth; on being expofed to the air it breaks into fmall die-like pieces.

From Mr. F.'s account of the manner of its acting, and more particularly from its appearance, I judged it to be a *brown marl*, rather than a *clay*; and, on trying it in acid, it proves to be ftrongly calcareous; effervefcing, and hiffing, more violently than moft of the *white marls* of *this* neighbourhood: and what is ftill more interefting, the *Hemsby clay* is equally turbulent in acid, as the *Norwich marl*; which is

VOL. II.   O   brought,

106.
FLEG CLAY.

brought, by water, forty miles into this country, at the exceffive expence of four fhillings a load upon the ftaith; befides the land-carriage. (But fee MARL, Vol. I.)

It is fomewhat extraordinary that Mr. F. fenfible and intelligent as he is, fhould be entirely tinacquainted with this quality of his clay; a circumftance, however, the lefs to be wondered at, as the Norfolk farmers, in general, are equally uninformed of the nature and properties of marl.

The quantity fet on by Mr. F. was about forty middling loads an acre, about twenty years ago:—it is now beginning to wear out; and he is of opinion his land will not bear claying a fecond time.

For want of mould he is fometimes obliged to ufe fome clay for the bottoms of his dung-hills; but he does not much approve of it, preferring good mould when he can get it.

THE FLEG
WORKMEN.

The Fleg farmers are noted for their quick difpatch of bufinefs; and for the great quantity of work they get done by a given number of fervants and labourers. Mr. F. made the obfervation, which is corroborated by Mr. E. (formerly of Fleg) who gives for inftance, that he has had twenty loads of tough fedgy muck

muck filled, daily, by a common day-la-
bourer !

Mr. Ferrier gave a ftriking inftance of the
fertility of the Hemfby foil. He has known
a farm driven by a beggarly tenant, who has
been fucceeded by another, who has ftill continued to drive it; yet, after all, it has retained its prolific qualities ; and has ftill continued to throw out abundant crops; efpecially if a full crop of *clover* can be obtained; a
thing which Mr. F. fpeaks of as an improvement almoft equal to that of a coat of muck.

CLOVER.

Mr. F.'s management of his *turneps* is very
judicious.—He begins with thofe which lie
fartheft from home; throwing them abroad in
the adjoining ftubbles and lays; but in winter
he brings his cattle into the yard ; which is a
very convenient one ; and is, I believe, efteemed
the firft in the country.

TURNEPS
IN FLEG.

It confifts of a large fquare : on one fide of
it ftand the barns ; and, on the oppofite fide,
a long range of troughs or mangers ; behind
which is a gangway for the feeder; and behind this (out of the yard) the turnep-houfe.

The turneps are tailed, and freed from the
principal part of the dirt, and put into the
troughs entire ; which Mr. F. efteems, upon

the

the whole, a better practice than chopping them.

The troughs stand on the highest side of the yard, upon a rising ground; so that the bullocks always stand clean to feed, while the urine settles down among the straw in the lower parts of the yard.

The posts which support the manger run up fence-height, and have a single rail passing from one to another, to prevent the bullocks from clambering over the troughs. (A shed under which the bullocks could feed and lie down warm and comfortable in rainy cold weather, would be a great improvement to this yard).

Turneps being now run up to blossom—Mr. F. mows off the tops with a sithe, giving these alone to his fatting bullocks; while his cows and lean stock have the bottoms given them entire. This judicious management has two good effects: the bullocks instead of receiving a check, as they are apt to do, when turneps are in this state, are pushed on, perhaps, faster than when the bottoms are in full perfection; and the flock-cattle, by not having had a taste of the tops, eat up the bottoms the cleaner.

How

How much preferable is this management to that of his neighbour 'Squire ———, who having turned twenty fine bullocks into a close of charming turneps, (such as would have been worth in this part of the country three or four pounds an acre) they have licked off the bloſſoms, and the better parts of the tops, and are now pining over the ſtalks and bottoms.

This piece of turneps, as well as the remains of Mr. Ferrier's, and the other remaining pieces in the neighbourhood, ſhew what noble crops of this valuable root are grown in the Fleg Hundreds.

Theſe and a thouſand other circumſtances are undeniable proofs of the richneſs of the Fleg ſoil : whilſt the univerſal foulneſs which overruns the crops of wheat and clover are proofs equally evident of the *uncleanlineſs* of Fleg farmers : from our leaving Happiſbro', Hempſtead, &c. until our return to Stalham and Brunſtead, we ſaw very few pieces either of wheat or of clover which did the owners any degree of credit.

Fences. In this neceſſary piece of huſbandry the Fleg huſbandmen excel ; while the hedges of Happing and Tunſtead, either from the nature

of

106.

HEDGES
IN FLEG.

of the air and soil, or from mifmanagement, or perhaps by old age, are greatly below par; the fences being mere mud-walls, with here and there an old ftunted thorn. Near the coaft the fea air may have fome influence; but in Fleg, equally near to the fea, the hedges are flourifhing and beautiful in a high degree. The Fleg farmers feem fully mafters of the fubject of live hedges. They plant the layer at a moderate height, and are aware of the utility of cutting it down to the ftub at four or five years old; facing and backing the ditch, and fetting on a new hedge. This fecures them a fence in perpetuity; for before the fecond dead hedge begins to fail, the quick is become a perfect fence. Another good practice is that of trimming off the young fhoots which fprawl over the ditch ; by which means their hedges become thick at the bottom. Add to this, they do not fuffer their quick to ftand too long before they cut it down to the ftub ; fo that an old overgrown hedge, or row of timber-like " bulls," is fcarcely to be feen. Their method of felling them, too, is much preferable to the practice of this part of the country; where the ftubs are ufually cut off fmack-fmooth with the face of the bank, and

many

many of them frequently buried in it, so as to be totally destroyed : whereas, in Fleg, the stubs, universally, whether young or old, stand six or eight inches out of the face of the ditch ; by which means a number of shoots is produced. The lately raised fences have most of them furze growing on the backs of the banks.

Feeding wheat. Throughout the journey, the wheat appeared to be almost universally fed by stock of every denomination; sheep excepted; of which stock we did not see a score either in the Happing or the Fleg Hundreds! but calves, young stock, cows, and even fat bullocks, and horses, were still to be seen in almost every close of wheat we passed. The spring of this year, however, is remarkably late; the turneps are gone, and the grass not yet come to a bite; so that wheats, this year, are more universally fed, and fed later, than perhaps was ever known. Mr. Ferrier seems almost the only exception to the practice : he never feeds his wheat, from a general idea that " the first fruits are the best."

It is observable, that let the Norfolk soil be ever so strong, it is not stubborn; and let it be even soddened by heavy rains, and rendered cold

and

NORFOLK
SOIL.

and livery by laying flat, it is no fooner expofed to the air than it becomes mellow and
friable, This peculiar quality is faid to be
principally owing to marl (or clay); by the
fertilizing quality of which, land that is
fufficiently ftrong for wheat, is rendered fufficiently tender for turneps and barley. Before
the ufe of marl and clay the Fleg farmers could
not grow turneps ; whereas now they excel in
that valuable crop. Mr. Ferrier, in one of
the ftiffeft of his pieces, put his toe upon a clod
to fhew me this excellent property ; and with
a flight preffure of his foot burft it to an almoft impalpable powder. This friability of
ftrong land is, perhaps, one of the beft crite-
rions of a good foil.

FARMERS.

Mr. B*ragnet*. The character of this man
is fo very extraordinary, that I cannot refrain
from fketching fome of its principal features.
He was, I believe, bred in the army ; ferved fome
time in the militia ; has fought two or three
duels ; quarrelled with moft of the gentlemen of
the county ; and, coming to a good paternal
eftate, difcharged his tenants and commenced
farmer.

He is now an occupier of 1700*l.* a year—yet
he has neither fteward nor even bailiff to affift
him ;

him: no wonder, then, he abuſes and receives abuſe from his work-people; or that he ſometimes frightens them away; his harveſt, perhaps, ſtanding ſtill, until his neighbours have finiſhed. He attends fairs and markets—ſells his own corn and his own bullocks; and even finds time to attend to the taking in giſt ſtock upon a very extenſive marſh—and this without any aſſiſtance; ſave that of his lady, who keeps his accounts.

My fellow-traveller being acquainted with him we rode through his farm-yard, and found him looking over ſome young cattle which had been brought up for his inſpection. His perſon is groſs and his appearance bacchanalian—his dreſs that of a ſlovenly gentleman.—There is a politeneſs in his manner; and his converſation beſpeaks a ſenſible intelligent mind; borne away, however, by a wildneſs and ferocity which is obvious in his countenance, and diſcovers itſelf in every word and action. Neverthaleſs, it is ſaid, that, in a polite circle, Mr. B. can excel in politeneſs.

The pariſh of Waxham is principally in his own hands; and the adjoining little pariſh of Horſey is entirely in his occupation.

The country round him is exceedingly flat and low, being nearly on a level with the ſea at high-

high-water, and defended from it only by the Marram Banks, which are broken into gaps at every two or three hundred yards ; so that in stormy weather the sea rushes through, and frequently does considerable damage by overflowing the country. Mr. B. told us, that he had four acres of very fine cole-seed swept down during the late tempestuous weather.

His land, however, which lies out of the water's way, is rich and fertile in a high degree ; and Mr. B. it is said, gets exceedingly fine crops from it ; so that it is probable, notwithstanding the irregularity with which his affairs are conducted, and that want of attention to minutiæ which must necessarily occur in such a boundless scene of business, Mr. B. does not injure his fortune by farming ; for it seems generally allowed that no farmer gets his work done *so cheep* as Mr. B.

Marram Banks. The country towards the coast from Happingsbro' to Winterton, about ten miles, is a dead flat ; and, to the eye, appears to lie lower than the sea at high water. By the side of the beach runs a range of broken, irregular hillocks, from five to fifteen or twenty feet high, and from fifty to upwards of a hundred yards in width at the base ; composed

posed entirely of sea sand; which, in some places, is pretty well overgrown, and bound together by a rush-like vegetable called, in that neighbourhood, "marram" (the *arundo arenaria* of LINNÆUS) which the poor people cut and sell for thatch.

These hillocks, however, do not serve the purpose of a secure embankment against the sea; they being, in many places, divided down to their bases, by sluices of different widths; namely, from five to fifteen or perhaps twenty yards wide, Through these inlets, in boisterous weather, and with an easterly wind, the sea rushes, and overflows the country.

The hills have a picturesque, though dreary appearance, and afford a romantic ride:—the traveller may in general pass either on the beach or the land side; winding through the openings at pleasure.

The manner in which these banks have been originally formed appears at first sight mysterious: how the sand should be blown up into heaps, and not scattered flat over the face of the adjoining country, seems inexplicable. The marram, it is true, may have assisted; but this, alone, seems unequal to the task.

Until we had passed Mr. B—e's marshes, the

106.

beach lay open to the country; so that the stock have free egress to the sea; on the edge of which they delight to lie in the heat of the summer; when they lie cool and free from the flies, with which the marshes are greatly pestered. But, having passed Mr. B——'s grounds, the proprietors of the next marshes are under the necessity of fencing against the beach; lest their cattle should stray into Mr. B—'s liberty, who is lord of the manor.

This is done by placing rows of faggots in the gaps, between the sand-hills; which, being steep on the side towards the sea, are of themselves a fence.

The effect of these faggot-fences are striking; for the sand being blown upon the beach in a similar manner to snow, it drifts in the same way; and, in some places, the tops of the faggots are only to be seen; the sand having drifted on both sides; more particularly on the side towards the country; so that the cattle might now almost walk over them: and it strikes me very forcibly, that from fences, to keep the marsh cattle from straying away upon the beach, have originated the Marram Banks.

But whether this is the fact or not, I am fully convinced that by faggots, or some other

more

more fubftantial fencing, Marram Banks might,
at a trifling expence, be converted into a barrier
not to be broken by the fea : for, notwithftanding the long and violent eafterly winds
which have lately blown, fuch as to violence
and continuance has fcarcely been known before, there is only one place in which the fea
has been able to move even thefe bramble-
faggots; and this has happened in a gap which
is wider than ordinary : the faggots, here, being
forced out and fcattered over the marfhes.

From the curfory view I have had, the
moft eligible way of joining the hillocks, fo
as to form a regular embankment, feems to be
this :—Make a double fence in each gap;
placing the two fences at, perhaps, twenty or
thirty yards diftance from each other; or,
more generally fpeaking, at five to ten yards
within the fkirts of the prefent bank. As
foon as the hollow fpace between the firft pair
of fences be filled up with fand, raife another
pair, a few yards within the firft ; and above
thefe another, and another, until the gap be
filled up, or be raifed to a fufficient height;
and then, on the top, propagate the marram
plant.

Two rows of faggots might be fufficient for
the narrow gaps ; and for the larger ones fhip-
wreck,

wreck, or other old ſhip-timber, might be uſed; more eſpecially for the foundation courſe.

If the ſea ſhould hereafter gain upon the banks, ſo, as, in proceſs of time, to endanger the whole, raiſe a fence on the land-ſide at ſome diſtance from the old banks, to catch the ſand blown over them; and thus from the wreck of one embankment another might be raiſed, and the country kept in perpetual ſafety.

Mr. B——e has attempted to make the embankment a public matter; but has not ſucceeded. It ſtrikes me, however, that it would be well worth his while to defend his own coaſt at his own expence: but he ſays, " It " is not for me to attack the German Ocean " ſingle-handed."

Mr. Anſon has hit off a very great improvement upon his eſtate near Yarmouth.

On the Suffolk ſide of the river, oppoſite the Key of Yarmouth, were ſome low grounds, let, I believe, as marſh-land. Theſe grounds have lately been divided into lots, and let on building leaſes of ninety-nine years, at the greatly improved rent of ſeven pounds an acre; beſides the advantage which will accrue at the expiration of the term.

Such.

Such a ftroke as this is a *real* improvement of an eftate; and there are few extenfive eftates which will not, if properly attended to, admit of being advanced, without fending the farmer to jail, or the cottager to the poor-houfe.

107.

MAY 12. WORSTEAD FAIR.—This fair is held on Old May-Day, and is called " May Fair." It has for many years been noted for fat bullocks. This year, however, there were not more than a hundred bullocks in the fair, and not twenty of thofe which were *fat*. There were about three hundred head of cattle; chiefly two-year-olds, and cows and calves, with fome few buds.

The Norwich butchers were the principal chapmen for bullocks.

108.

MAY 17. Laft year,—to render my refidence more commodious, as well as to gain fome information on the fubject of cheefe-making—an art I was then a ftranger to—I rented a fmall dairy of cows. I took them the rather as I had then in my fervice an ex-

cellent

108.

CHEESE.

cellent Wiltſhire dairy-woman; who, I was in hopes, might be able to make ſome improvement on the Norfolk method of making cheeſe; which, I had been given to underſtand, was execrable.

Having long conſidered this intereſting ſubject as being allied to experimental philoſophy, I placed it in that light, and paid as much attention to the different proceſſes as an active ſcene of employment would permit me.—What I have been able to do is only an eſſay; but it is ſufficient to convince me, that with leiſure and application, much might be done towards bringing this, at preſent myſterious, but important ſubject to ſome certain and fixed principles.

In regiſtering the information I have been able to obtain, it will be proper to digeſt it under the following heads:

1. The preparation of the rennet.
2. The coagulation of the milk.
3. The management of the curd. 219
4. The management of the cheeſe. 226

1. *Rennet.* The curd which happens to be contained in the ſtomach of the calf when butchered, together with the hairs and dirt which are inſeparable from it, are uſed by the

dairy-

dairy-women of *this* country to coagulate their
milk : hence, probably, the rancid flavor of
the Norfolk cheefe; perfectly refembling in
fcent the *parent* curd ; and *this*, as nearly as may
be, *its more matured felf.*

The rennet which I made ufe of was prepared in the following manner.

Take a calf's bag, maw, or ftomach; and,
having taken out the curd contained therein,
wafh it clean, and falt it thoroughly, infide and
out, leaving a white coat of falt over every
part of it. Put it into an earthen jar, or other
veffel, and let it ftand three or four days; in
which time it will have formed the falt and its
own natural juices into a pickle. Take it out
of the jar, and hang it up for two or three days
to let the pickle drain from it; refalt it; place
it again in a jar; cover it tight down with a
paper pierced with a large pin; and in this ftate
let it remain until it be wanted for ufe. In this
ftate it ought to be kept twelve months: it
may however, in cafe of neceffity, be ufed a
few days after it has received the fecond falting; but it will not be fo ftrong as if kept a
longer time.

To prepare the rennet for ufe; take a hand-
full of the leaves of fweet-briar,—the fame

quantity of the leaves of the dog rofe, and the like quantity of bramble leaves; boil them in a gallon of water, with three or four handfulls of falt, about a quarter of an hour; ftrain off the liquor, and, having let it ftand until perfectly cool, put it into an earthen veffel, and add to it the maw, prepared as above. To this is added a found good lemon, ftuck round with about a quarter of an ounce of cloves; which give the rennet an agreeable flavor.

The longer the bag remains in the liquor, the ftronger of courfe will be the rennet: the quantity, therefore, requifite to turn a given quantity of milk, can only be afcertained by daily ufe and obfervation.

When the rennet is fufficiently ftrong take out the bag; hang it up two or three days for the rennet to drain from it;—refalt it;—put it down again into the jar; and thus continue to treat it, until its virtues are exhaufted; which will not be until it has been ufed feveral times.

By fuffering one or more bags to remain in the liquor, the rennet thus prepared may be raifed to a very high degree of ftrength, as will appear in the following obfervations.

The leaves and the fpice, it is probable, have no other effect than that of doing away

the

the ill flavor of the maw; which, if ever fo
well cleaned, retains a faint difagreeable fmell;
whereas the rennet prepared as above, is perfectly well flavored.

It is, however, I find, an idea among the
Wiltfhire dairy-women, that the leaves correct
any ranknefs or evil quality in the milk, arifing
from a ranknefs of pafture: they being further
of opinion, that different paftures require different forts of herbs to correct them; and
fome of them, it feems, are, or pretend to be,
fo deeply verfed in this art, that they will un-
dertake to correct any milk, fo as to prevent
the rifing " heaving" or " blowing" of the
cheefes made from it; and, confequently, the
rancidnefs which ufually accompanies a porous
cheefe.

This is, no doubt, a grand object of cheefe-
makers; but it is not, I apprehend, to be obtained by fo fmall a proportion of vegetable
juices as pafs with the rennet into fo large a proportion of milk. Neverthelefs, it appears to
me highly probable, that this grand defidera-
tum lies within the reach of the chemical art;
and that, by a courfe of judicious experiments,
fome vegetable or mineral preparation, adequate to this valuable purpofe, may be difcovered.

P 2　　　　　2. Coagulation.

2. *Coagulation.* Next to the art of correct-ing the milk (an art as yet in its infancy) this seems to claim the attention of the experimen-talist.

It is known, from daily experience, that the warmer the milk is, when the rennet is put to it, the sooner it will coagulate, with a given quantity of rennet of a given strength.

It is equally well known that the cooler the milk, and the longer it is in coagulating, the more tender and delicate the curd becomes: on the contrary, if the milk be too hot, and the coagulation takes place too rapidly, the curd proves tough and harsh.

But it seems to be a fact, equally well esta-blished, that a cheese made from milk, which has been cooly and slowly coagulated, is lon-ger before it become marketable than one made from milk which has undergone a less deliberate coagulation; and which, being drier, and of a harsher texture, sooner becomes " cheesey," and fit for the *taster.*

Therefore, the great art in this stage of the process lies in—

The degree of warmth of the milk when *set;* that is, when the rennet is put to it; or, in—

The

The degree of heat retained by the curd when it *comes*; that is, when the coagulation has sufficiently taken place; or, in—

The length of time between the *setting* and the *coming*. Which length of time may be regulated either—

By the degree of the warmth of the milk when set; or—

By the state of warmth in which it is kept during the time of coagulation; or—

By the quantity and strength (taken jointly) of the rennet.—

To endeavour to gain some information on this subject, I made the following observations.

1781. *June* 5. Twenty-three gallons of milk, heated to ninety-six degrees of Farenheit's scale, with two tea-cup-fulls of weakish rennet, came in one hour; the curd delicate and good.

June 6. The same quantity of milk, of the same heat, with the same quantity of rennet, came in nearly the same time; the curd somewhat tough; owing, probably, to the milk having been " burnt to the kettle" in which it was heated.

June 7. Twenty-seven gallons of milk, heated to ninety-four degrees, with the same quantity of rennet, came in about two hours; the curd very good.

June

June 8. Twenty-six gallons of milk, heated to one hundred and two degrees, with one tea-cup-full of rennet, came in two hours and a half; curd very good,

June 9. Twenty-five gallons of milk, heated to one hundred degrees, with a tea-cup-full and a half of rennet, came in about one hour and a half; the curd good, but somewhat tough; owing, perhaps, to the milk being kept too warm in the cheese-tub, by being covered up close with a thick cloth.

Note, On the seventh and eighth, the whey retained a heat of about eighty-eight degrees, whereas the whey this morning was ninety-two degrees: so that, perhaps, it is not the heat when it is *set*, but the heat when it *comes*, which gives the quality of the curd.

June 10. Twenty-five gallons: ninety-six degrees; two cups; uncovered: came in two hours and a quarter: whey eighty-seven degrees: curd very tender.

June 11. Twenty-three gallons; one hundred degrees; more than a tea-cup: uncovered: did not come in two hours; owing to the rennet being lower in strength than before; therefore, added in a little more rennet; which brought it in about three hours from first setting:

ting: the whey eighty-feven degrees: the curd uncommonly delicate..

June 12. Twenty-four gallons of milk: one hundred degrees: two cups of rennet: uncovered: came in two hours: whey eighty-nine degrees: curd uncommonly *tender*.

June 13. Twenty-eight gallons of milk: ninety-two degrees: three cups (fay ftrongly renneted): covered up with a coarfe linen cloth: came in one hour and a half: whey eighty-fix degrees: curd very good, and of a very fine colour; though perhaps would have handled tenderer, if it had not ftood fome time after it came before it was broke up.

Perhaps much depends on its being broke up in the critical minute.

June 14. Twenty-eight gallons: one hundred degrees: two cup-fulls: uncovered: came in one hour and a quarter: whey ninety-four degrees: curd fomewhat harfh, but of a good colour.

The change of colour is therefore owing to the change of pafture.

Note, The milk fhould be covered to make it come together:—this came and grew hard at the bottom, half an hour before it was fet at the top.

June 15. Twenty-eight gallons : milk heated to ninety-five degrees : with two cups of rennet; and covered after it had stood three quarters of an hour : came in one hour and a half : whey eighty-nine degrees (the morning warm): curd very good and tender.

June 16. Thirty gallons of milk: heated to one hundred and three degrees ; but lowered by two pails-full of cold water to ninety-six degrees ; with two cups and a half of rennet ; and kept close covered : came in one hour : whey ninety-four degrees : curd pretty good ; but not sufficiently tender.

June 17. Twenty-eight gallons ; ninety-seven degrees : two and one-half cups : covered ; but not close : came in one hour and a half; whey not tried : curd somewhat tough.

Note, the toughness is owing, perhaps, to some milk of a new-calven cow being among it.

Note also, to try the exact heat of milk immediately from the cow, immerged a dish in the pail while milking. After it had lain long enough to receive a degree of heat equal to that of the milk in the pail, emptied it, and immediately milked into it from the teat (the cow being

being at this time about half milked); the heat
ninety-five degrees.

Note also, the cheeses of yesterday (the
16th of June) press remarkably elastic, and
spungy (like a fungus): *perhaps* owing to the
milk's coming too hot; or *perhaps* to two or
three of the cows being then a-bulling *; or
perhaps, being made thicker than usual, the
press was not heavy enough for them; or *perhaps* this ill quality is owing to the cold water
being put into the milk.

June 18. Thirty gallons: ninety-five degrees:
covered: came in one hour and a half: whey
ninety-two degrees : curd pretty good.

June 19. Thirty gallons : ninety-two degrees :
two cups covered: curd very good.

June 21. Thirty gallons: ninety-eight degrees;
lowered by half a pail of cold water to ninety-
five degrees : the curd good; but the cheeses
like those of the 16th press, hollow and
spungy.

* I afterwards found that the milk of a cow, on the day
of amour, retained, after having stood some time in the
pail after milking, ninety-eight degrees of heat. This shews
that the state if not the quality of the milk is altered by the
heat of the cow ; and a cautious dairy-woman always endeavours to keep such milk out of her cheese-tub.

There-

Therefore, it is *probable,* from thefe two incidents, that lowering the heat of the milk, with cold water, has an evil effect.

June 23. (Evening) Fifteen gallons of new milk warm from the cow, retaining a heat of ninety-two degrees, with two cups and a half of new weak runnet, and clofely covered, came in three quarters of an hour : whey eighty-eight degrees : curd very delicate and good.

June 25. Forty gallons of *half-fkim* milk, heated to eighty-feven degrees, with three cups of rennet, flightly covered, came in three quarters of an hour : whey feventy-nine degrees: curd remarkably good of *this* fort.

Sept. 8. In obferving the effect of fome remarkably ftrong rennet, I found that an ordinary tea-cup-full coagulated fufficiently upwards of forty gallons of milk, heated to only eighty-eight degrees, in thirty-five minutes.

From thefe obfervations it appears, that curd of a good quality may be obtained from milk heated from 87 to 103 degrees of Fahrenheit's thermometer ; provided the rennet be fo proportioned, that the time of coagulation be from three quarters of an hour to two hours and a half; and provided the milk be kept *properly* covered during the procefs of coagulation.

And

And from thefe as well as from a variety of other obfervations, which I made in the courfe of the fummer, but which are not minuted, it appears to me, at prefent, that from 85 to 90 are the proper degrees of heat; that from one to two hours is the proper time of coagulation; and that the milk ought to be covered fo as to lofe in the procefs about 5 degrees of its original heat.

But climature, feafons, the weather, and the pafture, may require that thefe bounds fhould fometimes be broken. A few obfervations, made in one feafon, and in one place, how accurately foever they may have been taken, are by no means adequate to the entire illuftration of this very abftrufe fubject.

3. *The curd.* — In Norfolk this ftage of the procefs is very fhort. Part of the whey being laded off, the remainder, with the curd, is poured into a cloth :—the whey drains through ; the curd is fhook in the cloth ; kneaded down into a vat; put under a light prefs, or perhaps under a ftone; the cloth once changed; the curd once turned; and lo ! a Norfolk cheefe appears. The cows are milked and the cheefe compleated in ten or twelve hours.

The

The practice in my dairy has been uniformly this.—As soon as the curd is come at the top, firm enough to discharge its whey, the dairy-woman tucks up her sleeves, plunges her hands to the bottom of the vessel; and, with a wooden dish, stirs the curd and whey briskly about : she then lets go the dish, and, by a circular motion of her hands and arms, violently agitates the whole ; carefully breaking every part of the curd ; and, at intervals, stirs it hard to the bottom with the dish ; so that not a piece of curd remains unbroken larger than a hazelnut. This is done to prevent what is called " slip-curd " (that is, lumps of curd which have slipped unbroken through the dairy-woman's hands), which, by retaining its whey, does not press uniformly with the other curd, but in a few days (if it happen to be situated toward the rind) turns livid and jelly-like, and soon becomes faulty and rotten. This operation takes about five or ten minutes ; or, if the quantity of curd be large, a quarter of an hour.

In a few minutes the curd subsides, leaving the whey clear upon the top. The dairy-woman now takes her dish, and lades off the whey into a pail; which she empties into a

milk-

milk-lead to ftand for cream, to be churned
for whey butter *.

Having laded off all the whey fhe can, without gathering up the fmall pieces of loofe
curd floating near the bottom of the veffel,
fhe fpreads a ftraining-cloth over her cheefe-
tongs, and ftrains the whey through it, returning the curd retained in the cloth into the
cheefe-tub. When fhe has got all the whey
fhe can, by preffing the curd with her hand
and the lading-difh, fhe takes a knife and cuts
it into fquare pieces, about two or three inches
fquare. This lets out more of the whey, and
makes the curd handy to be taken up, in order
to be broken into the vats †.

* This is a practice peculiar to the cheefe counties,
and forms no inconfiderable part of the profit of a dairy
in thofe counties. In Norfolk, the whey, even from new
milk, paffes from the cheefe-veffels immediately to the
hog-tub.

† A dairy fhould be plentifully furnifhed with vats;
and fome of them of different fizes; for when three or
four cheefes are made at each meal, a number of vats become actually in ufe; and if there are not ftill a number
empty, the dairy-woman becomes confined in her choice,
and cannot proportion exactly her vats to the quantity of
curd fhe *happens* to find in her cheefe-tub; and keeping
a little overplus curd from meal to meal frequently fpoils
a whole cheefe.

Having

108.

CHEESE.

Having made choice of a vat or vats, proportioned to the quantity of curd, so that the cheese, when fully pressed, shall neither over nor under fill the vat, she spreads a cheese-cloth loosely over the vat; into which she re-breaks the curd; carefully squeezing every part of it in her hands; and, having filled the vat heaped up and rounded above its top, folds over the cloth, and places it in the press *.

In autumn, when the weather got cool and moist, the curd was *scalded*, " to make the " cheese come quicker to hand," (that is, sooner saleable) and to prevent a white woolley coat from rising. It is done thus: If from

---

* Much depends on the construction and power of the press. The excellency of construction depends upon its pressing level: if it has too much play, so as to incline and become tottering or leaning one way or another, and do not fall perpendicular upon the cheese-board, one side of a cheese will frequently be thicker than another; and, what is still worse, one side will be thoroughly pressed while the other is left soft and spongy. Its power may be given by a screw, by a lever, or by a dead weight, and ought to be proportioned to the thickness of the cheese.

I had one constructed on the above principles; the power, a dead weight of stones, contained in a cubical box, moving in grooves so as to keep its bottom horizontal; the medium weight, 1 cwt. 2 qrs. but regulated, by the stones, agreeably to the thickness of the cheese or cheeses to be pressed.

new

new milk, fcalding water (boiling water with a fmall quantity of cold whey mixed with it) is poured over the whole furface of the curd as it lies at the bottom of the cheefe-tub : If from fkimmed or other inferior milk, the out-fides only are fcalded, after the curd is in the vat, by firft pouring the fcalding water on one fide, and then, turning the cheefeling, pouring it on the other. For if in this cafe the *curd* were to be fcalded, it would render it hard, and fpoil the tafte and texture of the cheefe. In fcalding the *cheefeling*, the curd is firft put into the bare naked vat, and the upper part fcalded : the cheefe-cloth is then fpread over it, and the vat being turned, the curd falls into the cloth : the curd, with the cloth under it, is then put into the vat; the outer edges pared off; the parings broke, and rounded up in the middle ; and the fcalding water poured upon it as before; the folds of the cloth laid over, and the vat fet in the prefs.

The whey, being pretty well preffed out, and the cheefeling (whether it has been fcalded or not) having got firm enough to handle, which it will be in about half an hour, the dairy-woman takes it out of the vat; wafhes the cloth in a pail of clean cold water; fpreads

it

it over the vat; turns the cheefeling upon it; fqueezes it gently into the vat; folds over the cloth; tucks in the corner with a wooden cheefe-knife; and replaces the vat in the prefs.

Suppofing the cheefeling to be made in the morning, it now remains in the prefs, un-touched, until the evening; when it is taken out, *falted*, put into a frefh dry cloth, and left in the prefs all night.

The method of falting is this:—The falt being well bruifed, and the lumps thoroughly broken, it is fpread plentifully on each fide of the cheefeling, fo as wholly to cover it, about one-tenth of an inch in thicknefs, more or lefs, in proportion to the thicknefs of the cheefe. If this be of a confiderable thicknefs, as fuppofe three inches and upwards, fome falt is put into the middle of it, by ftopping when the vat is half filled with curd, ftrewing on the falt, and on this putting the remainder of the curd.

Next morning, if the curd be rich, or has been cold-run, the cheefeling is turned into another dry cloth, and left in the prefs till evening: but if on the contrary the curd be from poor milk, or from milk which before

fetting

setting had acquired any degree of sourness, or if it has been run hot and quick, the cheesling should in the morning be "bare-vatted;" that is, be put into the vat without a cloth round it, and be put again into the press until evening.

The use of bare-vatting is to take out the marks of the cloth; and thereby evade a waste of labour in bringing the cheese to a smooth glossy coat. The reason for the above distinction is, therefore, obvious; for the harder the curd, the longer the marks of the cloth are in pressing out.

In the evening, that which was turned into the dry cloth in the morning, is now bare-vatted; and that which was bare-vatted in the morning, is now turned in the vat; and, having stood in the press until morning, the process is finished. The *cheeses* are taken out of the vats; and placed upon the shelf.

Thus, supposing the cheesling to be made on Monday morning, seven o'clock; it is, between eight and nine, taken out of the vat; the cloth washed; and immediately placed in the press again. On Monday evening, it is salted and, if wanted, pared * ; put into a dry

---

* A cheesling should never, in strict propriety, be pared after it has been bare-vatted.

cloth; and replaced in the prefs. On Tuefday morning it is bare-vatted, or the cloth changed; the cheefling, in either cafe, being turned, and again put into the prefs. On Tuefday evening it is again turned; and on Wednefday morning finally taken out of the vat and prefs.

4. *The cheefe.*—The objects of this moft laborious department of cheefemaking are, to preferve the cheefe *found* in itfelf, and to give it fuch an *appearance* as will recommend it to a purchafer.

Cheefes newly made, naturally acquire a white fcurfy coat; which, befides hiding, if not caufing, the defects of the cheefe, is at leaft unfightly, and is a certain mark of the flovenlinefs of its maker. This fcurf arifes more plentifully on a poor than on a rich cheefe. Cold moift weather encourages it; but, in warm weather, the oily exudation of a rich and well-made cheefe goes near of itfelf to eradicate the *white,* and bring on that defirable *blue* coat, which is at once a criterion of the goodnefs of the cheefe and of the fkilfulnefs of the dairy-woman.

The Norfolk dairy-woman, however, pays little regard to appearances; and, to fpeak truly of her, is equally ambitious to pleafe the eye

and

and the palate. Her method is this:—the cheese (or rather as yet a bundle of curd) being taken out of the press, is salted upon a large earthen platter, in the same manner a piece of beef or pork is salted; and, having lain some time in salt; it is put upon a shelf to dry and stiffen.

Being in a manner unpressed; never cleaned, and but seldom turned; it is no wonder, that in a short time the white scurfy coat gets full possession of it; or that its surface should appear bloated and wrinkled; or that its rind should be divided by innumerable fissures.; or that its appearance, altogether, should be that of a sugared plumb-cake, rather than of a cheese.

However, with respect to appearances, the Norfolk dairy-woman may plead in excuse that her customers are familiarized to the *sights* which she prepares for them: but when she follows a practice which subjects her produce, if not sold off while yet in an unripe state, to almost inevitable destruction; she is highly culpable.

Cheeses made in this country are attacked by an enemy little dreaded, or wholly unknown, in the cheese counties; namely, a species of

maggot,

108.

CHEESE.

maggot, whofe unlimited mifchievoufnefs feems to be confined to this part of the kingdom.

The fly, which is the caufe of this ferious mifchief, is of a fpecies fomewhat fmall, flender, black, and fhining; very much refembling the fmall winged ant. Wherever it finds a crack or other defect in the rind, be it ever fo minute, it turns its tail towards the aperture; and, by the infertion of a flender fheath not unlike the fting of a bee, there depofits its eggs. If the fiffure be fufficiently large and deep, it enters its hind-parts alfo: if ftill deeper, it crawls backward into the cheefe; leaving only its head in fight, and thus injects its eggs to a confiderable depth.

As the maggots rife into life, they travel ftill farther into the fubftance of the cheefe; and, if it happens to be porous, foon pervade every part of it; in a few weeks working its total deftruction: for not only the parts they immediately inhabit, but the whole cheefe becomes bitter, and entirely inedible; except by fome of the good people of the country, to whom cuftom has rendered even the maggots grateful.

Laft year (1781) being remarkable for flies of every fpecies, there were, in this neighbourhood,

hood, many dairy-women who had not, even in September, one thoroughly found new-milk cheefe in their dairies.

A remedy for this evil would be a valuable difcovery to the Eaft Norfolk farmer: for although Eaft Norfolk is not properly fpeaking a dairy country, there are a great number of cows kept in it; not only for its home confump-tion of butter and cheefe, but for the pur-pofe of rearing bullocks for the London market.

The only remedy practifed here, in com-mon, is to place in the cheefe-chamber large boughs, on which the flies fettle. The boughs being loaded with flies, are taken into another room, and beaten upon the floor; by which means numbers may be deftroyed; numbers, however, are ftill left behind; and while there is one fly in the room, a defective cheefe is not fafe.

This mifchievous animal, whether in its fly or maggot ftate, is very difficult to be de-ftroyed, without actually crufhing it. *By way of experiment*, fhut up the cheefe-chamber as clofe as poffible; and burnt in it not lefs than four or five ounces of fulphur; caufing a fume powerful enough to have ftifled an elephant;

but

108.
CHEESE.

but not a fly suffered by it.—*Again*, put a slice of cheese affected by the maggot, into some boiling water, immediately from the tea-kettle: let it lie a few minutes in the water: took it out and broke it: the maggots were, to every appearance, as much alive as if they had not been in the water!—It is in vain, therefore, to think of destroying the animal; for, although the fly may be easily killed by hand or otherwise, and, with a little pains, the dairy and cheese-chamber might for a moment be cleared; yet, from the numbers which are bred in the neighbour-hood, the very air is filled with them; and the room, of course, presently replenished: therefore, the only way left of avoiding the loss is to endeavour to find out some means of defending the cheeses themselves against the attacks of these destructive ene-mies.

These means, I flatter myself, are fully pointed out in the practice I am now register-ing.

The first week or ten days, the new-made cheeses are carefully turned once a day; great care being had not to break the yet tender rind in turning; nor to suffer it to be cracked by

too

too free an admiffion of a dry, parching air.

As foon as they are become firm enough to be handled with fafety, they are cleaned in this manner: fome fkimmed whey being put into a milk-lead, or other broad, fhallow veffel, fo as to cover the bottom of it half an inch or an inch deep, the cheefes to be cleaned are taken from the fhelf and placed in the whey. One fide being thoroughly moiftened, the other fide is placed downward: the edges too are wetted with a cloth, fo as to make the whole coat of the cheefe foaking wet. The dairy-woman then takes a hard brufh, and brufhes every part of the cheefe; frequently dipping her brufh in the whey, to eradicate the white coat more readily and more effectually. This done, fhe places them again on the fhelves; but before they be quite dry, while their coats are yet moift, fhe rubs them over with a cloth, on which a piece of whey, or other common, butter has been fpread. This keeps the rind fupple, and free from cracks; checks the fcurfy coat from rifing; and, by ftopping the pores and fiffures of the coat, prevents the fly from depofiting her eggs. If the rind be rough, from the marks of the cloth or other caufe, fhe fcrapes them with a knife, or other inftrument:

Q 4   this

108.
CHEESE.

this laſt operation, however, is as yet performed with great care and delicacy.

Having thus waſhed and ſcraped them two or three times (in the courſe of about a week from the firſt cleanſing) ſhe removes them from the dairy-ſhelves into ſome ſpacious airy room, with a firm even floor, which ſhe firſt rubs plentifully with green ſucculent nettles, ſo as to give it a temporary greenneſs, and then places her cheeſes in rows upon the prepared floor. She now waſhes them no more; but, if the coat be yet rough, and the ſcurf continue to riſe, ſhe ſcrapes them more freely than before; and, as the rind gets harſh, ſoftens it with butter; thus continuing to treat them, and ſtill continuing to turn them once a day, until they acquire a rich golden poliſh, and the *blue coat* begin to ſhew itſelf.

This criſis, namely, the appearance of the blue coat, is not altogether regulated by the age of the cheeſe, but depends on its quality and the ſtate of the weather. Perhaps it may appear before the cheeſe be one, perhaps not until it be more than two, or even three, months old; therefore, no certain number of cleanings can be fixed; theſe rules, however, may be obſervable: ſcrape and rub them, until they be

per-

perfectly fmooth; mellow the rind with butter, whenever, for want of natural exudation, their coats get dry and harfh; thus continuing to keep them fmooth yellow and gloffy, until the blue coat begin to make its appearance, voluntarily; and then, but not before, begin to encourage the blue coat.

This ingenious procefs is thus conducted: Having rubbed the floor thoroughly with frefh nettles, the dairy-woman places fuch of the cheefes upon it as fhe judges to be ready for "coating;" and upon the top of each cheefe puts three or four vine-leaves; or, for want of thefe, a cabbage-leaf. This, if the cheefe be good, will in a day or two bring up the defired veftment: but an inferior cheefe will take a longer time in coating; and as the leaves lofe their greennefs and fucculence, fhe replaces them with frefh ones; and as fhe turns the cheefes, which is now done every fecond or third day, fhe re-covers the upper fides with leaves; but wipes their edges hard with a clammy cloth; fo that the *edge*, and a narrow ring round each fide, ever retain the polifhed yellow hue.

When the cheefes were properly coated, and their edges had got fufficiently firm, they were

placed

placed on edge in a cheese-rack *, and, without further care, (except once a week moving them a little round, and now and then wiping their edges) there remained until the time they were sent to market,—which was yesterday.

The *soil* from which these cheeses were made is a sandy loam, but lies cooler, and is of a better quality than are Norfolk soils in general.

The *herbage* principally rye grafs (*lolium perenne*), oat grafs (*bromus mollis*), and white clover (*trifolium repens*), being principally new-lays of three to five years old.

---

* *Cheese-racks* fave labour in turning,—collect the cheese into a small compafs, - and put it out of the way of vermin. They may be variously conftructed. The plate-rack, with four or five tier one above another, feems to be the beft form. If the cheefes be nearly of one fize, the rack fhould be made the fame width at the top as the bottom : but if they be of different fizes, it ought to be made narrower at the top than at the bottom ; and if they be of different thicknesses as well as of different diameters, the spaces for the respective cheefes fhould likewife be varied. A fmall rack may be flung with a rope and pullies at each end ; fo as be to drawn up and lowered down at pleafure : but a large one is difficult to fling, in a common room, in that manner ; it ought therefore to ftand on legs about two feet high, with a broad bafe-board projecting over the legs, fo as to prevent vermin from climbing up into the rack. Mine was on the latter conftruction.

The

The *cows* of the Lancashire *breed* *, and of different *ages*.

The *cheese*, in quality and appearance, refembles very much that of inferior Warwick-shire, or the two-meal cheese of Gloucester-shire; being lean and dry, considering the species of milk; which was neat, or nearly neat, from the cow.

This inferior quality is probably owing, in a great measure, to the quality of the soil; and perhaps, in some degree, to the method made use of in separating the whey.

With respect to the *fly*, not one cheese in a hundred (after the mischief was first discovered) suffered from it. There cannot be a greater proof of the eligibility of the method in this case practised, than that of my being able to preserve the principal part of the dairy to a time when there is not, generally speaking, another Norfolk cheese in *this* part of the county †.

If

---

* That something considerable depends on the breed or *variety* of cow is evident from an experiment I made with the milk of the Alderney cow; the produce from which was of a texture almost as close and firm as bees-wax, and nearly as high-coloured; as different in quality and appearance from the produce of the long-horned cows, as if they were two distinct *species* of animals.

† On the Suffolk side of the county, about Harleston

and

108.
CHEESE.

If from one year's experience I might venture to dictate in the art of making cheese in
Norfolk, it would be in this way.

1. To make use of a clean well-flavoured
rennet.

2. To pursue the method now in use of separating the curd from the whey : for, although
the method above described may be eligible
on rich land (and is practised in the counties
of Wiltshire, Gloucestershire, and Warwick-
shire), yet, on a leaner soil, it may be prudent
to preserve as many of the butyraceous particles
as possible in the curd, rather than to suffer
them to escape from this, and pass through the
whey into butter * ; *provided cheeses of a sufficient contexture to secure them from the attacks of
the fly, can be produced by the method of separating
the whey now in practice in Norfolk.*

3. To let the cheeses remain in the press
until they have acquired a sufficient degree of

and Difs, the method of making cheese partakes of the
Suffolk practice ; which, though *not celebrated*, is a degree
above that of East-Norfolk.

* It is, however, observable in this place, that, in point
of *neat profit*, it is highly probable that the *certain* advantage arising from the butter would more than overbalance
any *probable* advantage which the quality of the cheese
would receive by retaining in the curd *a part* of this
butter.

firm-

firmnefs, and their rind fuch a degree of toughnefs, that they may, on being taken out, of the prefs, be fafely handled, without danger of cracking.

4. To keep their coats fupple and clean; the firft, to prevent, as much as poffible, their cracking afterwards in turning; and the latter, to difcover with greater readinefs, and to remedy with greater eafe when difcovered, any flaw which, through accidents or overfight, may happen.

5. If through accident or neglect the fly fhould be fuffered to make an impreffion (which is eafily difcoverable by a dimple in the rind and its foftnefs to the touch), cut out the part affected (perhaps not yet larger than a walnut), duft the wound with pepper, fill it up with butter, and clofe it with a piece of foft paper: thus forming an artificial rind, which will fecure it from further injury, until it has acquired an age fufficient to recommend it to a purchafer.

By thefe rules, *I am of opinion*, that cheefe of a middle quality as to richnefs, and fecure againft the fly, might be produced in Eaft Norfolk; *provided the prefent method of feparating the whey, will give the cheefling a fufficient degree of texture to be handled with fafety* *.

* My doubts, refpecting this matter, arife not more
from

108.
CHEESE.

If not, *I am certain*, that by adhering clofely throughout, to the practice above regiftered, a *wholefome* good cheefe, palatable to men in general, and *proof againft the fly*, may be made in Eaft Norfolk, with a great degree of certainty.

from the loofe crumbly texture of Norfolk cheefes in general, than from the following practice; which, likewife, ftrengthens my apprehenfions of the richnefs of the cheefe in queftion being lowered by the curd having been broken too finely in the whey.

A gentlewoman, who lives in this neighbourhood, who pays a perfonal attention to her dairy, and whofe abilities in matters of houfehold are indifputable, fays, that when fhe wifhes to make a cheefe of a fuperior degree of richnefs, for her own table, fhe takes the curd and whey out of the cheefe-tub very gently, with a fleeting difh (before they have been any way difturbed) and puts them immediately into the vat; upon which fhe places a broad hoop; by means of which fhe is able to pile up a fufficient quantity of this wheyey curd to fill the vat when preffed. She then folds over the cloth, and lets the prefs down upon it, very gently and gradually; fo as to fqueeze out the whey, and at the fame time retain that rich milky liquor which is mixed among the curd, and which by much breaking before it be put into the vat, is loft among the whey. With care, fhe fays, the whey may be drawn off quite green and clear; leaving the "buttery" particles behind in the cheefe. By this means, fhe fays, fhe has made cheefes which have toafted as fat as Gloucefterfhire cheefe: but adds, that *great care is neceffary in handling a cheefling thus made; for if it crack, no preffing will ever clofe it again.*

109.

109.

MAY 17. In the course of last summer I BUTTER.
likewise paid confiderable attention to the art
of making butter; regiftering, at the time of
obfervation, the minutiæ of the different pro-
ceffes.

In the production of good butter, much no
doubt depends on *foil* and *herbage*; and fomething, perhaps, on the fpecies of *cow* :—much,
nevertheless, depends upon *management*.

The different ftages of the art are,

1. Milking the cow.
2. Setting the milk.
3. Preferving the cream.
4. Churning.
5. Making up the butter, for prefent ufe.
6. Putting it down, for future ufe.

1. *Milking.*—Cleanlinefs is the bafis of the
whole art.—A dairy-maid fhould not be fuffered
to fit down under a cow with a pail which a
fine lady would fcruple to cool her tea in; nor
until fhe has wafhed the teat of the cow and
her own hands : and for this purpofe clean water and a cloth fhould always be at hand.

A cow

109.
BUTTER.

A cow fhould be milked at regular and ftated hours; and, if poffible, always by the fame perfon : for cows, in general, will not give down their milk fo willingly to a ftranger as to one with whom they are intimate. The confequence is, the richeft and beft part of the milk is left behind in the udder, and the cow which is not clean-milked becomes *dry* prematurely.

2. *Setting the milk.* Much depends on the cleannefs of the veffel, the degree of heat of the milk when fet, and its depth in the veffel.

In fummer it is difficult to fet milk to cool : —in winter no time fhould be loft in getting it as foon as poffible into the pan or milk-lead. Should it be fet too hot in fummer, " the cream does not rife fo fmooth and rich, nor in fo large a quantity, as when it has been fet of a due degree of warmth :—it is apt to come up *frothy* ; and does not, in this cafe, prove well in the churn."

Judicious dairy-women, therefore, in fummer, pour their new milk firft into a large earthen jar or other veffel, there letting it remain half an hour ; or until it be nearly cool, and the *froth* be funk ; and then put it into the lead or

pan

pan, in which cold water has, until that time, ſtood.

If it be ſet too cool in winter, the cream will not riſe ſo thick as when ſet immediately from the teat, or has had a little hot water put into the milk; viz. about a pint of water to a gallon of milk, or as much as will make it new-milk warm : that is, ninety to ninety-five degrees.

The depth of the milk ſhould not exceed two inches : from one to two is a proper depth. If the milk be ſet too thick, the cream does not riſe ſo freely ; nor, conſequently, in ſo large a quantity in a given time. If ſet too ſhallow, it is difficult to ſeparate the cream from it.

3. *Preſerving the cream*—The great art here lies in keeping the cream free from ranknefs, to a proper age.

Freſh cream affords a well-flavoured butter ; but yields a leſs quantity than ſtale cream ; it being a received opinion among dairy-women, that age, and a ſlight degree of *aceſtency* in the cream, increaſes the quantity, without injuring, ſenſibly, the quality of the butter ; but that the ſmalleſt degree of *rancidity* in the cream ſpoils the flavour of the butter.

In winter, cream may be eaſily kept free from any degree of acidity ; but, in ſummer, it requires fome care to keep it entirely free even from ranknefs.

A quantity of cream, though ever fo judicioufly taken off the milk, will, when put into a veffel, and fuffered to ftand fome time, let fall a greater or fmaller quantity of milk.

It has been difcovered that this milk, or dregs of the cream, which fubfides at the bottom of the veffel, becomes rancid much fooner than the cream itfelf; and that, being fuffered to remain at the bottom of the veffel, it prefently communicates its rancidity to the cream : and further, that if it be permitted to mix again with the cream in the churn, the butter takes that marbled half-cheefe-like appearance under which we too frequently fee it.

Therefore, a judicious dairy-woman never fuffers thefe dregs to remain any length of time under the cream. She has two means of preventing it; namely, repeatedly ftirring them together to prevent them from fubfiding too frequently; and, when a proper quantity is fubfided, pouring off the cream into a frefh veffel, leaving the dregs behind. In fummer, a good dairy-woman ftirs her cream-jar every time (generally fpeaking) fhe

goes

goes into the dairy; and shifts it every morning (and in close muggy weather every evening) into a fresh, clean, well-scalded jar, or other vessel.

To take off the rankness of cream produced from turneps, the *Norfolk* dairy-women sometimes scald their cream : this however is allowed to lessen its productiveness of butter; and I was told by a lady, whose attention to her dairy entitles her to credit in this case, that putting a quart of boiling water into each pail of milk before it be set, is a more effectual and less wasteful remedy.

4. *Churning.* The principal art in churning lies in keeping the cream of a due degree of warmth in the churn; and in giving it a due and regular agitation. Warmth and a rapid motion makes it come quick : coolness, and a gentle motion, brings it slowly. If butter come too quickly, it is soft and *frothy*, and soon turns rancid; nor does it part from the butter-milk so freely, nor yields so large a quantity, as when it has been a proper time in churning. If it come too slowly, there is labour lost; besides the butter losing its flavour and texture. From one to two hours is a proper length of time in churning.

If

109.

BUTTER.

If the weather be hot, the churn ought to be chilled with cold water before the cream be put into it, and fhould be placed in a cool fituation: if cold, fcald the churn with boiling water, and endeavour to churn in a warm room. If in either cafe thefe be not fufficient, add hot or cold water to the cream during the time of churning.

If the cream be inclined to get *frothy* in the churn, open its mouth for a few minutes, to let in the air, and give the froth time to diffipate; and the butter will generally come fooner than it would have done had the agitation been continued: for, while the cream is in a ftate of *frothinefs*, the butter will not feparate. Reverfing the motion has fometimes a good effect *.

---

* It is this ftate of *frothinefs*, (fermentation it cannot be called) which fometimes gives inexperienced dairy-women much fatigue of body, and anxiety of mind. In the days of witchcraft the caufe was readily afcribed; and the witch was often fuccefsfully burnt-out, with a red-hot poker. The devil, to this day, is now and then fubjected to a fimilar treatment; and with equal fuccefs: for while the poker is heating the froth fubfides; and, in cold weather, the warmth communicated to the cream renders this ftroke of heroinifm doubly efficacious. There may be other caufes (than the frothinefs of the cream) of that obftinate delay which not unfrequently happens in this important operation; which well deferves a philofophical inveftigation.

If

If the butter come in small particles which are slow in uniting, strain off part of the butter-milk; and the butter in general will sooner gather. Reversing the motion generally gathers the butter quickest +.

5. *Making up the butter.* When the butter is sufficiently gathered in the churn, which is known by the largeness of the lumps, and the cleanness of the *dashers*, it is taken out; kneaded in a bowl, or other shallow vessel, to let out the butter-milk; spread thin over the inside of the bowl, and clean cold water poured over it; kneaded, broken, and re-spread in the water; the water poured off; the butter beaten, in large lumps or handfulls of three or four pounds, against the side of the bowl; re-spread; salted; the salt worked in; re-washed; and re-beaten, until the water come off unsullied; which it will do after two or three washings. It is then broken into pound-lumps; re-beaten against the bowl; and printed, or otherwise made up.

But before the dairy-woman begins to take the butter out of the churn, she first scalds, and then plunges immediately into cold water, every vessel and thing which she is about to make use of; in order to prevent the butter

+ A horizontal or barrel-churn is here to be understood.

from

109.
BUTTER.

from fticking to them. In fummer, when the butter is very foft, it is fometimes neceffary to rub them after fcalding with falt, which greatly affifts the wood in retaining the moifture.

She alfo puts her own hands into the hotteft water fhe can bear them in; rubs them with falt; and immediately plunges them into cold water:—this fhe repeats as often as fhe finds the butter ftick to them.

There is a *finifhing* operation, which is fometimes given in the neighbourhood of the metropolis, and perhaps in fome few provincial diftricts: in general however this excellent finifh is omitted;—either through want of knowledge, or want of induftry, or through *policy:* for its ufe being to give not only firmnefs and a wax-like evennefs of texture to the butter, but to extract from it entirely the butter-milk and the water in which it has been wafhed, the quantity is thereby leffened; for fo many ounces of milk and water extracted, fo many ounces fewer of butter go to market: this however is the beft proof of its utility; and butter cannot ftrictly be faid to be marketable, until it has undergone this operation: which is thus performed.

The bowl or tray being wetted to prevent the butter from fticking to it; and a cheefe-cloth

cloth ftrainer or other cloth being wafhed in clean cold water and wrung as dry as poffible; a pound-lump of butter is placed in the bowl; and, with a ftroke of the hand proportioned to the ftiffnefs of the butter, is beaten with the cloth. As the pat of butter becomes flat and thin, it is rolled up with the cloth, (by a kind of dexterity which can only be acquired by practice) and again beaten flat; the dairy-woman, every three or four ftrokes, rolling up either one fide or the other of the pat, and moving it about in the bowl to prevent its ftick-ing. As the cloth fills with moifture (which it extracts from the butter and imbibes in the manner of a fpunge) it is wrung and re-wafhed in clean cold water. Each pound of butter requires in cool weather four or five minutes to be beaten thoroughly, but two minutes are at any time of effential fervice.

In warm weather it is well to beat it two or three times over; as the coolnefs of the cloth affifts in giving firmnefs to the butter *.

* 1781, JULY 23. Weighed a lump of butter before and after being beaten with a cloth. Before beating it weighed fixteen ounces and a quarter; after beating fifteen ounces and three quarters; juft half an ounce of butter-milk and water being abforbed by the cloth, during about three minutes beating. The cloth was wrung equally hard before and after the operation : a confiderable quantity of milk and water was wrung out of it.

6. *Putting*

6. *Putting down.*—The more pure the butter is when put down, and the more perfectly it is afterwards kept from a communication with the outward air, the longer it will retain a state of perfect *sweetness.*

The purity of butter consists in its being free from internal air, moisture, filth, and a rankness of flavour.

The preservation of butter therefore depends principally on the *pasture* and the method of *making.* If the pasture be rank, whether through *soil, manure,* or *herbage,* it is generally injudicious to put down butter from it. But if the pasture be sweet; and the cows be properly milked, the milk judiciously set, the cream carefully kept, and properly churned; and the butter well worked up, with an additional quantity of salt; there is little art necessary in *putting it down* so as to preserve it sweet for several months: nevertheless the more judiciously it is put down, the *longer* it will retain its sweetness.

There are various vessels used for putting down butter. When a length of carriage is necessary, wooden firkins are the safest: gla-zed earthen-ware, however, is preferable when it can be made use of with safety and conveni-ency: for, out of this, the external air may be entirely secluded.

The

The figure or fhape of a butter jar fhould be that of the lower fruftum of a cone ; namely, wider at the bottom than the top : refembling the ftanding or upright churn : the top of it being made fufficiently wide to admit of its being filled conveniently ; but not wider.

109.

BUTTER.

This form prevents the butter from rifing in the jar, and effectually prevents the air from infinuating itfelf between the jar and the butter ; whofe natural elafticity preffes it, in this cafe, ftill clofer to the fides of the containing veffel : but, were the form of this reverfed, the fame propenfity of expanfion in the butter would feparate it from the fides of the jar, fo that towards the top a knife might (as it frequently may) be drawn round between them, and the air of courfe have free admiffion.

The method of putting it down is this : — The butter having lain in pound-lumps twenty-four hours, the dairy-woman takes two or three of the lumps, joins them together, and kneads them in the manner in which pafte is kneaded. This brings out a confiderable quantity of watery brine ; which being poured out of the bowl, the butter is beaten with a cloth as before ; and the jar having been previoufly boiled, or otherwife thoroughly fcalded, and

having

109.
BUTTER.

having ſtood to be perfectly cool and dry, the butter is thrown into it, and kneaded down as cloſe and firm as· poſſible, with the knuckles and the cloth alternately; being careful not to leave any hollow cell or vacuity for the air to lodge in; more particularly round the out-ſides, between the butter and the jar:—and for this purpoſe ſhe repeatedly draws her finger round by the ſides of the jar; preſſing the butter hard, and thereby uniting intimately the jar and butter.

It is fortunate when the jar can be filled at one churning; but when this cannot be done conveniently, the top is left level; and, when the next churning of butter is added, the ſurface is raiſed into inequalities, and the two churnings united into one maſs.

The jar being filled with butter to within two or three inches of the top, it is filled up with brine; made by boiling ſalt and water (in the proportion of a handful to a pint) ten mi-nutes or a quarter of an hour; ſtraining it into a cooling veſſel; and, when perfectly cool, putting it upon the butter, about one and a half or two inches thick. If a wooden bung be put upon this, and a bladder tied over the mouth of the jar, butter thus preſerved, from a good

paſture

pasture, will remain perfectly sweet for almost any length of time; provided the jars be placed in a *dry* and *cool* situation.

110.

MAY 18. (See MIN. 97.). There is not now less than four pounds a head difference between these two parcels of bullocks! yet Mr. ———— is deservedly reckoned a good farmer; and has treated his heifers in the common way of throwing turneps to them; first on his wheat stubbles, and afterwards on his ollands.

There was one thing, it is true, very much against Mr. ————: his best piece of turneps lay detached from his farm; except from a part which was too wet to be thrown upon; and although he got a neighbour to let him throw upon an adjoining piece of young clover (giving him the teathe for the conveniency) yet he had no other "shift" than that of his turnep-close itself; drawing from one part and throwing upon the part already bared; and this spring being unmercifully wet and cold, the bullocks stood to their dew-claws in dirt; and, what was worse, had no other place to lay down on. This was undoubtedly against them.

Ne-

Nevertheless it is obfervable, that bullocks in general, this year, have not done better than thefe. Mr. ———'s have not done better; he had three under-done ones " turned out" of Smithfield laft Monday: and Mr. ——— is not an inferior grazier.

Yet notwithftanding the badnefs of the feafon, and the much-complained-of badnefs of turneps, this year, Mr. Baker's heifers have done extremely well. For, although they were bought-in on very high terms, they will, if they meet with a fair market, nearly double their firft coft.

I have ftill continued to attend particularly to the fatting of thefe heifers; which was thus conducted. They have had plenty of turneps and a " clean trencher" every day; with plenty of followers to lick up the crumbs; fo that the fatting bullocks only picked and chofe the prime of the turneps: and in this feems to confift the excellency of the management. For thefe heifers were fatted abroad, where they remained night and day; with ftraw fcattered under the hedge. Toward the fpring, however, when the turneps began to lofe their goodnefs, they had *hay* inftead of ftraw.

This practice, which is not peculiar to Mr. B. is very judicious; for the bullocks are

thereby

thereby led on from turneps to grafs, without receiving a check between them.

The above is not the only inftance of Mr. B.'s fkill in grazing. Laft year, he fold two Galloway Scots for near fifty pounds. Thefe however he had kept "over-year;"— that is, from October 1779, to May or June 1781; eighteen or nineteen months.

But, a few years ago, he fold five Scots, in May-June, which he had bought in, at St. Faith's fair, the preceding October, for twenty pounds a piece. The lot confifted of ten:—the other five he fold at feventeen, eighteen, and nineteen, pounds each. This half fcore did not coft him quite nine pound ten fhillings a head; fo that, in about feven months, he doubled his money.

But what is ftill more, about four or five years ago, he bought nine *Irifh* bullocks at St. Faith's; namely, feven at feven guineas each, and two at fix pound fifteen fhillings each. Thefe he finifhed by the beginning of June, and fold (in Smithfield) four of the fmalleft at fixteen pounds a piece; the remainder at eighteen pounds or upwards. This is probably the greateft grazing that ever happened in the county.

Much,

Much, however, may depend on the choice of a bullock for fatting. The Norfolk farmers know, or pretend to know, whether a bullock will *grow* during the time of his fatting; and it is the bullock which grows and fats at the same time, which leaves moſt profit to the grazier. If one may judge from Mr. B—'s ſucceſs in grazing, he is deeply verſed in this myſtery; indeed, the heifers before-mentioned are a ſtriking proof of his judgment in this particular. For they have grown very conſiderable, as well as fatted kindly; whilſt the principal part of Mr. ————'s, out of which thoſe were drafted, ſeem, as to carcaſs, the ſame as they were laſt October.

A thick ſhin is a favourite point in a Highland Scot; and there may be other points ſymptomatic of a growing bullock; but I am apprehenſive that a good grazier forms his judgment from general appearances, and from intuitive impreſſions, rather than from particular marks and ſigns: and I am of opinion, nothing but continued practice and cloſe attention can make a man a judicious grazier.

111.

MAY 25. Yeſterday Mr. ———— ſhewed me another account for eleven more of his heifers,

heifers, which happened to go up to a good
market laſt week. They neated 104*l.* 17*s.*
10*d.* ½, or 9*l.* 11*s.* a head. They coſt about
6*l.* 15*s.* and therefore left a profit of 2*l.* 16*s.*
a piece, only; but, conſidering the high price at
which they were bought-in, and the untoward-
neſs of the ſeaſon, they have not done amiſs.
He may thank, however, the fluctuation of
Smithfield market.

III.
BULLOCKS
AT
TURNEPS.

The preceding week there was an uncommonly full market. Smith alone drove ſeven
ſcore. The demand was glutted and the prices
low. (A farmer in the neighbourhood ſent up
three, which were ſold for what he had expected for two of them!). This frightened
the grazier; ſo that, laſt week, the market
was thin, and they ſold well.

SMITHFIELD
MARKET.

A week or two at the finiſhing of the turneps ſeems to be an injudicious time to ſend
bullocks to Smithfield and St. Ive's:—there is
generally a glut about that time. If, therefore, bullocks are fit, they ought to be ſent
off a week or two before; if not, they ought,
if poſſible, to be kept two or three weeks
longer.

112.

DISTRICT.

112.

May 28. Yefterday morning, fet out, early, for Ingham fair—by way of the fea-coaft.

Made the coaft at Munfley, and kept it to. Haibro'; fometimes riding above, fometimes below cliff.

There being a large fleet of fhips, clofe in land, fteering to the northward, with a gentle breeze upon the quarter, and the morning mild and pleafant, the ride became delightful; though fometimes rendered awful by the height of the cliff, and the narrownefs of the path immediately upon the brink of it; more efpecially as the cliff itfelf is of an earthy crumbling texture, and liable to " fhoots," whereby many acres are every year fwallowed up by the fea.

SEA-CLIFFS.

Mr. Baker (who rode with me) fhewed me the remains of a field, which men, now living, remember to have been twelve acres; of which there is now only a corner of two or three acres remaining. Had this piece lain parallel with the line of the cliff, every rod of it muft have long fince difappeared.

The lofs is the greater, as the foil is rich and prolific in a fuperior degree. Noble crops

rife

rife clofe to the edge of the cliff; except in
fome places where the fea-fand is blown up in
too great quantities; which it is, moſt particularly toward Munſley; where the cliff is not
leſs than one hundred feet high ; more than at
Haſbro',where it does not rife ten feet from the
beach.

In going above-cliff we faw two large heaps
of marl, which have been got out of the face
of the cliff.

This, it feems, is a common practice of the
farmers whofe lands lie next the coaft. It is
fometimes drawn up by a wince, which they
call "davying" it up; or elfe run up in
wheelbarrows, in oblique paths, made in the
face of the cliff; in which manner thefe heaps
appear to have been got up: but neither the
place where it has been dug from, nor even
the path or gangway, except juſt at the very
top, are now to be feen ; the whole having, in
a few weeks, crumbled into the ocean.

Further along the coaft, towards Haſbro',
the farmers throw up a clay, out of the face
of the cliff, which is here very low : and near
the village of Haſbro' is found a white brick-
earth eſteemed the beft in the county.

VOL. II.   S   I have

112.

I have examined the three different earths, and tried them in acid.

The "marl" is a white gritty chalky Norfolk marl; effervefcing very ftrongly.

The "clay" is of a browner darker colour, but interfperfed with fpecks of a white chalky fubftance: this effervefces very confiderably, but not fo violently as the marl.

The "brick-earth" is of a dufky-white, or ftone-colour. It is lefs harfh than the other two fpecimens; eafily burfting between the fingers to a fmooth impalpable powder; and effervefces ftrongly in acid. This did not furprife me, as I had enquired particularly into whether it was "good for the land;" for I have not *yet* found a clay which has been fet on as a manure with fuccefs, which has not been ftrongly calcareous. I had, however, conceived that bricks could not be made from a calcareous earth. But the fact is, that this earth is calcareous, and that the Walfham brickmakers give 3*s*. a load for it upon the fpot, and carry it fix or feven miles, to make white bricks and pavements of.

The farmer knowing, with a degree of moral certainty, that his land next the fea will fhoot down into it, why does he not, at once,

cart

cart away the rich top-mould for bottoms of
dunghills, &c. and caft, at his eafe, the marl
or clay which lies beneath it? I faw no trace
of a regular plan of this kind, either in this
ride, or in the journey to Yarmouth.

Going below-cliff gave me an opportunity
of feeing more fully the nature of the marram
plant. The leaves proceed from a fmall crown;
from whence, downward, proceeds a long fimple
hollow toot, with verticils of fibres at different
diftances; according to the depth; the upper
ones being only two or three, but the lower
ones eight or ten inches, afunder. I meafured
one root eight feet long; and I apprehend the
length is generally equal to the depth of the
fand-bank. In mowing marram for thatch,
the workmen keep their fithes an inch or
more under the furface of the fand. Marram
upon a cultivated foil (a ditch bank) grows
with a broad flat blade, and does not take that
rufhlike form which it appears in upon the fand-
banks.

Norfolk Hufbandry. In a large inclofure near
Ingham were thirty fine Scotch bullocks (belonging to a capital grazier in that neighbourhood); fome fat, others fatting; weighing from
fifty to fixty ftone a bullock; confequently

112.

MARKETS.

worth from three to four hundred pounds.—
What a fight is this in an arable country!

Ingham Fair. There were three or four hundred head of cattle, and more fat bullocks than there were at Walſham and Worſtead jointly; and theſe, too, finiſhed in a ſuperior ſtyle. The farmers in that country are, like their ſoil, ſtrong in hand; and even now, bad as times are, are ſaid to be getting money.

There were a good many buyers; but the ſellers were unreaſonable in their demands. They did not aſk leſs than five ſhillings a ſtone for beaſts that were tolerable meat. There might be from fifty to one hundred ſold.

Very little young ſtock I apprehend was ſold. There is indeed very little in the county; and now the farmers having, from the wetneſs of the ſeaſon, a proſpect of graſs, they are unwilling to ſell, except at extraordinary prices.

A farmer of South-Reps ſold eight, two-year-olds, forward in fleſh, and very pretty ones, for 5*l.* 10*s.* a head. This is paying him very well, though they have been at full keep ever ſince they were dropt.

FATTING
CATTLE.

It may be ſaid that fatting cattle at two years old is nipping bullocks in the bud; ſo it may; but

but if this farmer, for inftance, were to keep his
bullocks till three years old, he would bring up
calves in proportion; fo that from a given
quantity of land the community has the fame
or a fimilar quantity of beef.

Ingham fair reaches four or five miles
round on every fide. We breakfafted at
Hafbro', baited at Ingham, and dined at Brun-
ftead; a circuit which Mr. B. and his friends
take every year among their relations and acquaintances. This fpecies of fociability and
hofpitality is not peculiar to Ingham : Walfham, Worftead, South-Reps, Alboro', St.
Faith's, &c. &c. have their fairs, more famed
for their hofpitality than the bufinefs tranfacted
at them ; except the laft, which is one of the
largeft fairs in the kingdom.

Yorkfhire has its *feafts*; other countries their
wakes; and Norfolk its *fairs*.—

113.

June 1. This morning went to fee Mr.
Baker's fix heifers go off for Smithfield-market,
with five under-done fteers of Mr. D.

The heifers are beautiful; one of them
more efpecially : fhe is "full every-where"—no
point higher finifhed than another; and is, to
ufe the grazier's phrafe, as firm as wax, and

S 3   ap-

113.

SELLING
BULLOCKS.

appears fo compleatly ftuffed within, that fhe feems to walk with difficulty. There is another appears, *to the eye*, to be fatter than this; but fhe *handles loofe*; and will probably wafte much in travelling; whereas Mr. B. has no doubt (and he fpeaks from experience) but that the former will *fhew her points* better in Smithfield market than fhe does now; adding, that a " right-fat bullock does not fhrink in travel- " ling nearly fo much as one which is only " meaty."

BUYING
BULLOCKS.

Enquiring, of the drover, as to who has fent up the beft bullocks this year; he faid, that Mr. Rackham, of R———— Hall, had fent the beft lot he had driven this year. Ah! fays Mr. B—, " Peter always buys a good bullock. If a man " don't buy a good thing, he can never expect " to have any thing capital; he does not mind " a few fhillings at St. Faith's:" adding, that " we think nothing of a difference, at this time " of the year, of three or four pounds a bul- " lock; but look as much at fhillings on Fay's " Hill, as we do at pounds in Smithfield."

This dropt fpontaneoufly·from Mr. B. and is, no doubt, the principle and grand bafis of his own practice. For he always buys the beft bullocks he can lay his hands on; and he is,

and

and has been for fome years, efteemed very juftly the beft grazier in *this* neighbourhood.

It is obfervable that bullocks have got on very faft at grafs this fpring. Mr. B. gives for a reafon, that the weather is cool; and altho' it has been wet, rainy weather does not hurt bullocks fo much as it does fheep. Hot weather, he fays, is the worft for bullocks; "it "fets them a-gadding;—makes them cock their "tails and run about the clofes; and nothing "checks them more."

114.

JUNE 1. How helplefs are the Norfolk far- mers on a wet foil! If the water do not run through it like a fieve, they are at a ftand: if it lodge on the furface, they are loft.

This uncommonly wet fpring has embarraffed them. Mr.————, one of the oldeft and beft arable farmers in the neighbourhood, came to me the other morning to defire I would let him have a little wood to "bufh-drain" a piece of land, which he wanted to fow with barley; but which he could not get on to; it being under water!

I reafoned with him on the impropriety of under-draining a piece of land while it lies

S 4   fopped

fopped in wet, and which was to be immediately
trodden with the plow and harrow-horfes.   I
could not, however, convince him of his
error; and, hoping that it might hereafter be of
fome ufe, as well as to prevent a clamour, I
this morning went and fet him out fome alders
(juft broken into leaf!) and went to fee his
operations; which are in fome forwardnefs.

The clofe is nearly a fquare of ten acres;—
lying with a moft defirable gentle defcent;
and the little quantity of water which ftood
upon it was towards the bottom of the piece;
in the place where the water-furrow is ufually
made; but where he is making a trench for
a fub-drain!

The foil is a ftrongifh fandy loam; lying on
a perfectly found abforbent brick earth; but
which, from three or four months continual
rain, had become fatiated: and all that could
be poffibly wanted, at prefent, was a furface-
drain to carry off the fuperfluous water.

His fon, who I found was a principal in
the bufinefs, though defervedly efteemed one of
the beft hufbandmen of his years in the county,
went with us.—He feemed to think that
the water might have been got off, but then
how were they to have plowed and harrowed
without

without filling up the drain? I told him, that if he had put one horse in a plow and drawn each furrow (the soil lying in five-pace warps), and afterwards had taken two and cut a deep crofs-furrow; then fet on one man to fhovel out the crumbs, and another to open the eyes of the interfurrows with a hoe, every drop of the ftanding water might in a few hours have been got rid of: and—the land having lain in this ftate until a day or two of fine weather came—if he had then began to plow on the upper fide of the clofe,—and worked towards the outlet, at the lower end of the crofs-furrow,—he could have had no more trouble with the furface-water.

115.

JUNE 7. Fence-walls, carried to a proper height, are warmer and more durable than *battons*; the cuftomary farm-yard fence of this country. (See BUILD. and REPAIRS, Vol. I.).

But, if walls are not raifed to a proper height, they afford little fhelter, and are continually liable to be uncoped by the cattle. The yard of Antingham-Hall farm is a fufficient inftance of the former, and various inftances

of

115.

YARD-
FENCES.

of the latter occur on different parts of this estate.

A fence-wall to a farm-yard should not be less than six feet high; the coping is then out of the reach of the stock. Where dung is laid against it, the height ought to be still greater.

Battoning is very expensive, and frequently out of repair.

Posts, rails, and kids are, in many points of view, preferable.

116.

BUILDINGS.

June 8. It is very dangerous to run up *sea-stone walls* too quick. Mr. —— had one shot down the other day at Antingham, and nearly killed one of the workmen. The weather was wet, and the bricklayer run up the wall, at once, without stopping, at intervals, to let it settle. The stones, being already saturated with wet, could not absorb the moisture of the mortar;—the air being also moist, the mortar, of course, remained pappy; and sea-stones, being globular, have no other bond or stay than the mortar; which being unable to hold them together, the super-incumbent weight crushed down the whole.

Had

Had the bricklayer proceeded by stages, letting the lower parts get sufficiently firm before the upper parts had been laid on, the mortar would have had time to stiffen, and the wall would have stood.

If the stones and air be dry, one halt, when the wall is a few feet above the foundation, is generally found sufficient.

116.
SEA-STONE
WALLS.

117.

June 13. This afternoon, went to see the Smithfield drover pay off his "masters," at his chamber, at the Angel, at Walsham (Market-day—Thursday).

SELLING
BULLOCKS.

The room was full of "graziers," who had sent up bullocks last week, and were come to-day to receive their accounts and money.

What a trust! A man, *perhaps*, not worth a hundred pounds, brings down twelve or fifteen hundred, or, perhaps, two thousand pounds, to be distributed among twenty or thirty persons, who have no other security than his honesty for their money:—nay, even the servant of this man is entrusted with the same charge; the master going one week, the man the other: but so it has been for a century past; and I do not learn that one breach has been committed.

The

The bufinefs was conducted with great eafe, regularity, and difpatch. He had each man's account, and a pair of fmall faddle-bags with the money and bills, lying upon the table : and the farmers in their turns took their feat at his elbow. Having examined the falefman's account; received their money ; drank a glafs or two of liquor ; and thrown down fixpence towards the reckoning, they feverally returned into the market.

Laft Monday's market being what is called a " whipping market," the room was filled with chearfulnefs and fatisfaction : there was only one long face in the company. This was a farmer who had fent up three bullocks, for which he had twenty-four pounds bade at Walfham fair ; whereas the falefman's account from Smithfield, notwithftanding the goodnefs of this week's market, was only twenty-two pounds.

Such is the uncertainty of Smithfield-market ; and fuch the misjudgement or partiality of the Smithfield falefmen. If thefe bullocks were worth twenty-four pounds at Walfham fair, they ought after three weeks or a month's grafs, and confidering the market and the expences incurred, to have fetched twenty-feven, twenty-

twenty-eight, or thirty pounds, in Smithfield; but they will not neat twenty-one pounds. From twenty-two pound, the grofs fale, deduct the expences, feven fhillings and one-penny half-penny a head; there remains only twenty pounds eighteen fhillings and fevenpence half-penny: little more than two-thirds of their value.

Laft week, it is true, this farmer had the beft end of the ftaff: four bullocks, belonging to four feparate graziers, were fold in one lot; and the falefman divided the lot equally; though it was allowed that this farmer's bullock was not worth fo much by two pounds as fome of the lot!

Mr. Baker received for his fix heifers. They fold uncommonly dear; far exceeding what we had laid them at; for inftead of five fhillings, they fetched nearly fix fhillings a ftone. One of them which we had laid at forty-eight ftone fold for fourteen pounds*.

The

---

* Among thefe heifers was a feventh — a "foul-dugged" one: namely, an open heifer, which had dropt her calf in coming from Scotland; and was given to Mr. B. by one of the drovers, to make him amends for a hard bargain of laft year: an inftance, this, of generofity in the drover.

This heifer was treated the fame as the other fix; among which fhe was fatted; and was, as to fatnefs, on a par with the reft; was fomewhat larger; and would, no doubt, *prove* nearly as well: neverthelefs, Mr. B. knowing the difadvantageous predicament fhe ftood in, did not lay her

at

117.

SMITHFIELD
MARKET.

The under-done steers, which went up with these heifers, (see Min. 113.) sold for nothing. They did not fetch above eleven pounds a-piece, one with another, notwithstanding they weighed considerably more than the heifers.

This shews the absurdity of sending bullocks to Smithfield before they be fat : Mr. B.'s were " right-fat," and fetched six shillings ;—Mr. D.'s only " meaty ;" and did not fetch four shillings and sixpence, notwithstanding the extraordinary market.

118.

DISTRICT.

June 17. On Saturday last set out for the Blowfield Hundred, and the Yarmouth Marshes, in company with Mr. John Hylton, of Felmingham, who formerly resided in that district.

We passed through the following Hundreds and Parishes.

at more than ten pound. But following these heifers to London, and falling in company (on the eve of the market) with a butcher, to whom he related these circumstances, he got twelve pound ten shillings for her : a striking instance, this, of the advantage of following bullocks to Smithfield : and, in similar cross cases, or when the lot sent up is extraordinarily large, it may sometimes be prudent for a Norfolk grazier to attend the market in person ; but, in general, *perhaps*, it is three or four guineas, and three or four days, *unprofitably* spent ; provided the grazier can depend upon the *uprightness* of his salesman.

HUND.	PARISHES.	IN GOING. SOIL.	HUSB.	HUND.	RETURNING. PARISHES.	SOIL.	HUSB.
North Erpingham.	Gunton	sandy loam	good	South Walsham.	Marshes	wheat land	middling
	Antingham	ditto	ditto		Wickhampton	ditto	ditto
					Free Thorp		
South Erpingham.	Felmingham	light	passable	Blowfield.	Cantley	very good	good
	Swanton	good wheat loam	good		Haftingham	ditto	ditto
	Score Ruston	ditto	very good		Southwood	ditto, with heath	ditto
	Coltishall	various, and common fields	middling		Buckingham	wheat land	ditto
	Belaugh	ditto and ditto	ditto		Scrumshaw	ditto, and common	middling
Taverham.	Wroxham	pretty good	middling		Lingwood	ditto	ditto
	Salhouse	light	ditto		Blowfield	good land	ditto
South Walsham.	Monsehold Heath	heath	—		Birlingham, St. A.	tolerable wheat land	ditto
	Hemlington	part heath	—	South Walsham.	South Walsham	ditto	ditto
Blowfield.	Blowfield	good wheat land, and hops	good		Ranworth	ditto, and marshes	ditto
	Bradstone	ditto	ditto		Bastwick	ditto	ditto
	Scrumshaw	various, and common	various	Tunstead.	Honing	light, and heath	middling
	Lingwood	wheat land, and common	ditto		Hofton	heath, and very good	good
South Walsham.	Beighton	wheat land	middling		Tunstead	good wheat land	ditto
	Birlingham, St. E.	ditto	ditto	South Erpingham.	Scottow*(asbefore)	ditto	ditto
	Moulton	ditto	ditto		Swanton		
	Havergate	ditto	ditto		Felm. &c.		
	Marshes						

* The lands of Scottow, Score Ruston, Tunstead, Hostess, &c. if one may judge from the present black luxuriant crops of wheat, are nearly equal to those of the Happing Hundred.

118.

SOIL OF
BLOWFIELD.

The *foil* moſt prevalent in the BLOWFIELD HUNDRED is a rich dark-coloured loam, of a good depth; the farmers plowing from five to ſeven or eight inches deep; and affect to laugh at the ſhallow plowing practiſed by farmers in *this* part of the county:

MANURES
OF
BLOWFIELD

There is no *marl* in the Hundred; but, the river Yare running by the ſide of it, the farmers get marl very reaſonably from Norwich; and ſet on about ten loads an acre: Dung they alſo get by water from Yarmouth and Norwich.

HOPS IN
BLOWFIELD

The firſt thing which ſtruck me in Blowfield Hundred was a tolerably large hop garden:

We called upon a perſon in the village of Blowfield; who is owner of this and two or three more patches; he being the principal grower in the pariſh. Enquiring as to the quantity of hops grown in this neighbourhood, he ſaid that, three or four years ago, there were ten acres of hops in the pariſh of Blowfield; which, he added, is more than can be collected in the reſt of the county. At preſent, however, there are not more than five acres, and the quantity is every year declining. Hops have lately been low, and the crops have not anſwered the expence. There are two or three drying-houſes in the town, but they are, except one, going to decay.

The

The principal crops of the Blowfield Hundred are wheat, barley, peas, and firſt-year's clover.

The *Wheats* are in general very promiſing, and mark the goodneſs of the ſoil, and the plentifulneſs of the manure of Norwich and Yarmouth:

Saw ſeveral pieces of dibbled wheat, which made an uncommonly beautiful appearance : but the practice is by no means general.

The *Barleys* have alſo a promiſing appearance; and

The *Peas,* which it ſeems are ten-fold more numerous this year than uſual (owing to the preſent low price of barley), are luxuriant and very forward; conſidering the ſeaſon. A large proportion of them " ſet ;" that is, dibbled in.

The *Clovers,* where they have taken, are fine ; but the *Rye-graſs,* in general, hides the ſmall quantity of clover, even of the *firſt year :* and as to *two-years lays,* there is ſcarcely a piece to be ſeen in the whole Hundred : the ſoil is ſaid to be "quite tired" of this crop. The ſeedling-plants are in general ſufficiently numerous, and look very promiſing the firſt autumn ; but go off in the courſe of the winter.

Their *Turnep-*crops, too, have failed them of late. Mr. Batchelor, of Bradſtone, (a ſen-

118.

fible intelligent farmer, at whofe houfe I flept) fays, that twenty or thirty years ago, he never could get ftock enough for his turneps : he has finifhed forty or fifty bullocks in a year : now, he does not know how to buy few enough; and does not finifh more than twenty or thirty : the roots do not come to any fize; and have no " tack" or proof in them.

The Blowfield farmers in general fat their *bullocks* in fheds, or in bins in the yard.

Some of their *bullock-fheds* are large expenfive buildings. Mr. Batchelor has a very good one : it confifts of a center building, thirty-fix feet long, nineteen feet wide, and about eleven feet high to the eaves; with a pair of wide folding-doors at each end ; and with a lean-to on each fide, the whole length of the building, and eleven feet wide.

The center building is the turnep-houfe; the lean-tos, fheds for the bullocks; which ftand with their heads toward, or rather in, the turnep-houfe; from which they are parted by a range of mangers only; having the full freedom of breathing in its fpacious area. By opening the doors at each end, a fufficient degree of air and coolnefs may be given in the clofeft weather; while, behind, the eaves of the fheds are

brought

brought down to within five feet of the ground, and are boarded with rough boards (excepting an opening at each end for the bullocks to *creep* in at) to prevent too great a coldnefs in fevere weather; thus preferving a due temperature.

This fhed holds twenty bullocks, ten on each fide, faftened by the neck, with chains, fwivels and rings, playing freely upon pofts, feven feet high. At each corner of the turnep-houfe is a triangular bin for the topped-and-tailed turneps.

In autumn, the entire building is fometimes ufed as a temporary barn, for buck, peas, &c. and in fummer, the center part is an excellent waggon-fhed : had the doors been made a foot and a half higher, it would have been an admirable refuge for loads of corn or hay in a fhowery harveft.

The main building is covered with reed, the lean-tos with tiles.

At Ranworth I faw a ftill more expenfive bullock-fhed than Mr. B.'s; it being all clofe boarded and painted : the entrance for the bullocks are folding-doors, which fhut clofe like the back-doors of a barn. The doors to the turnep-houfe, however, are I think ftill fmaller than Mr. Batchelor's. The conftruction is

T 2　　　nearly

nearly the fame as that of Mr. B.'s, which is a more fubftantial though rougher building.

The *turneps* are drawn into the houfe in carts, and fhot down in the area; where they are topped and tailed.—The roots are given to the fatting bullocks whole; and the tops given to the cows and lean ftock.

The man who tends the bullocks, tops and tails the turneps; in doing which he ufes a very large knife and fork, made for the pur-pofe; it having been found from experience that a man, who ftands perhaps fifteen or fix-teen hours in a turnep-houfe, cannot *handle* them in cold weather without injury to his hands. It is confidered as a much more fevere employ-ment than that of drawing them in the field.

The MARSHES were a new world to me. They form a vaft level, containing many thou-fand acres, of a black and fomewhat moory foil; formed, perhaps, originally of fea-mud: it being highly probable that the whole level has once been a gulf of the German Ocean.

Until about twenty years ago, this valuable tract lay principally under water; except in a dry fummer. But during that fpace of time a number of windmills have been erected, which throw the water into main drains, formed for
the

the purpofe. By this means the principal part of the marfhes are freed from furface-water early in the fpring; fo that cattle may now be turned into them about the beginning of May, and are kept free long enough to permit them, in general, to remain there until near Chriftmas.

The Marfhes, taken collectively, are, though nearly *level*, not perfectly *fmooth*; being furrowed into inequalities by fwamps; which, in their natural ftate, feem to have been the main drains of the mud-banks.

Thefe fwamps, or "reed-ronds," in fome places of confiderable width, are now the main drains to the Marfhes; from the graffy drier parts of which they are detached by banks of foil; which at once ferve the purpofes of roads, fences, and embankments.

In the beginning of fpring, the water is thrown from the grazable parts into thefe reed-ronds;—which, in their turn, are alfo drained; and mown for thatch, hay, &c. fo that, by the affiftance of the mills, every part of the Marfhes now become productive.

The grazing parts are divided into inclofures, of various fizes and figures, by means of water-ditches, of different widths, from five or fix to eight or ten feet wide.

T 3　　　　Thefe

Thefe water-fences, running in all directions, and being of various widths, makes it probable that the principal part of them were the fmaller furrows, or partial drains, which carried off the rains, back-water, &c. in a ftate of nature.

The inclofures, or " marfhes," run from ten or fifteen to forty or fifty acres each ; belong to a variety of owners; and are rented by a ftill greater number of occupiers; almoft every farmer, within fifteen or even twenty miles, having his marfh.

The *herbage* of thefe marfhes is various, even in the fame inclofure : for the individual marfhes are far from being level; they being more or lefs fcooped out into hollows ; where the water lodges a confiderable time after the higher parts are dry. On thefe grow a rich luxuriant herbage, compofed of the choiceft meadow-graffes ; while on the moifter parts grows a long wiry kind of grafs, which I think the marfhmen call " flat ;" and which the cattle are very fond of. But none of the graffes being yet in blow (the *poa annua* excepted*)* and the aquatic grafs not having yet formed its fruit-ftalk (the feafon being unufually backward), I could not afcertain the fpecies.

Marfh-worms.—The Marfhes are infefted by a grub, which laft year deftroyed many acres of grafs,

grafs, by eating off the roots about an inch below the furface. This year, the damage is trifling; there are, however, ftripes to be feen in almoft every marfh, which look nearly as brown as the foil itfelf. The grafs is totally dead; and by ftriking off the furface, with the heel of the boot, the grubs may readily be found. They are from an inch to an inch and a half long, and about the thicknefs of a goofe-quill. Their colour is a dark dufky brown, with a black head, and two whitifh lines waving irregularly from the head along the back to near the tail. They are generally believed to be the grub of the cock-chafer; but I cannot learn that any one has accurately traced the metamorphofe.

The *ftock* of the Marfhes are principally young cattle, lean Scots, and old and young horfes. There are, neverthelefs, a confiderable number of fatting bullocks; and fome fheep.

I do not learn, however, that the Yarmouth marfhes are equal, in their fatting quality, to thofe on the Thames, or to Romney marfhes. Bullocks, neverthelefs, which have been at turneps, and have had the fpring-bite of clover, receive no check on being put into thefe marfhes; but, on the contrary, get, in a few months, a very confiderable improvement.

T 4

If

If they were properly drained from the puddles of furface-water which ftand on them till late in the fpring; their faces fmoothed by levelling; and kept fo by the harrow and rol-·ler; their quality might be much improved.

But, as to improvement, they are totally neglected: the cattle are permitted to poach them in winter; and the tuffocks which they tread up remain ftumbling-blocks to them all the fummer: while the dung, collected by the marfhmen, is fold to the upland farmers.

The landlord finds mills, opens the fence-drains, and hangs the gates; the tenant, who generally rents them from year to year, and frequently for only one year, turns in his flock as foon as the furface is freed from water, and keeps them in until the water, or the feverity of the weather, obliges him to draw them off.

The flock are under the care of *marfh-men*, who live in cottages fcattered over the Marfhes; —each having his diftrict, or " level of " marfhes," to look after. His perquifite is a fhilling upon the pound-rent, which is fome-times paid by the landlord; but more gene-rally by the tenant.

The marfh-men alfo keep cows, which pick about in the fwamps, roads, and uninclofed parts,

in

in fummer; and for which they mow winter-fodder from the reed-ronds, &c. They carry their butter to Yarmouth, and in winter generally fell their *bay*-butter above the market-price of *turnep*-butter;—the univerfal produce of the county in that feafon of the year.

We entered the Marfhes at Havergate, which ftands on a bold fwell, from whence there is a very extenfive view of this great level; which, to the left, is terminated by Yarmouth (diftant about nine miles); to which in fummer there is a tolerable road, acrofs the Marfhes.

At the foot of the fwell, the Marfhes commence. For nearly the firft mile, we rode to our horfes knees in water. This watery part is common to Havergate, and there are two reafons for its being overflowed: It is no perfon's bufinefs to drain it; and, what is remarkable, it lies lower than the middle of the Marfhes; which, it feems, is the higheft, and the beft, land.

The firft marfh we entered was Mr. Batchelor's (who went with us). It contains about thirty acres:—his ftock are fixteen fine bullocks; but it would carry three or four more; the grafs being now footlock deep. Thefe bullocks were at turneps laft winter; at clover

iq

in the spring; and are now doing very well. Part of them are already sold to the butcher, and the rest will be ready by harvest. This is a fair specimen of the present *quality* of these marshes.

We then went over Mr. Hylton's: his stock chiefly two-year-olds, and colts; with three or four three-year-olds, which he expects will be finished by harvest.

We afterwards rode through a variety of marshes belonging to their acquaintances and relations; and having seen a marsh-mill, we made a sweep towards the middle of the level, and came up at Wickhampton, where the entrance is almost free from water.

Marsh-mills.—The proprietor of a level of marshes either builds a mill himself, or pays so much an acre to a neighbouring mill; which engages to draw off the superfluous water.

The construction of these mills and the principle they act upon are beautifully simple. The body of the mill is built of brick, about twenty feet high, with sails similar to those of a corn-mill, but somewhat smaller. Upon the axis of the sails is fixed a cogged wheel, of about five feet diameter. This turns a horizontal wheel of the same, or nearly the same size;

size; fixed upon the mill-post, or upright beam; which reaches from the top to the bottom of the mill. Near the bottom of this beam is fixed a similar horizontal wheel; which turns a vertical one, fixed to the axis of the efficient wheel. *This*, as to construction, is a small under-shot water-mill wheel; but, in its manner of acting, is directly the reverse; for instead of being forced round by a weight of water lying above it, it gathers up, by the means of its floats, the dead water among which they work, and forces it up into a drain resembling a mill-dam. This wheel works in a case of wood or stone, nicely formed to the floats; and at the head of the drain is a valve-gate, to prevent the water from receding when the mill stops; it therefore, in every respect, re-sembles a water-mill reversed.

The mill which I examined raised the water about three feet; which is fully adequate to the draining of the adjacent marshes.

119.

June 22. (See Min. 39.). Yesterday Mr. Robert Bayfield told me, that he has finished the sale of those nine bullocks.

One of them sold for ten pounds, and the rest for about nine pounds a piece; so that in

less

119.

FATTING CATTLE.

lefs than feven months, taking the par of time, they have more than doubled their coft.

Suppofe that he kept them, one with another, twenty-eight weeks; and that he cleared four pounds ten fhillings a head; they paid him three fhillings and twopence halfpenny a week; which, notwithftanding the high prices given this year, is great work for a bullock of lefs than forty ftone; and fhews,

BREED OF CATTLE.

in a ftriking manner, the value of the Norfolk breed of cattle.

120.

MANURE.

JUNE 30. Obferving, the other day, a dunghill, which a judicious hufbandman was fetting about for turneps, covered with afhes,—I afked him the reafon of it. He faid, that the muck being pretty long when it was turned over, and the weather fince having been dry, there was much long ftrawy muck at the top, and on the outfides, which would have been in the way of the harrow, and would have kept his light land too hollow; he therefore fet it on fire.—A new idea; and, in this inftance, well applied.

121.

121.

June 30. It is very obfervable, that after the late cold wet fpring, wheats on *fcalds* are affected in a manner fimilar to what they fuffer by a dry hot fummer! looking yellow and puny.

But it has been faid, it feems, by an old man, who was the oracle of his neighbourhood, that " nothing is fo cold as fand wet."

If this be a fact, it may account for this very remarkable incident.

122.

August 8. This year, the fpring being moift and the weather fine, the young turnep-plants got out of the way of the " fly," which ufually attacks them in their feed-leaf ftate, with very little injury; and a fairer profpect of a general and full crop of turneps has not been feen for feveral years.

Many farmers had begun to fet out their plants with the hoe; little fufpecting they were throwing away their labour, and putting their crops in the way of immediate deftruction.

The alarm, in this neighbourhood, was given about a month ago at South-Reps; where an
early-

122.

TURNEP
CATER-
PILLARS.

early-fown piece of turneps, through which a footpath lies, was obferved, by paffengers; to be covered with the fufpected flies.

The report of this circumftance was carried immediately, by a farmer's fervant, to the coaft, about Backton and Walcot; where, the turneps being ftill forwarder, the farmers (who on that part of the coaft either did not obferve the flies, or, if they did, were not aware of their evil effects) were bufy hoeing; and received the intelligence with a fmile; congratulating themfelves on their better fortune; for not a fly was to be feen in their fields: but, on turning up the under-furfaces of their plants, they found them fwarming with young caterpillars; and immediately ftopped the hoe.—In the courfe of ten days or a fortnight the entire fea-coaft was ftripped; and the country in general, if reports may be credited, has already fuftained an injury which may be felt for many years.

Notwithftanding, however, the flies had efcaped notice on the part of the coaft above-mentioned, they were too numerous and too confpicuous to pafs unobferved on other parts of it; more efpecially about Cromer; where they were obferved, feveral days, before they

were

were feen in this neighbourhood; and where

the obfervations made this year ftrongly corroborate the idea of their being brought acrofs the fea during a continuance of north-eaft wind.

Mr. Howfe, of Overftrand, (who lives near the beach, and who is a man of good credit) declares, he faw them arrive " in clouds, fo " as to darken the air;" and the fifhermen of Beck-hithe have made the fame affertion: while, from the reports of feveral perfons who live upon the coaft, they were feen in fuch numbers upon the cliffs, and in the adjoining grounds, that, being apparently fpent with their flight, they might have been " taken " up by fhovel-fulls *." Even in the abovementioned foot-path piece at South-Reps, three miles from the fea, they were defcribed as refembling " flights of bees."

The 28th July, I walked over this piece with Mr. John Baker, its proprietor. In about

---

* Afterward, hearing a perfon (unknown) relating this circumftance, I afked him particularly as to the thicknefs the flies might lie upon the ground; he faid, in fome places he believed they lay two inches thick; adding, that they might have been raked up into heaps of almoft any fize. Perhaps, had fire been put to them in this critical ftate (which perhaps was not altogether a ftate of reft but of copulation), numbers might have been deftroyed.

ten

ten days after the appearance of the flies, the young caterpillars began to appear on the under fides of the leaves of the plants; and, at the time I faw them, which was about ten days more, the plants were entirely eaten up; nothing but the fkeleton or ftronger fibres of the leaves being left: except upon a fmall patch or two towards the middle of the clofe; and except on a border, round the outfide, under the hedges, of a breadth proportioned to the height of the hedge or tree adjoining.

On the weft fide of this clofe there was a ftriking inftance of this circumftance. One end of the fence is free from trees; the white-thorn hedge, here, rifing 10 or 12 feet high: under this part, the border was fomething more than the height of the hedge. The other end of the fence is full of pollards, with tops from 18 to 20 feet high; and there the width of the border was in due proportion. The firft pollard marked the difference with the greateft exactnefs !

Almoft every inclofure has a fimilar border; and, in fome fmall pightles fet round with high trees, the plants have almoft entirely efcaped.

Large open fields, and fmaller inclofures which lie open to the fea-ward, have fuffered moft.

moſt.—The hangs of hills dipping from the ſea have ſuffered leſs;—owing, perhaps, to the flies overſhooting them in their flight.

The ſhade of the trees, or the inſtinct of the animal, may likewiſe account for the borders round the incloſures; but why one patch of a field ſhould be leſs affected than another, ſeems ſomewhat myſterious. Perhaps, the inſects, being naturally gregarious, may hang together in bodies, even while they are depoſiting their eggs.

Theſe patches and borders however, though they eſcape the fly, do not long eſcape the caterpillars; for no ſooner have they devoured their foſter-plant, than they begin to travel in queſt of a freſh ſupply of food; and one ſide of the piece being finiſhed, they with a wonderful inſtinct travel in bodies towards the other. The whole field being finiſhed, the gateway and the adjoining roads have, it is ſaid with great confidence, been ſeen black with them.

They ſeem to neglect entirely the graſſes and every other plant, turneps and charlock (*ſinapis arvenſis*) only excepted. The laſt they are ſaid to devour with greater avidity than they do the turneps themſelves.

Mr. Baker inſtances a corner patch, which, for want of hoeing, had got up almoſt knee-high : the turneps were much eaten, but the charlocks were ftripped to the top.

Various experiments have been tried for their deftruction.

Mr. Baker tried *lime,* fowing it in the middle of the night, when the plants were moift with dews, but without effect.

He alfo tried *rolling.* This checked them, efpecially if two or three times repeated, but did not fave the plants. It is obfervable, however, that the plants under the hedges, though they had been run over two or three times with a heavy roller, did not appear to be injured by the operation.

Mr. Chandler, of Munfley, is faid to have tried *foot* without effect.

Ducks have been tried by feveral, and with univerfal fuccefs.

Poultry are faid to be equally beneficial; and, if one may judge by a fingle circumftance,

Rooks are highly ferviceable. A large piece of turneps lying in an open field has efcaped in a remarkable manner; it lies near a rookery, which is a general rendezvous for thefe birds; and I recollect to have feen this piece, more than once, covered with them.

Where

Where the plants have been hoed out, many persons have *hand-picked* them; but this is tedious and expensive, where the numbers are great. I have myself counted twenty caterpillars on a plant, not much larger than my hand. Mr. John Joy declares, that he has reckoned " sixteen score " upon one turnep; but it was a large plant, which had been hoed some time.

It has been almost a universal practice among farmers, when one part of a close was cut off, and the caterpillars were marching to attack another part which was less infested, to draw a furrow between them, deepening it with a spade into a kind of a *trench*, making the side towards the plants to be defended as upright as possible; or, if the soil would stand, somewhat overhanging, in order to prevent the caterpillars from scaling it. This, if well done, had generally a good effect; and it was not uncommon to see the bottom of the trench entirely covered with them.

I have seen a trench across a gateway between two turnep-pieces for the same purpose.

Another expedient practised by many for checking the caterpillars was, to draw a *cart-rope* over the plants, in order to shake them

off, but cannot learn that it ever proved effectual.

A labourer tells me, that in the " canker
" year," about twenty years ago, the beſt contrivance that was then hit upon was a kind of
bruſh made of *furze*; by fixing the branches to
a long pole or axle-tree, with a wheel at each
end, of ſuch a height that the furze bruſhed
the plants without pulling them up by the
roots. This not only bruſhed the caterpillars
off the plants, but numbers of them were
ſtabbed and deſtroyed by the prickles of the
furze. This, in theory, is very plauſible, and
might be good in practice; but I have not ſeen
it, nor heard of its being uſed, this year.

The expedient which has this year caught
popular attention moſt, is that of bruſhing
the plants with twigs of *elder* tied upon a
waggon-rope.

Yeſterday, having heard much of the ſucceſs of this expedient, I called upon the
farmer * who had gained the moſt credit by
it, to learn from himſelf the particulars; and
to ſee the plants.

The bruſh is judiciouſly made of the ſtraight
luxuriant ſhoots of this year, about the thick-

* Mr. Jonathan Bond, of South-Reps.

neſs

nefs of the finger, and from two to three feet long. Thefe are tied upon the cart-rope with rope-yarn, about four to fix inches apart, and about eighteen or twenty feet long upon the rope. It is drawn by two men, and takes half a ten-pace warp (about a ftatute rod) at once. The men lay hold near the twigs: —the two loofe ends of the rope being tied together, and drag at a diftance behind the elder.

The circumftances attending the piece of turneps faid to be faved by this contrivance, were thefe : part of the clofe had been fown early, and the plants were in rough leaf when the yellow flies firft made their appearance : —the other fide of it was not fown until after that time. The forward part being entirely cut off, the ground was plowed and fown a fecond time ; but the plowing and harrowings did not kill all the caterpillars :—thoufands were feen on the furface of the ground tra-velling towards the backward-fown part ; the plants of which had then got to a confiderable fize.

The farmer perceiving this, drew a furrow and made a trench between the two parts ; and he and his man three times a day (viz. in the

U 3   morning

morning before they went to their day's work, at noon when they came home to dinner, and at night when they returned from work) drew the elder-brush over the plants. The piece is about three acres, and it generally employed them about an hour and a half; especially in the morning, when the dew made the elder drag heavy. He has used the brush about ten days, in which time he has renewed the elder three times; and it is now nearly worn out.

After looking attentively for some time among the plants, I saw only two caterpillars; and so healthy a piece of turneps I do not re-collect to have seen : they have been sown only three weeks, yet they are now fit for the hoe.

In riding towards North Reps, I saw a similar machine ; but this is made of the rough boughs, not the twigs. It is a large aukward unmanage-able thing :—the woody crooked boughs, some of them almost as thick as the wrist, drag up or lacerate the plants ; whereas the straight twigs, lying flat and evenly upon the ground, shake them in a most effectual manner, without doing them the smallest injury ; every plant is kept in a quivering motion from the time the rope touches it until it be passed by the last leaf: and, perhaps, in this consists the merit of the invention.

The

The received idea, however, is, that the el-der is in its nature noxious to the animal. But this I much doubt : indeed, the experiments which I have made convince me that the idea is erroneous.

The evening before laſt, I took ſome freſh elder-leaves, bruiſed them between the hands, broke them in the middle, and put them with a caterpillar into a ſmall tin-box; ſhutting it up cloſe with the cover. Yeſterday morning, it was as briſk as when it was put in.

Yeſterday, I took a turnep-leaf and whipped it with a twig of elder, and afterwards preſſed them together between the hands for ſome ſe-conds, and then put the turnep-leaf into a box of freſh-gathered caterpillars. This morning nothing but the fibres were left,

Among another parcel of caterpillars I put a freſh-gathered turnep-leaf untouched—another whipped, &c. with elder; and a charlock-leaf alſo freſh-gathered. This morning the elder-leaf was not only conſiderably eaten, but one of the animals was repoſing itſelf upon it,

The leaf of charlock had only one perfora-ſion :—the untainted turnep-leaf had ſeveral.

It ſeems therefore evident that elder, ſo far from being fatal to theſe animals, is not in any

U 4   degree

degree difagreeable to them. The merit there-fore of the elder-brufh (if it has any) lies in its effectually fhaking off the caterpillars with-out injuring the plants.

But it appears to me highly probable, that it was the trench, and not the elder, which faved the plants abovementioned. For if Mr. Thomas Shephard, of North-Reps, be accurate in the relation of an experiment which he made twenty years ago (and I have no reafon to doubt his accuracy), brufhing off the caterpillars is of little ufe. He relates, that he had a two-acre pightle run over with a cart-rope, day and night, uninterruptedly, for fome days, without any de-gree of fuccefs; for, fmall as the piece was, the plants on one fide of it would be covered with caterpillars before the men reached the other fide. Indeed, if we obferve how foon they begin to crawl after being thrown down, and how faft they travel when upon their legs, it feems very probable, that being fhook from the plants they may regain the leaves, fo as to begin feeding again, in five minutes. It feems therefore in vain to expect any effential benefit from brufhing them off the plants; for while they have life, they will encounter many dif-ficulties to preferve it.

But

But whether the plants above fpoken of were
or were not preferved from the caterpillars by
the elder-brufh, I am very much of opinion,
that in regard to their growth and healthful-
nefs, they received fome benefit from it. The
exercife of the wind, it is well known, greatly
accelerates the growth of turneps ; and it feems
not unreafonable to fuppofe, that the exercife of
the elder-brufh produced a fimilar effect. The
plants in queftion are peculiarly fine, and the
incident appears to me to be worth preferving.

Towards the fea, where the vermin were
very numerous, the plants were ftripped in a few
days ; fo that if the farmer had had fkill, he
had not time, to fave them. His only refource
was, to plow up the ground and fow it a fecond
time : and it is probable, that two-thirds of the
turnep-grounds in Eaft Norfolk have been fubjected to this treatment.

But what is ftill more unfortunate, fome of
the farmers, who plowed up and refowed, have
loft their fecond crop ; for, being willing to
fave the borders and patches which had fared
better than the main body of the clofe, they
left them ftanding : but, the plow and harrow
not being equal to the deftruction of the whole
of the caterpillars, thofe which furvived crawled

to

122.

TURNEP
CATER-
PILLARS.

to the plants which were left; which support-
ing them until the young plants got up, they
returned and prefently eat up the fecond crop.

Some few men are hardy enough to let the
ftalks and fibres remain ftanding; hoping that
they will fhoot again; and that they may by
this means fave their crops, as well as the trouble and expence of refowing.

AUGUST 15.—In my rides to Wroxham,
Baftwick, Staninghall, and Norwich, this week,
I find that fome hundred acres of turneps have
been faved by DUCKS.

Mr. Samuel Barber had, at one time, upon
his farms, at Staninghall and Woodbaftwick,
near four hundred ducks at work: and, thro'
their induftry, has faved a principal part of
his crop:--had he begun to employ them
fooner, he believes he fhould have faved the
whole.

The different detachments (fome of them
near one hundred ftrong) were kept by a boy
or girl. They were regularly driven to water,
and refted three or four times a day: but had
no corn nor any other food given them. After
having drank, they would difgorge the caterpillars in great abundance; fo that they foon fell
to again with frefh appetites.

                              Half

Half or three-quarter-grown ducks are preferable to old ones, which are lazy, and will
fooner eat the turnep-tops than run after the
caterpillars.

It is very amufing to fee the young ones dart
at their prey : thefe, however, when the caterpillars grow fcarce, take to the turnep-tops,
and after they have reduced the vermin to a
certain ebb, do the turneps more harm than
the caterpillars themfelves do.

This has been ufed as an argument againft
employing ducks ; and, in refpect to old ducks,
it may have its weight : but if the caterpillars
are fo few as to tire the young ducks in looking for them, the plants cannot fuftain any material injury from them.

The fact feems clearly to be, that where one
acre of turneps has been faved by any other
means whatever (hand-picking excepted) an
hundred have been faved by Ducks.

Poultry may be equally good (and perhaps
without the evil attendant of eating the plants);
but their ufe does not feem to have been difcovered, or attended to, until too late.

Alfo, when a piece of turneps has been in
danger from the enemy in the neighbourhood;
but not already infefted ; cutting a trench has
per-

122.
TURNEP
CATER-
PILLARS.

perhaps been very beneficial : filling the bottom of it with ſtraw, and, when the caterpillars were in ſufficient numbers among the ſtraw, ſetting fire to it, ſeems to be a late, though an ingenious improvement.

TENTHREDO
OF
THE TURNEP

Aug. 20. The firſt of this month I gathered, alive, eight or ten of the yellow flies ſuppoſed to produce the turnep-caterpillars, alſo a parcel of the caterpillars themſelves.

The flies were eaſily caught by beating them from the leaf on to the ground, where they lie, apparently lifeleſs, time enough to be picked up. Brought them home in a ſmall box, and put them into a drinking-glaſs, covered with perforated paper.

Before I could get a third fly into the glaſs, the two firſt, happening to be a male and female, were in the act of copulation; and before I could get in the whole, two more were in the ſame amorous ſituation. The party conſiſting of nearly an equal number of males and females, an almoſt inceſſant ardour prevailed, till the cloſe of the evening; and, ſetting them in the ſun the next morning, their amours were renewed.

Suſpecting them to be of the genus *Tenthredo,* and being willing to diſcover the two
ſerrated

ferrated laminæ mentioned as the diftinguifh-
ing character of that genus, I put one of the
females to a flight degree of torture, expecting
fhe would have unfheathed them as a weapon;
but I was difappointed : I therefore (that her
pain might be as momentary as poffible) fevered
her head from her body ; thinking that in the
agony of death fhe might difclofe them ; but
I was ftill left in the dark : for, to my aftonifh-
ment, inftead of death enfuing immediately
the decapitation, her body feemed to experience no great degree of inconveniency from it.
She ran upon the table. I turned her upon her
back : fhe recovered her legs as nimbly as ever;
fpread out her wings, and actually made an attempt to fly. Three hours after her head was
fevered, her body was to appearance perfectly
alive ; and how long fhe lived afterwards I know
not ; for, conceiving that without the head
the body could not be fenfible of pain, I did
not preferve or deftroy it.

My curiofity, however, was afterwards gratified in a manner I had not expected; for
putting a frefh turnep-leaf into the glafs, as
food for fome caterpillars which were alfo in
it, I perceived one of the female flies peculiarly bufy in examining the different parts of
the

the leaf; and obferving her to be partial to a part which was fortunately on the outer fide of the leaf towards the eye, I took a magnifier, and placing it againſt the outſide of the glaſs, ſaw her very diſtinctly unſheath her inſtruments; inſinuate them into the edge of the leaf, to a depth equal to their fulleſt length; and, having feparated them ſo as to form a channel or pipe between them, placed her pubes to the aperture: remained in that poſture a few feconds; deliberately drew out the inſtruments; ſheathed them; and immediately went in queſt of another convenient nidus. Standing by a window on which the fun ſhone ſtrongly, and holding the fubject between the eye and the light, I ſaw the operation very evidently.

The inſtruments are brown, refembling in colour the ſting of the bee, but much finer, and appear to be flatted; but whether they are or are not ferrated, I cannot be poſitive. In the courſe of two or three minutes I ſaw her make three or four depoſits;

One of thefe flies lived eleven days; other two, eight or nine; the reſt, feven or eight days.—The females died firſt.

What their food is I am not certain.—The only thing put to them in the glaſs were green

turnep-

turnep-leaves. I fancied more than once I could perceive them feeding on the finer hairs of the plant; but am not clear as to the fact *.

In the clofe of the evening they take their ftand, hanging down their heads, and putting their antennæ down to whatever they ftand upon; remaining in this pofture, and apparently in a ftate of fleep or ftupefaction, until they become enlivened by the fun the next morning.

Their fœces are of the colour and confiftence of cream, but dry to a white powder.

The female is confiderably larger than the male, and, when upon the wing, appears to be of a brighter yellow colour.—On examination, however, their colours are fimilar.

The following is a pretty accurate defcription of each fex.

FEMALE FLY. *Antennæ*, or horn-like feelers; —confifts of nine joints; the third joint from the head longer than the reft; meafure one hundred and twenty-five thoufandths of an inch long; are clubbed; and black.

---

* I have, fince, frequently feen them drink the fap oozing out at the end of a broken fibre of a turnep-leaf; and I have, lately, difcovered that diffolved fugar is a favourite food. *Jan.* 1787.

Head.

Head, with the eyes, and two ear-like appendages, black.

Tentacula, or mouth-feelers,—four; amber-coloured.—Mouth whitish.—

Wings—four; deflex; thirty-five hundredths of an inch long; light-coloured membrane, with black nerves. Upper wings with ftrong, black, clubbed nerves along the outer edges :—under wings, lefs nervous; projecting one-twentieth of an inch behind the apex.

Legs—fix; amber; with black feet, and five black articulations. Hind legs, three-tenths of an inch long.

Body (from the neck to the apex)—thirty-five hundredths of an inch :—bright orange; except two diamond-fhaped fcutuli, or patches on the fhoulders, black.

Thorax—lefs than one-third of the length of the whole body.

Abdomen—more than two-thirds of the body; and fixed to the thorax, *without any infection.* Its form is between the cone and the cylinder (the greateft diameter about half its length) compofed of eight fegments on the upper fide; and fix on the under fide. Under the two imperfect fegments lies the—

Pubes—which opens under the laft perfect fegment of the abdomen ;—and the—

Sting

Sting *—compofed of *three* † hanger-like Inftruments, with a fpiral wrinkle winding from the point to the bafe; making ten or twelve revolutions :—length about one-twentieth of an inch. Inclofed in a *fheath*; opening longitudinally; and reaching from the pubes to near the point of the tail, where it ends in a black fpeck. This fheath ftands edgeway to, and projects fomewhat below, the body; but is fituated principally in a recefs in the abdomen.

MALE FLY.—The fame as the female; except that its antennæ meafure only one-tenth of an inch in length,, — its legs twenty-five hundredth,—its body two hundred and feventy-five thoufandth,—and except that beneath the two imperfect fegments lies a plain fcale, covering the

Penis—which is inclofed in a cloven-hoof-like capfule; which forms the point of the tail.—In the act of copulation, the two claws of the hoof expand, and, in fome meafure, embrace the female.—The penis is cylindrical, fhort, and of a tranfparent, cartilaginous fubftance.

---

* Improperly fo termed; its ufe not being that of a weapon, but an inftrument wherewith the female forms her nidufes.

† But fee forward.

In copulating, fometimes the male, fome-times the female invites. The male leaping the female; and curling his tail beneath her's; they become united; and, turning tail to tail, remain about a minute in the act.

After feparation, the female walks off with feeming unconcern; but the male remains fta-tent for fome time. No fooner, however, has he recovered himfelf, than he begins to drefs for another amour, by cleaning and burnifhing his body, and antennæ, with his legs; and, in about five minutes, becomes engaged in an-other embrace.

The CATERPILLAR, when full-grown, is about half an inch long, and one-tenth of an inch in diameter near the head; the body be-ing fomewhat fmaller: twenty legs, fix of them long (probably anfwering to the legs of the fly), and fourteen very fhort (perhaps, mere-ly adapted to the caterpillar). The entire animal of a jetty black; (except a whitifh line on each fide, juft above the fetting on of its legs) with many wrinkles, but without hair.

Having arrived at fome certain period of life, it fixes its hind parts to a turnep-leaf or fome other fubftance, and, breaking its outer coat near the head, crawls out; leaving the flough fixed to the leaf.

It

It is now fomewhat diminifhed in fize, being lefs than half an inch in length, and thick in proportion; its colour, too, is altered from black to a blueifh or lead colour; with a black line waving along its back; and with two fmall black eyes, which now are become confpicuous. It is ftill covered with wrinkles, and appears in every other refpeſt the fame animal as before.

It is entertaining to fee (through a magnifier) the caterpillars eat. The avidity and voracity with which they feed are fimilar to thofe of a hungry cow turned into a frefh pafture; and the motion of the head and mouth is not unlike that of the quadruped. If a caterpillar begins in the middle part of the leaf, it firft takes off the furface, towards it; and does not, at once, break through the leaf; but, having cleared a round part half-way through, it makes a perforation, and prefently difpatches the other furface of the leaf: nor does it afterwards eat the two fides together, but grinds them down fingly; until having made a circular hole of from one-tenth to two-tenths of an inch in diameter, it leaves this for another perforation.

It feems probable that thefe round holes are not the effeſt of the caprice, but of the

X 2   in-

inftinct, of the animal, and that they are intended by nature for the conveniency of the female in depofiting her eggs.

When the caterpillar is apprehenfive of danger, he coils himfelf up in a circular form, putting his head and his tail together. If the plant on which he is feeding be fhook, he immediately coils himfelf up and falls to the ground; where he lies to appearance inanimate, until he thinks the danger over; when he unfolds himfelf and foon remounts the plant.

AUGUST 21. Yefterday morning, going into a field, where fome plants which had been ftripped by the caterpillars, had been left ftanding to wait the effect, (to obferve the progrefs thefe plants had made), I perceived fome of the yellow flies among them. Being anxious to procure fome, I went eagerly to the purfuit, and found them fo abundant, that in half an hour I caught near forty, notwithftanding they were remarkably wild. Their alertnefs ftruck me; they being now more difficult to take than I had found them three weeks ago. This led me to the idea that they are the produce of the caterpillars which deftroyed the plants above-mentioned; for the
ground

ground being left unftirred, the chryfalifes met with no interruption, but were left to the bent of their nature.

Wifhing to trace this infect from the egg to the caterpillar ftate, I this morning took up a fmall turnep-plant with a ball of earth to it, and put it into a garden-pot, fet on a faucer of water. Having a number of the flies in the receiver of an air-pump (fomewhat bell-fhaped, about eight inches high and feven in diameter) I put this over the plant with the flies fticking to it:—they prefently quitted the infide of the glafs, on which they were refting, for the plant; and the fun being warm, they feemed much delighted with their fituation.

I looked with impatience to fee the females begin to depofit their eggs, but could only perceive one which feemed any way inclined to the operation, and this did not go deliberately to the edge of the leaf and unfheath her inftrument in the manner I had before obferved.

AUGUST 22.—On Thurfday the 15th inftant, I put fix blue caterpillars (bedewed with moifture exuding from their bodies) into a box, and (by way of drying them and placing them in a ftate fomewhat refembling their ftate in nature) put fome common garden-mould to them;

X 3   covering

covering two of them up with the mould, and leaving the other four uncovered; some of them being upon the bottom of the tin box; some upon a turnep-leaf, also purposely put in the box.

Friday the 16th.—The whole had disappeared.

Saturday the 17th.—Moving the turnep-leaf, found one under it, alive, but naked.

This morning, to satisfy myself as to the state of the other five, as well as to endeavour to procure a chrysalis, I searched among the mould with the point of a large needle; and turning up one, which stuck pretty hard to the bottom of the box, found it crusted with mould on every side, except that which was next to the box; on which there was a hole large enough to see the animal perfectly alive.

Being willing to collect all the authentic information I could respecting this interesting subject, I went down this day to Beck-Hithe, to enquire of the fishermen, there, whether they had seen the flies arrive in cloud-like flights, as had been reported they did.

Old Hardingham, and his partner, declared to me, and old Gregory had before declared to Mr. Robert Bartram, who went down with

me,

me, that they have this year feen repeated
flights fly over their heads as they lay at a diftance from the fhore :—that they have alfo feen
them upon the fea, as well as upon the beach
wafhed up by the tide :—and further, that they
have feen thofe which the tide had left, begin,
on the fun's fhining upon them, to crawl ; and,
having recovered themfelves, afterwards take
wing and fly away : and, moreover, feem to be
of opinion that they fometimes light upon the
water to reft themfelves, and then renew their
flight.

' This appearing to me improbable, I have
tried the following experiments.—I took one of
the flies, and placed it gently on a bafon of water. It lay upon it, with its legs regularly
ftretched out, as if lifelefs. Having remained
in this pofture fome time, I agitated the water
in the bafon : this roufed it : and, having got its
wings fomewhat wetted, it raifed its tail, and
when the water had fubfided, very deliberately
dried them with its hind legs; which having
done, and having otherwife properly adjufted itfelf, it with the utmoft eafe took wing, and flew
to the edge of the bafon. This experiment I
repeated with the fame refult,

I then took another between my fingers, in
fuch a manner as not to injure it, and plunged

X 4

122.

TENTHREDO
OF
THE TURNEP

it into the water; wetting it thoroughly, its wings and body being by this means loaded with water, its utmost efforts to dry them were in vain :—it still, however, kept upon the surface, and made regular efforts in swimming; by which means reaching the water's edge, it crawled out, dried its wings, and took flight, without having received any apparent injury from the ducking.

Thus the fishermen may be right : in a smooth sea the flies may rest themselves upon its surface, and renew their flight ; but, being once thoroughly wetted by the waves, they either perish, or are brought by the wind and tide to the shore; where, if alive, they gain foot-hold, dry themselves, and fly to dry land *.

* Being doubtful as to the genus to which this species of insect belongs ; and being, *under the above date*, in possession of some living flies, also of some caterpillars and chrysalises, I embraced the opportunity of conveying one of them in each state to Doctor Morton, (principal librarian of the British Museum, from whom I had been happy in receiving more than one mark of disinterested friendship) in order that the species and its history might be ascertained ; and, towards this intent, *as far as my observations had then enabled me*, as well as to apologize in the importance of the subject for the liberty I was taking, I accompanied them with the *substance* of the *foregoing minutes* on this subject. Dr. Morton was pleased to shew them

AUGUST 24.—Being ſtruck with the before-
mentioned incident of the fly living ſeveral
hours without its head, I this morning, (Sat.) a
quarter before ſeven, cut off the head of a female
fly, which appeared very briſk and ſtrong, dividing the neck cloſe to the head, ſo as to leave
the two black appendages fixed to the body,
without maiming the legs. The body immediately recovered its legs, and ſtood as firmly
and to appearance as free from pain as if its
head had been ſtill joined to it. I turned it on
its back in order to view the different parts of
it, and left it lying on its ſide; but it preſently
ſprung upon its legs, and began to adjuſt and
clean its wings with as much dexterity as if
nothing had happened to it; continuing in that
act for ſeveral minutes; and, when it left off,
placed its legs regularly, firm, and upright as
uſual.

Mr. John Baker ſaw it at nine o'clock ſtanding
in this poſition; and the Rev. Mr. Parkinſon
favoring me with a call between twelve and
one, ſaw the ſame. It had, however, by this

them to Sir Joſeph Banks, (Preſident of the Royal Society)
and, through Sir Joſeph's liberality and diſintereſtedneſs,
the letter has the honor of appearing in the Philoſophical
Tranſactions, Vol. LXXIII. Part I. for 1783, page 217.

time

122.

TENTHREDO
OF
THE TURNEP

time moved a few paces from its firſt ſtanding-
place, and got its head and antennæ, which lay
by it, under its body! It continued upon its
legs all day, and at bed-time I left it ſtanding.

On Sunday morning, found it in the very
ſame poſture. In the courſe of the morning
it had a regular diſcharge of the fœces. Wanting the ſtand of the microſcope on which it
ſtood, I made it walk on to a piece of writing-
paper. This it performed without a ſtumble;
and the inſtrument by which I urged it forward
having ruffled its wings, it with the utmoſt propriety and compoſure adjuſted them, and took
its ſtand as before.

Between four and five on Sunday afternoon,
wiſhing to move it more into the middle of
the paper on which it ſtood, and being willing
to try its ſtrength, I put a large needle under
its body, to lift it from the paper : it immediately laid hold of the needle with all its legs,
and not only hung to it, but kept itſelf perfectly
upright; and might, I believe, have been carried to any diſtance. Replaced it on the paper,
when it took its ſtand as uſual.

In the cloſe of the evening it began to drop
its body nearer to the paper, reſting its tail
upon it : but on examining the other flies in
the

the evening, I find that to be the very posture in which they all repose themselves *in the night!*

Monday morning, six o'clock.—In the same posture; but had moved upon the paper in the night. *In the day*, it stood on its legs as usual! At two in the afternoon Mr. Samuel Barber saw it.—About five, it cleaned its wings; and this afternoon seemed more alert than it had been since its head had been taken off.

Tuesday morning—As much alive as before. About nine it cleaned its wings, and seemed remarkably brisk. About two, I found it upon its back;———endeavoured to place it upon its legs; but it could not expand them, though it was still evidently alive. Nine in the evening, it appears to be quite dead. But, astonishing to reflect on, this fly has lived upwards of three days without its head! during which time several of its cotemporaries have died with their heads on; so that it may be a moot point, whether cutting off its head shortened or lengthened its days!—Its life must have been merely vegetative; and the care of its wings pure instinct *.

---

* Wednesday morning, the whole dead, except five or six. Thursday morning, not one alive!

August

August 25. This morning, to my great fa-tisfaction, I at laſt ſaw another female depoſit; and in a different direction to that in which I had formerly ſeen them. The fly had her tail di-rected towards me;—the only direction I could ſee her in. In this point of view I could not ſee her draw her ſting, its edge being towards me; but ſaw the end of the caſe open, and, at firſt, ſtand expanded; but, as the inſtru-ment entered the edge of the turnep-leaf, (which ſhe ſtrode) the ſheath began to cloſe; and, having reached her fulleſt depth, became entirely ſhut. Having remained a while in this poſture, ſhe, with great deliberation, drew out her inſtrument; and, having reſheathed it, ſtood motionleſs for ſome time, as if overcome with fatigue.

She was not leſs than two minutes in the operation, owing, I believe, to the age and ſtuntedneſs of the turnep.

I ſaw her withdraw her inſtrument very evi-dently; but, in the direction of my eye, it appeared ſingle; whereas, in a ſide-view, it had appeared double.

August 26. On Thurſday the twenty-firſt, gathered ten or twelve caterpillars, one or two of them remarkably long, namely, ſix-tenths or

more,

more. All eat till Sunday the twenty-fifth. One left off about noon.—Placed it on a piece of paper, and covered it up with a little dry mould;—it crawled out not apparently by de-sign; but it seemed to want more mould to root in: covered it half an inch thick with moister mould, taken from the garden (the weather moist): it kept moving under the mould for some time, but in lefs than half an hour the motion was not perceptible.

This morning the mould still undisturbed. About four o'clock in the afternoon, searched for it among the mould with the point of a needle, and found it sticking to the paper: blew away the loose mould, which now was become dry, and saw the coat perfectly formed, and ad-hering firmly to the paper.

AUGUST 27. On Sunday afternoon, 25th of August, put three caterpillars to the live turnep in the garden-pot; two black, one blue.—One of the black ones soon mounted the turnep, but the other seemed neither to have fight nor in-stinct towards it.

Perceiving the blue one near the root of the turnep, in an upright posture, I apprehended it was also going to feed; but on observing it more closely, I found that instead of the head

being

being afcending, as I had thought, towards the plant, its head and part of its body was buried in the mould ; and, by the motion of the part in fight, I found that it was in the act of burrowing.—In about half an hour it had compleatly buried itfelf ; and had clofed up the mouth of the hole fo judicioufly, that no trace of it remained on the furface of the mould.

Yefterday morning, eight o'clock, placed three more blue caterpillars on the mould in the garden-pot :—they had remained in a fmall clofe-fhutting tin-box until they were as wet as moifture could make them, and feemed to be almoft in a ftate of diffolution ; fo that I was afraid to touch them with the pliers. One of them, however, the livelieft, immediately took to the mould, and buried itfelf in lefs than an hour ; the other two appeared fickly ; but at twelve o'clock they had got a confiderable way into the ground. About one, their tails were only to be feen: before four o'clock in the afternoon they had compleatly buried themfelves.

AUGUST 28. Yefterday morning examining the nature of the female inftruments more attentively, I difcovered *four* hanger-like divifions ;

not

not only in a fly which I then diffected for the
purpofe of further inveftigation; but in the very
fubject from which I wrote the above defcrip-
tion, and which I had preferved; one of the
three being double.

They are fo extremely thin and tranfparent,
that without a good light and a ftrong magnifier, it is difficult to diftinguifh between a
double and a fingle *blade*.

I am now, however, fully fatisfied as to
their number and fituation. —— By putting the point of a fine needle into the orifice of the pubes, and drawing it towards
the point of the tail, I feparated the compound inftrument into two extremely fine lan-
ceolated laminæ, each of which are evidently
divifible into two fomewhat hanger-like inftruments, making in the whole four; one of
which is placed on each fide the pubes, and
the other two on its lower margin towards the
tail:—when united, they take the foim of a
lancet.

By cutting off the lower part of the abdomen juft above the pubes, and drawing the
part on to the point of a very large needle,
the fting fprings out of the fheath, and is
easily

easily separated in the manner above-mentioned.

The two sides of the sheath are not united at the back, as I had imagined, but are two distinct valves or pieces, until they incorporate with the coats of the abdomen.

N. B. I have repeatedly dissected the female instrument (by drawing the lower part of the abdomen on to the point of a pair of compasses) for my own satisfaction, as well as that of my friends, and have always found them exactly as above described.

123.

August 28. Cawston-Sheep-Show.—This fair is held the last Wednesday in August, for sheep, solely; principally lambs, brought by the West-Norfolk breeders, and bought up by the East-Norfolk " graziers ;" in order to pick among their summerlies, and their stubbles, after harvest; to follow their bullocks in winter; and to be finished the next summer on clover, or the ensuing winter on turneps.

The West-Norfolk ewe-flock farmers also bring their crones to this fair; which the East-Norfolk men buy to put to the ram; and, having followed the bullocks and fatted their
lambs,

lambs, are themfelves finifhed for " harveft
beef." To-day, there was, alfo, feveral pens
of fheerling-wedders, brought by the Weft-
Norfolk farmers, who keep what are called
wedder-flocks (that is, buy wedder-lambs one
year, and fell them as fheerlings the next), to
be bought by the eaftern or weftern farmers, to
finifh with turneps the enfuing winter: alfo
confiderable quantities of ftock-ewes, two and
three fheer; brought by thofe who are over-
ftocked, or are throwing up their ewe-flock,
and bought by thofe who are increafing, or
" fetting" a ewe-flock.

Sheep of all forts were very dear; nearly double the prices they were laft year, at this fair.
Laft year good lambs were bought for five
fhillings and fixpence, or fix fhillings a head:
this year, ten to twelve pounds a fcore was
the current price. Mr. Durfgate, who is now,
fince Mr. Mallet's death, efteemed the richeft
farmer in the county (having, it is faid, made
thirty thoufand pounds by farming), was bade
twelve fhillings a piece for his whole pen (about
three or four hundred): but he refufed the
offer. His and Mr. Martin's (alfo a capital Weft- Norfolk farmer) were the " top of
" the fair;" and they both of them afked

123.

fourteen pounds. Seven and eight shillings were asked for the diminutive "heath-lambs" (from the Brandon side of the county), not much larger than rabbits. Last year they were sold at three, or three and a half,—four the outside price. Notwithstanding, however, the high prices this year, a principal part of the lambs were sold.

There are several reasons for the high price of Norfolk lambs this year: the low price which they have borne for some years back has greatly reduced the size and number of ewe-flocks: another, there being no market for long wool, while Norfolk wool bears a high price, the Lincolnshire farmers are getting into the short-wooled breed of sheep; and have, it is said, bought up considerable numbers of Norfolk lambs, and stock-ewes, this summer: and another reason, the first sowing of turneps having been cut off by the caterpillar, the second sowing will produce better food for sheep than for bullocks.

Stock-ewes were sold from twelve to fifteen shillings a head; sheerling-wedders fourteen or fifteen shillings; and even a parcel of crones were sold so high as twelve shillings, but they were singularly good ones; in general,

ral, about feven to nine pounds a fcore : laft
year they were bought for four to five
pounds.

Sheerling-wedders were the cheapeft, and
lambs the deareft ftock. How a farmer could
bid twelve fhillings for lambs, when he might
have bought wedders, of almoft twice the fize,
for fourteen fhillings, is fomewhat remarkable *.

This is entirely a fair of bufinefs : fcarcely
a woman or a townfman to be feen in it.
Many of the firft farmers in Norfolk were there
to-day ; this being, I believe, the greateft
" fheep-fhow " in the county.

124.

August 30. On Sunday the 4th inftant
put one black and one blue caterpillar into a
box with a turnep-leaf : the black one died ;
the blue one laid itfelf up in a fold of the
leaf, which it fixed to the bottom of the box.
Laft Sunday, the 25th, I fancied I could fee
the antennæ of the fly playing at one end of
the chryfalis ; and not being able to fee it af-

---

* My reafons for giving the minutiæ of the bufinefs of
fairs appear at the clofe of the article MARKETS, Vol. I.

terwards, or to difcover any progrefs which
was made, I began to fear that the leaf was
too tough for the fly to difengage itfelf: I
therefore, yefterday morning, wetted it with
dew, and fet it in the fun ; but in the evening, perceiving no appearance of life, I cut the
chryfalis from the box, and found the animal
perfectly alive : not in the ftate of a fly, but
to all appearance in the very ftate in which it
laid itfelf up. The part of the leaf which
lay between its body and the bottom of the
box was converted into a fine tranfparent lamina, and fo faft glued to the box that I was
obliged to feparate them with the edge of a
knife; or rather, to cut off the chryfalis coat
clofe to the box (with which the chryfaline
matter feems to be incorporated), making a
hole in the bottom of the coat. Replaced it
as nearly as I could in the pofition I had taken
it from.

This morning, I find, it has got its tail out
of the coat, and has given me a full opportunity of examining it. It is ftill the fame
blue caterpillar with a black ftreak down its
back ; appears quite healthy ; and indeed remarkably plump and fleek. I am afraid,
however, that by laying open the cell prematurely,

.turely, I have caufed an abortion : it is neverthelefs a fatisfaction to know the exact ftate in
·which they appear after having been laid up
·near a month.

AUGUST 31. On Thurfday the 29th procured
a frefh parcel of flies. Yefterday put a group
.of young turnep-plants into a garden-pot. To-
day put the flies under the glafs-receiver.

Being nearly an equal number of males and
females, and having been fhut up in a dark
box for two days, they began, on being placed
.in a hottifh fun, to copulate with a degree of
lafcivioufnefs I had not before obferved. The
males not only remained longer in the act
(from one to two minutes), but neglecting to
.drefs themfelves, in the manner I had before
noticed, flew from embrace to embrace, with
very little intermiffion. Three or four couple
were generally engaged at once, and the females
which did not happen to be in the act were
venting their fury on their more fortunate fifter-
hood; half a dozen of them, fome double
fome fingle, being frequently engaged at once
in battle-royal. Their furor lafted about an
hour ; after which they appeared flat and
fpiritlefs.

I now put three of the females upon the

Y 3   young

young turnep-plants, and foon found my expectation gratified in the fulleft extent; for
the plants being fucculent and tender (the
rough leaves about an inch in diameter, and the
feedling-leaves ftill remaining), they immediately began to depofit their eggs. I had put
the glafs over them, left they fhould fly away;
but this was unneceffary: I therefore took it
off, and made my obfervations without re-
ftraint. The leaves were thin and tranfparent;
the fun fhone full upon them; and the flies
were fo tame that I could obferve the operation in any point of view I pleafed: even
touching them gently while in the act did not
difturb them. I faw not lefs than twelve or
fifteen depofits; and Mr. Robert Bartram calling upon bufinefs, while I was obferving them,
alfo faw three or four.

I put them upon the plants between nine
and ten o'clock in the morning; and leaving
them between ten and eleven, did not return
until paft one, when I found them ftill bufy
in the act of depofiting. My worthy and
fenfible friend, Mr. Parkinfon, calling at that
time, obferved two or three operations. They
foon afterwards, however, began to droop, and
entirely left the plants.

I have now no longer any doubt as to the
opera-

operation. Having tried the texture of the
leaf, and its fitnefs for her purpofe (by piercing
it repeatedly with the point of her inftrument),
and having chofen fome convenient part on its
edge (the choice of which feems frequently to
puzzle her), the female adjufts herfelf for the
operation, by placing one, two, or three of her
feet on the upper, and the reft on the under,
fide of the leaf; but always clafping it with
her hindmoft legs, without which fhe cannot,
with any degree of conveniency, perform the
act.—Having taken her ftand, fhe begins to
feel for the middle of the edge of the leaf,
which fhe finds by the help of her fheath,
placing one of its valves on one fide, and the
other on the oppofite fide; by which means
the point of her inftrument eafily hits the middle way. She then fplits the edge of the leaf,
and having made a fhallow fiffure about twice
the breadth of her inftrument, fhe begins to
infinuate this downward, into the margin of
the leaf; not in a line perpendicular to the
edge, but obliquely backward; feldom making
an angle of more than 45°. with the line of
the edge, and frequently of lefs than 20°.
running it almoft parallel with it. Having got
the inftrument to near its fulleft depth, fhe

Y 4   begins

begins to defcribe a fegment of a circle, bringing it round with a fweep until it almoft reaches
the margin of the leaf on the oppofite fide of
the orifice; and thus, cleaving the leaf, forms
a purfe-like nidus within it.

This creates a work of confiderable labour,
in executing which fhe employs her four inftruments with a fkill and dexterity which is
delightful to look on, but difficult to defcribe.
The two in front fhe makes ufe of as hand-
faws; while the two hinder ones are employed
as fprings to impel them forward, and make
them lay hold of the work. What feems to
make the operation go on fmoothly and plea-
fantly to the eye, and with apparent eafe to
the animal, is, the manner in which fhe works
her front inftruments; which are not drawn
up and pufhed down together, but alternately,
and feparately, one of them rifing while the
other is preffed downward; as is evidently
feen by their wrinkles or ferratures; efpecially
if viewed through a delicate tranfparent leaf,
held between a good glafs and a ftrong light.

The nidus being formed, the fly lets her
inftruments recede towards its center, where
they remain motionlefs until the time of labour
comes on; which is generally many feconds,
often

often half a minute, after the nidus is finished: but the body having undergone a fpafm-like agitation, the orifices of the pubes and the nidus, which are now intimately connected, become fwelled out with a femi-tranfparent whitifh matter, which is feen to glide flowly down between *two* laminæ (feparated and formed into a funnel-like pipe) until having got near to their points, it drops from between them, and falls deliberately to the bottom of the nidus; where it plainly fhews itfelf of an oval form. The points of the inftruments being ftill carried farther backward, until they are fafely freed from the ovum, they are carefully and leifurely withdrawn (nearly in the direction in which they were infinuated); fheathed; and the operation compleated.

SEPTEMBER 1. To make myfelf completely mafter of this fubject, I put a fly, this morning, upon the fame plants I had obferved from yefterday; and finding her fo tame that I could place her on any leaf I pleafed, and even turn it to the light while fhe was in the act, I cut off one of the tendereft leaves, took it between the finger and thumb, placed the fly upon it, and holding them between the

glafs

glafs and the light, faw five or fix compleat
depofits in about twenty minutes : all exactly
in the manner above defcribed.

If the fly diflike the part of the leaf fhe has
begun to work upon, fhe withdraws her inftruments, and feeks for a more commodious part.
Sometimes I have feen her begin at an angle,
where fhe had not room for a nidus; at others,
the leaf being curled, fhe has found her inftruments getting too near one fide of it ; and again,
have feen her begin fo near a former nidus that
her inftrument has broke into it : in either of
thefe cafes fhe defifted from going any farther.

It is very obfervable, that fhe refufed entirely
the fmooth tender feedling-leaves, for thofe
which are rough and apparently more difficult
to work upon : but inftinct, no doubt, and not
eafe, directs her in the choice ; for the feedling-
leaves are of fhort duration, and would probably wither before the caterpillar became perfected.

To-day, looking carefully to fee if I
could perceive any progrefs made in an egg
which I faw depofited, laft Sunday, in the
edge of the live turnep-leaf, and which I then
marked, I obferved, to my great fatisfaction,
a young caterpillar feeding on the under-
fide

fide of the leaf; and, on examining the edge, attentively, found a number of nidufes; from three or four of which the animals had obvioufly efcaped; they being empty, with a hole on their under-fide, proportioned to the fize of the young animal; and looking diligently on the under-furface of the other leaves, I found four more infant caterpillars.

In the afternoon, I difcovered a fixth caterpillar, which, I apprehend, had efcaped in the courfe of the day. The flies, I find, were put upon the leaves the twenty-firft of Auguft, and it is probable that fome of the young caterpillars were perfected, and left their nidufes, yefterday; fo that they remained ten days in the egg-ftate.

Their form is that of the full-grown caterpillars:—their fize, one-tenth of an inch in length:—their thicknefs in proportion:—their colour, a dirty white; except the head, which is of a jetty fhining black.

They begin to feed on the under-furface of the leaf, as foon, I apprehend, as they efcape from their confinement; and fome of them were, this afternoon, ftout enough to accomplifh a perforation.

Being femi-tranfparent, their food may be plainly feen paffing through their bodies; their

vifcera

viscera appearing to confift of one ftraight
paffage from the mouth to the anus.

They feem to have a perfect ufe of all their
limbs and faculties; and cling fo clofe to the
leaf that it is difficult to fhake them off.

SEPTEMBER 2. Yefterday, to try whether it
be a univerfal faculty belonging to flies in
general to live in a ftate of difcapitation,
or whether it be peculiar to the Tenthredo of
the turnep, I feparated the head of a common
large blue houfe-fly, about a quarter before
two o'clock. It immediately rofe upon its
wings, two or three inches high, and falling
upon its back, fpun round for fome time:
lifted it up by its legs, and letting it fall, it
made ufe of its wings and lighted upon its
feet, on which it now ftood motionlefs. About
feven it was ftill alive. Neglected to obferve
it later. This morning it is dead.

Thus it feems probable, that all flies have a
faculty of living fome length of time without
the head; but that fome flies will furvive
the decapitation much longer than others.

SEPTEMBER 2. To-day, put a female fly on to
a fucculent leaf of rape (*braffica napus*). She
tried it over and over, both on the fide and
on the edge; but would not attempt to infinuate

nuate her inftrument; and flew away from it. Put her, immediately, on to a young turnep-leaf: in three minutes fhe made a depofit.—Replaced her on the rape-leaf:—fhe appeared to be dif-gufted; and would not offer to make a nidus:—but fuffering her to walk on to the turnep-leaf again, fhe feemed much pleafed; and there being a large perforation, fhe put one foot through the hole, and made a depofit; the firft I had feen made on the margin of a hole in the leaf. She feemed to ftand aukwardly for the operation; but, neverthelefs, twifted her inftrument in fuch a manner as to hit the middle of the leaf very accurately.

Saw the fame fly, afterwards, make three feparate depofits in the edge of a fmooth feed-ling-leaf; but, perhaps, the edges of the rough leaves were already occupied.

Placed a caterpillar upon the rape-leaf; but it immediately walked off:—put it on again, and fhut them up in a box; it eat very freely.

September 5. The caterpillar lived upon this leaf until yefterday noon, when the leaf was become dry.

Put it on to the live turnep to pall its hun-ger; and then fhut it up in a box with two

very

124.

TENTHREDO
OF
THE TURNEP

very tender leaves of fow-thiftle (*fonchus ole-raceus*).

This morning untouched, except a flight rafure on each leaf.—Returned it to the tur-nep-leaf;—it eat immediately.

SEPTEMBER 6. Yefterday, put two leaves of garden-muftard and two of garden-crefs (fmall fallading) into a box with a caterpillar, covering it up with the crefs-leaves, and lay-ing thofe of the muftard at a diftance. In the evening it had left the crefs untouched, and had got upon the muftard. This morn-ing found it refting itfelf upon one of the muftard-leaves; but it had not eaten any percep-tible part of it. Put it on to the live turnep; it eat a little, but did not quite finifh one per-foration; it having, I apprehend, almoft done feeding: this experiment, therefore, is not quite decifive.

SEPTEMBER 6.—This morning, obferving the ftate of the nidus which I marked the twenty-fifth of Auguft, I perceived the young cater-pillar had juft come forth; its tail ftill upon the nidus. This, therefore, laid in the egg-ftate eleven days.

The nidus appears fmall, comparatively with the animal; which muft lie coiled up in a very
com-

compact manner. The body nearly white, and the head, except the eyes, also whitish.

SEPTEMBER 7. This morning I find two of the oldest of the young caterpillars have shed their exuviæ; having left them fixed to the leaf of the turnep. What surprised me much was, to find them of a deeper black than they were before they cast their first coat; which had, within this day or two, become blackish; but this second coat is almost a jetty black.

One of them seemed but just disengaged from its slough; yet was remarkably lively, and appeared to be feeding; but, on touching the leaf somewhat roughly, it fell to the ground. This somewhat surprised me: because, before they shed their coats, it was almost impossible to shake them off. Small as it yet is, however, it had activity enough to regain the plant in less than ten minutes.

They are now six days old; one of them three-twentieths—the other four-twentieths of an inch long.

125.

SEPTEMBER 7. The seasons, during the last nine months, have been much behind the sun. Autumn lasted until the middle of January; Winter

124.

TENTHREDO
OF
THE TURNEP

SEASONS;

Winter till the beginning of May; Spring until the month of July; and, now, we are in the height of Summer! I have been ftrolling about the neighbourhood this morning, and find the farmers in the throng of wheat-harveft! They did not begin, in general, until about a week ago.

Stock remained in the ftubbles and paftures until after Old Chriftmas; fome until February: indeed, the grafs continued growing until December; and a frefh fhoot was, in fome places, obfervable in the middle of January.

Daifies began to appear about Chriftmas; honey-fuckles, in general, foliated the firft week in January; and the hazel catkin, having received no check, began to blow about the feventh of January: and, what is extraordinary, continued to blow, in intervals of fine weather, until the beginning of April; until which time the graffes, and wheats, were entirely at a ftand, by a fucceffion of cold, ftormy, wet weather; but without much froft or fnow.

The uncertainty of feafons in this country will appear by the following regifter of the advancement of the laft and the three preceding fprings.

The

	1779. Surrey.	1780. Surrey.	1781. Norfolk.	1782. Norfolk.
The primrose blowed -	Feb. 7	Mar. 9	Mar. 15	Apr. 10
The hazel blowed -	Feb. 10	Mar. 10	Feb. 10	Mar. 31
The gooseberry foliated -	Feb. 20	Mar. 25	Mar. 20	Apr. 1
The sallow blowed - -	Feb. 20	Mar. 30	Mar. 20	Apr. 10
The elder foliated - -	Mar. 1	Mar. 21	Mar. 25	Apr. 23
The wild rose foliated -	Mar. 4	Apr. 10	Mar. 28	Apr. 14
The hawthorn foliated -	Mar. 20	Apr. 18	Apr. 15	May 10
The floe blowed . -	Mar. 25	Apr. 28	Apr. 17	May 12
The nightingale beg. to sing	Mar. 28	Apr. 24	Apr. 17	May 4
The hazel foliated - -	Apr. 1	Apr. 29	Apr. 21	May 22
The birch foliated - .	Apr. 7	Apr. 30	Apr. 22	———
The elm foliated - -	Apr. 7	May 1	Apr. 23	June 12
The cuckow began to call	Apr. 16	Apr. 23	Apr. 18	Apr. 20
The maple foliated - -	Apr. 12	May 4	May. 1	May 26
The cowslip blowed -	Apr. 20	May 4		
The swallow returned -	May 8	Apr. 23	Apr. 18	Apr. 21
The oak foliated - -	Apr. 20	May 20	May 17	June 4
The ash foliated -	Apr. 25	May 22	May 29	June 10
The haw blowed . -	May 1	May 25	May 27	June 15
Wheat shot into ear -	June 1	June 21	June 15	July 2
Wheat harvest in gen. beg.	July 28	———	———	Aug. 29
Turneps in full blow -	Mar. 25	———	———	May 12

In May, we had loud claps of thunder, with lightning, and a succession of rain and tempest, throughout the month! The farmers were distressed, even upon the light lands of Norfolk, to get in their barley: many acres, probably many hundred acres, were sown in the month of June! In the wet land countries, it is said, a considerable share of the grounds intended for spring-corn could not be sown; and much of that which was got in rotted in the ground.

The summer continued wet (excepting two short intervals) until the twenty-first of August,

when

125.
SEASONS.

when the weather took up; and the laſt ten days or a fortnight have been extremely fine and ſummer-like :—foggy mornings and hot parching days :—a finer wheat-harveſt never happened.

But the barlies are ſtill backward, ſome of them quite green,—ſcarcely a ſwath cut in the neighbourhood.—Neverthelefs, the crops look well; eſpecially the late-ſown ones! a ſtriking proof, this, that the farmer, in his time of ſowing, ought to conſult the *ſeaſon* rather than the *ſun* *.

TIME OF
SOWING.

* *Oɛˋober* 10. A piece of barley which fell more particularly under my notice (fee M.114.) was ſown the fourth and fifth of June; and was cut the twenty-fixth and twenty-ſeventh of September : the crop not quite thick enough upon the ground; but remarkable " top-corn !" twenty-eight to thirty or thirty-two grains on a ſpike. And what makes this incident a ſtill ſtronger evidence in favour of attending to the ſeaſons for the proper time of ſowing—this piece of barley, though ſown later by ſeveral days than any other piece upon the farm, was (where it had not been chilled by the ſtanding water) the *ſtouteſt*, beſt barley upon it. Had this piece of barley been ſown on the ſame days, in an early ſpring, it is more than probable that, inſtead of being the beſt, it would have been the worſt, upon the farm. The ſtoutneſs of the ſtraw, the length of the ears, and the plumpneſs of the grain (a ſpecimen of which I have preſerved), are proofs that it was *ſown in ſeaſon*, the fourth and fifth of June.

For general remarks on this ſubjeɛt, fee *Experiments and Obſervations on Agriculture and the Weather*, p. 171.

126.

126.

SEPTEMBER 7. Laſt year, I put a ſwarm of bees into a wooden hive, of a particular conſtruction. They took it remarkably well, and in the courſe of the ſummer laid up an ample ſtore. But the mildneſs of the autumn, and the length of the ſpring, were fatal to a principal part of the bees in the country; and to theſe among the reſt. Nevertheleſs, through inattention, I let the hive ſtand in its place, with the empty comb in it.

Paſſing by it on the twenty-fourth of July, (the height of ſwarming-time this year!) I ſaw ſeveral bees about the mouth of the hive: but in the evening they diſappeared. Next morning they returned; and, at noon, were followed by a very large ſwarm; which took poſſeſſion of the hive; and, in a few hours, began throwing out the dead, and clearing their new habitation: a work which employed them that and the enſuing day.

Perhaps, this was a ſtray flight, which had ſettled upon ſome neighbouring tree; and the firſt were out-ſcouts, ſearching for a hollow tree, or a fiſſure in a rock.

Or, perhaps, they came immediately from ſome hive in the neighbourhood. I have been

fince

126.

BEES.

since told that this circumstance frequently happens; and that it is reckoned unneighbourly, if not unlawful, to let a " dead stock" remain upon the stand. A labourer, it seems, followed one, this year, immediately from his own to a farmer's garden in the neighbourhood.

These are circumstances in the history of this petty but pleasing object of rural economy, which, though they seem to be well understood in this part of the kingdom, are not, I believe, generally known.

127.

MANURING GRASSLAND.

SEPTEMBER 7. Last year I made two accurate experiments on the *time* of manuring grassland. One of them was made the thirtieth of *July*, presently after the hay had been carried off: the other in *October*.

The first was very decisive: the benefit was evident; though the whole crop was extremely good; at least two load an acre: but, where the dung had been set, the grass was lodged, and the swath obviously larger than it was on the unmanured parts.

But the benefit arising from that set on in October was by no means obvious; indeed, on

a close

a clofe infpection, I could not fee any fhade of
difference; although the crop was in this cafe
very moderate; not a load an acre.

128.

SEPTEMBER 7. (See M. 62.) Another exceedingly fine afh, which ftood in the neighbourhood
of that before mentioned, and which had alfo
been difbarked, entirely round, by the deer, was
blown down by the high winds of laft fpring.

The roots were entirely rotten, and the bottom of the ftem appeared, as it lay with its
butt on, to be decayed; but the topwood and
the bark of the ftem had a healthy and found
appearance.

Neverthelefs, on cutting it up, the ftem proves
rotten at the heart, for twelve or fifteen feet up;
and is, at the bottom, a mere fhell.

Therefore, notwithftanding the afh may appear healthy and flourifhing after it has been
barked; it is, neverthelefs, decaying in the moft
effential part; and ought not, in point of profit,
to be fuffered to ftand *.

---

* The rottennefs of this tree could not be owing to a
natural decay; as it had every appearance of a healthy,
growing tree; and ftood in a grove, which probably is
not more than fifty or fixty years old; and whofe trees, in
general, are now in full vigour.

Z 3　SEPTEM-

TENTHREDO
OF
THE TURNEP

129.

SEPTEMBER 7. The young caterpillars are partial to the leaf they are bred in. Observ-ing one juft excluded from a leaf which is be-come old, withered, and yellow, with only here and there a green fpeck, I cut off the part on which it was feeding (thinking that a younger leaf would be more acceptable) and laid it upon a frefh young plant, in fuch a man-ner that the animal lay at its eafe between the two leaves : neverthelefs, it ftill kept feeding on the old leaf, for many hours; and, when it left it, did not begin upon the top of the ten-der leaf, but went down to the leaf-ftalk. But on reflection, this is in confonance with nature : the animal had been nourifhed, while in the nidus, with the juices of the old leaf; and after its enlargement, the fame juices, and thofe of a fimilar nature, were moft fuitable to its acquired habit. Inftinct, therefore, led it to feed upon its fofter plant; and to prefer the rigid to the tender part of the young leaf.

SEPTEMBER 9. The eggs depofited on Saturday the thirty-firft of Auguft, are beginning to come forth to-day; which is only the ninth day from the time of their being de-pofited : the leaves young, healthy, and fuc-culent:

culent: there is, however, only one as yet excluded (fix o'clock in the evening) and another which seems ready to burst forth: —the nidus, on the under-fide of the leaf, being fwelled to the ftretch; and fomewhat on one fide is a large black fpeck; over which the leaf has a fhining gloffy appearance. Cut off the margin of the leaf, and fhut it up in a box.

SEPTEMBER 10. This morning it is come forth, and has eaten a pit in the leaf large enough to bury itfelf.

Examining the leaves in the garden-pot, I find them fwarming with young caterpillars, which have been excluded laft night; fo that ten days may be taken as a mean continuance in the egg-ftate.

Examining thefe leaves ftill further, I perceived one of the animals in the act of exclufion.—Cut off the part of the leaf it was in, and faw it crawl out under the glafs. It began feeding in lefs than two minutes.

Seeing feveral more in, or near, the fame ftate, cut them off with a pair of fciffars, and laid them on a microfcope-ftand, placed in a warm fun. One, whofe head was already bared, prefently made its efcape, and actually fed, or appeared to feed, while its tail yet remained in the nidus.

Z 4 Having

129.

TENTHREDO
OF
THE TURNIP

Having not yet had an opportunity of seeing any of them in the act of breaking the shell of the nidus, I began to apprehend that the perforation was made by a simple solution of the leaf, by means of the glutinous moisture with which their heads appear to be covered (and which, no doubt, gives the leaf its glossy transparency); for in the two acts of exclusion which I had seen, the head appeared passive, with its upper part protuberant, and its mouth within the nidus; until bringing its mouth and two of its foremost feet without the orifice, it began to struggle, and soon made its escape. But, casting my eye on a neighbouring nidus, I saw a faint working within it, and presently saw its coat pierced by a tooth, or some other appendage of the mouth of the animal; which was obviously in the act of eating its way out.

Having made a perforation large enough for its purpose, it placed its head in the position above described, as if to rest itself after the fatigue it had undergone in making the doorway. In a few minutes it began to struggle, and having got its fore legs without the orifice, crept out with ease.

I afterwards observed two more perform the same operation, in the same manner, and minuted

nuted them both :—one of them was fifteen
and the other twenty minutes, from the firft
vifible act to the final exclufion, namely, about
ten minutes in making the perforation, and
the reft of the time in refting, and in the labour of extricating themfelves.

I am clearly of opinion, neverthelefs, that
the moifture, abovementioned, affifts them
materially in the operation, by refolving the
coat of the nidus into a jelly-like matter, ·foft
and inviting to the infant tooth; for one
which, on being placed in a hot fun, began to
make the perforation before the coat had fufficiently received its femi-diffolution; that is,
before the livid patch was large enough; could
not extricate itfelf, but ftuck with its fore-
head out; while its tentacula, and fore legs,
were bound in by a part of the coat, ftill
green and rigid; and it died in this ftate.

130.

SEPT. 11. The *Midfummer fhoot* of the
oak, this year, has been more obvious than I
recollect to have feen it. It has, however, I apprehend, been made much later than ufual: it
was not obvioufly general until the beginning
of Auguft. Many oaks have fhot upwards
of a foot in length.

The

130.

MIDSUMMER
SHOOT.

The Midfummer fhoot and the Midfummer barking-time have always ftaggered my
opinion relative to a uniform motion of the
fap, on Dr. Hales' principles : nor have they,
I believe, ever been fairly accounted for ; but
remain an unanfwered argument in favour of
a *circulation* of the fap *.

Being ftruck with this year's ample fhoot,
I was led into a train of reflection upon this
interefting fubject.

The fpring run of the bark and the fpring
fhoot are the acknowledged confequences of
the rife of the fap ; but how fimilar effects
fhould take place about Midfummer, when an
extraordinary rife of fap cannot eafily be
proved, may feem difficult to explain.

If, however, we conceive a regularly afcending ftream to commence on the approach of
fpring, and to continue rifing, uniformly, until the wane of Autumn ; and trace, with
clofe attention, the effects which muft necefla-
rily be produced upon the tree by fuch a uniform rife of fap ; we fhall find them to be
exactly thofe which annually occur in nature :
namely, a fpring run of the bark, fucceeded
by a fpring fhoot, with leaves, &c. a Midfummer run, with a fucceeding fhoot, &c.

* The *arterial* fap, if it may be fo termed, which flows
immediately from the root, is here to be underftood.

and,

and, perhaps, what every year occurs in a greater or smaller degree, a Michaelmas run of the bark, with a Michaelmas shoot.

. This procefs of nature might be illuftrated in the following manner.

Suppofe four elaftic veffels to be connected in regular feries, with narrow communications between them; each channel of communication being furnifhed with an elaftic valve, requiring a degree of force to open it; but, being over-come by fuperior preffure, its elafticity weak-ening, until entirely fpent.

Suppofe this feries of elaftic veffels ftretched flat upon a table (reprefenting the tree), and covered with a board (reprefenting its bark). This would refemble the winter ftate of the tree, when the bark and the wood are in their neareft degree of contact.

Suppofe further, a regular ftream of water to be injected into the firft veffel. As the water continued to flow, the veffel would fwell; the board be lifted by flow degrees from the table; and in this ftate reprefent, fufficiently, the *fpring run of the bark.*

. The veffel being filled to the ftretch, the firft valve would begin to yield; the buds of the tree would burft, the leaves expand, and the *fpring fhoot* be protruded.

But

But the spring shoot being compleated; every twig and every leaf having received its limited size; and the stream still continuing to flow; *a second surcharge* naturally takes place; and the bark becomes, a *second time*, separated from the tree.

The stream still flowing, the second valve is opened; and a second, called the *Midsummer shoot*, necessarily follows.

The autumn proving fine, and the current of sap still continuing to rise, the second shoot arrives at maturity, and *a third overflow of sap* takes place; the third valve is burst open, and a third or *Michaelmas shoot* is the consequence.

But winter setting in, the supply of sap is stopt; and that which has already been raised, being spent on the younger shoots, carried off by perspiration, or having fallen back again to the root, the bark closes upon the wood, and the tree returns again to its winter state.

131.

SEPTEMBER 21. *Hog-cisterns*, in this country, are principally built with bricks and *terrace*. But *this* is expensive: yet a hog-cistern is among the first conveniences of a farm-house. Wooden vessels are incommodious, and leaden ones dangerous.

This

This fummer a receptacle for water in a brick-yard being wanted, I had one built of bricks, laid in *clay*, and furrounded with a coat of the fame material : it holds water perfectly.

Afterwards, I built a hog-ciftern in the fame manner. This morning, on enquiry, I find that not only the tenant, but his wife and her maids, are fully fatisfied with it.

It was built in this manner—A pit five feet and a half long, by four feet wide, and five feet deep, was funk in the place moft convenient to the dairy, kitchen, and hog-yard jointly.

The bottom of the pit was bedded with fome extraordinarily fine clay, fetched from the fea-coaft for this purpofe ; moiftened and rammed down ; and its furface fmoothed over with a trowel. On this flooring were laid three courfes of bricks, in clay-mortar (the beft of the clay being taken for this purpofe), and in fuch a manner, that the joints of one courfe fell in the middle of the bricks of the courfe below ; the whole being laid long-ways ; not croffed, in the ufual manner.

The fides were carried up half a brick thick (that is, a brick in width) with mortar of fine clay; and, in a vacancy left between the brick-work and the fides of the pit, moift clay was firmly

ram•

131.
CISTERNS.

rammed; fo as to unite as much as poffible the bricks, the clay, and the fides of the pit into one folid mafs; carrying the brick and clay work up together; and beating back fuch bricks, into the clay, as were forced forward by ramming.

The ciftern when brought up level with the furface of the ground meafured three feet long, two and a half feet wide, and three and a half feet deep; confequently the furrounding feam of clay is not more than four inches thick; and the ftratum at the bottom is about the fame thicknefs.

Above-ground, a nine-inch wall was raifed on each fide, two feet high, with a gable carried up at one end; and, on thefe, a fpan or pitched roof was fet, and covered with tyles; the other end being left entirely open as a doorway.

This is an admirable covering for a ciftern. A *flap* (whether it lie horizontally or floping) being continually expofed to the weather, lets in rain-water; foon rots; and, from the manner in which it hangs, is liable every day to be fplit, and its hinges forced off, by the heedlefsnefs of fervants: whereas a *door*, having only a gentle fall, and being always under cover, will laft a number of years.

132.

132.

SEPTEMBER 21. Yefterday evening, between five and fix o'clock, faw a young caterpillar flip its flough. What ftruck me moft, was its head being of a filvery white; except its eyes (very fmall), which are black, as was the body. Watched the head to fee it change its colour. In about half an hour, it began obvioufly to change to a lead-colour : at eight o'clock (two hours and a half) it was become quite dark : this morning it is entirely black.

SEPTEMBER 22.—One of the caterpillars (full feven-tenths of an inch long) excluded the firft of September (the only one living) took ground to-day : exactly three weeks from the firft exclufion (two hours and a half in burrowing).

It fhed its coat about the feventh, and another time, laft Friday, the twentieth; and probably another intermediate time, about the thirteenth : for thefe excluded the ninth fhed theirs about the fifteenth, and are now fhedding them a fecond time :—four flipped yefterday; three to-day :—one of them I faw flip its flough :—the head white as above-mentioned.

SEP.

SEPEMBER 28. Thofe excluded the ninth began to fhed their laft coat laft night (five fhed), which is only nineteen days from their exclufion. But they have been fhut up in a warm box, and regularly fed.

Thefe, I am pofitive, have fhed their coats three times, at about fix days diftance.

Put them upon a pot of mould :—they would not take it, nor would they eat; but feemed defirous of being releafed from their confinement. I therefore gave them their liberty. They were remarkably active; crawling much fafter now than at any preceding period of the caterpillar-ftate. Hitherto their bufinefs of life has been eating; now, they are in a buftle to provide themfelves convehient lodging-places.

OCTOBER 16.—To try whether rain, or other water, coming in contact with the chryfaline coat, injures the animal; or, whether the coat is water-proof; I fuffered a caterpillar to burrow in a garden-pot, and let it remain about thirty-fix hours undifturbed. I then watered the furface plentifully, almoft covering it with a fheet of water, and put a quantity into the faucer on which it ftood. This

I have

I have several times repeated; so that if the coat be not water-proof, it must in this time be injured, and the animal drowned.

Searched for it this morning (Mr. Parkinson present); found it intire, and the coat as firm and as tough as parchment, notwithstanding the mould round it was in a state of mortar. Put it into a glass of water to wash off the loose mould: the chrysaline coat now shewed itself of a delicate silky texture, and of a cylindrical form; rounded at both ends, which were perfectly closed and exactly alike.—With some difficulty (occasioned by its toughness and tightness) I made a breach at one end; and found the animal perfectly alive, perfectly dry, and of a healthy appearance.

The season being now far spent, I despair of seeing any of the chrysalises come to the flystate this autumn; their present state is this:

That laid up in the fold of a turnep-leaf the fourth of August, still retains its plumpness and curvature; and still, I apprehend, retains its chrysalis life.

Of the six laid up the fifteenth of August among mould, four now remain fixed to the bottom of the box.—On separating one of them, I find the coat very tender and somewhat

VOL. II. A a broken,

broken, with only the skin of the animal remaining; not entire, but divided longitudinally; one of the divisions, or sides, being very entire, the other broken. *Query*—Has the fly escaped from this unnoticed (for during the first two or three weeks the box was frequently left open to receive the rays of the sun); or has some other animal entered the coat, and devoured the entrails of the caterpillar?—Loosening another, I find it very perfect, containing a plump, sleek, healthy-looking chrysalis.—Separating a third, it proves a fine large coat, curiously lined on the inside, with a smooth silvery lamina; but without any remains whatever of the animal, which has obviously escaped through a perforation at one end of the coat. *Query*—Did it escape in the caterpillar or the fly state? I am of opinion it made its escape presently after it had formed its coat, and was that which I found under the turnep-leaf (see back); for there were only six caterpillars put into the box, and there have been six coats formed: it is, therefore, probable, that each formed its respective coat, and that two of them made their escape. The other coat, seemingly perfect, and, I apprehend, containing a chrysalis, still remains fixed to the bottom.

That

·· That formed the twenty-fifth of Auguſt, with mould upon a ſlip of paper, ſtill remains a perfect coat, adhering cloſely to the paper.

Thoſe which burrowed in the garden-pot: while warm weather continued, the pot was placed in the ſun: it has ſince ſtood near the fire; ſo as to receive a conſiderable degree of warmth; but nothing, I believe, has yet come forth. Two or three of them being marked, I have ſearched for them, by digging up the earth carefully, and breaking the lumps between the fingers: this I have found a nice and difficult buſineſs, and the firſt I unfortunately cruſhed between my fingers.

On ſeparating and adjuſting the parts, however, I can clearly perceive the head with its antennæ folded back; its palpi, and legs, perfectly formed; its ſcutuli (or black ſhields upon the ſhoulders) of their full ſize and proper colour; as is the head; but the antennæ and legs and palpi are ſtill white, and appear limber, and not yet hardened. I cannot, however, find any traces of wings: there are ſome fragments of a hardiſh ſubſtance, green within, and brown without; which may be the wings ſtuck to the ſlough of the caterpillar; but I am not certain.

Being

Being willing to facrifice another to my curiofity, I have fearched for and found another coat; but only one-half of the flough of the caterpillar remains; divided longitudinally as before.

The garden-pot now contains— one burrowed on Sunday twenty-fifth of Auguft; one on Monday twenty-fixth of Auguft; and three or four which have burrowed fince that time, not minuted. I now put the pot by, with the glafs over it to prevent efcapes *.

From thefe circumftances, from the frefh flight of flies which appear to fpring up in the middle of fummer, as well as from the affertions of more than one farmer, who fay, that having fhut the caterpillars up in boxes they came to flies (the particulars I have not learned); it appears to me more than probable, that the early broods pafs through the feveral changes, and arrive at the fly-ftate, in the courfe of the fummer : while, from the ftate in which feveral of the chryfalifes above-noticed ftill remain, as well as from the fcattered flights of flies which every year are obferved to make their appearance in the fpring,

* Leaving the country, a fhort time afterwards, I had not an opportunity of noticing the event.

it

it appears to me equally probable that the latter broods lie in the chryfalis ftate through the winter; and that fuch as efcape deftruction from birds, infects, and the uncertainty of feafons in this climate, rife in the fly-ftate the enfuing fpring. Further, it feems probable, that in the more northern climates, where the fummer is fhort, the entire brood lie in the chryfalis-ftate through winter; which being rigid, and the fpring ufually fetting in abruptly, the chryfalifes are locked up free from injury, and the flies at once rife upon the wing; forming thofe cloud-like flights, which, when the wind happens to blow a fufficient length of time invariably from the northeaft, have been feen to arrive, or which may with every degree of probability be brought, upon the eaftern coaft of this ifland.

It is, I believe, known that Tenthredos in general are gregarious; hanging together in flights: from repeated obfervations I know that the fpecies under confideration will live from five to ten days without food.— The diftance from the fouthern cape of Norway to the coaft of Norfolk is not five hundred miles.— It has been calculated that a balloon has been carried, *by the wind alone*, at the rate

A a 3   of

132.

NTHREDO
OF
E TURNEP

of fifty miles an hour : confequently, a flight of infects, even fuppofing them to make no ufe of their wings to impel them forward, might be brought from Norway to this coaft in ten hours. In one week they might, provided their wings could bear them, be brought to us from the moft eaftern confines of the Ruffian empire.

If no exotic flights arrive, the few which furvive the winter, here, efcape in a manner unnoticed, and the plants receive no perceptible injury : but, when to thefe the foreign fwarms are added, their progeny become too powerful for the plants ; and the devaftation becomes confpicuous and alarming ; producing that dreadful calamity to this country, " A CANKER YEAR *."

* Were an apology for the length of this and the foregoing Minutes on this fubject to be required, I fhould make the following : Finding, on the perufal of thefe Minutes, that I was poffeffed of a minutial detail of facts, relative to the hiftory of an infect, which has been imperfectly attended to by naturalifts ; but which is of the greateft importance to the agriculture of this country ; more efpecially of the Diftrict whofe practice I wifh to defcribe with accuracy and minutenefs ; I did not hefitate in my determination to publifh them entire. I determined with greater readinefs as I have found, fince thofe obfervations were made, that the deftruction caufed by this alarming infect, has, in fome well-cultivated diftricts, thrown a
damp

133.

133.

October 16. (See Min. 13.) To endeavour to afcertain the truth of this opinion, I had a fmall bufh of the *berbery plant* fet, in February or March laft, in the middle of a large piece of wheat.

I neglected to make any obfervations upon it until a little before harveft; when a neighbour (Mr. John Baker, of South-Reps) came to tell me of the effect it had produced.

The wheat was then changing, and the reft of the piece (about twenty acres) had acquired a confiderable degree of whitenefs (white wheat); while about the berbery bufh there appeared a long, but fomewhat oval-fhaped, ftripe, of a dark livid colour, obvious to a perfon riding on the road at a confiderable diftance.

The part affected refembled the tail of a comet, the bufh itfelf reprefenting the nu-

damp upon the cultivation of a valuable object of rural economy, which will not readily be removed. And I flatter myfelf that the expedients, here regiftered, for checking or removing the evil, will not be lefs ufeful to the agricultor, than a fedulous adduction of facts, relative to the migration and propagation of infects, will be interefting to the admirers of the economy of nature.

A a 4 cleus;

cleus; on one fide of which the fenfible effect reached about twelve yards; but on the other, not more than two yards; the tail pointing towards the fouth-weft: fo that probably the effect took place during a north-eaft wind.

At harveft, the ears near the bufh ftood erect, handling foft and chaffy; the grains flender, fhrivelled and light.—As the diftance from the bufh increafed, the effect was lefs difcernible, until it vanifhed imperceptibly.

The reft of the piece was a tolerable crop; and the ftraw clean, except on a part which was lodged; where the *ftraw* nearly refembled that round the berbery; but the *grain* on that part, though lodged, was much *heavier* than it was on this, where the crop ftood erect.

The grain of the crop, in general, was thin-bodied; neverthelefs, ten grains, chofen impartially out of the ordinary corn of the piece, took twenty-four of the berberied grains, chofen equally impartially, to balance it! fo that, fuppofing the crop in general to be worth five pounds an acre, the part injured by the berbery would barely be worth forty fhillings; the quality, as well as the quantity, being much inferior.

To try whether the vegetating faculty of thefe grains was deftroyed or not by the damage

damage the farinaceous part of them had received; I fowed, Wednefday fourth of September, three grains of the heavy, and as many of the light, in a garden-pot. Thurfday nineteenth of September, one of the light grains came up; but none of the other until Thurfday the twenty-fixth, when one of the heavy ones made its apperance: and on Tuefday fecond of October, another of the heavy grains broke ground.

To-day, turned the mould out of the pot: found the other heavy grain, and *one* of the light ones; both of them fprouted.

It is, therefore, proved that, notwithftanding the injury done to the farinaceous part of thefe grains, their vegetative virtue is not *wholly* deftroyed.

133.
BERBERY PLANT.

134.

OCTOBER 26. *Bullock-fair of St. Faith's.* Bullocks, this year, have been dearer than they were even laft year (fee MIN. 27.). The firft day of this fair (the 17th inftant), ten to twelve pounds a head was afked for bullocks; but good ones have fince been bought for feven to nine pounds. Bullocks which will fat to fifty ftone, may now be bought for feven pounds.

MARKETS.

This

133.

This morning, I saw ten two-year-old Isle-of-Sky Scots, drawn out of a lot of two hundred, at two guineas and a half a head. Very small: not larger than the ordinary yearling-calves of the larger breeds of cattle.

135.

FENCES.

OCTOBER 28. This morning, I observed some workmen fencing a rick-yard with furze-faggots, alone :—a species of fence I have not met with before.

In a trench, about eighteen inches wide, and six inches deep, they set the faggots, as close as possible, upon their ends ; spreading the bottoms; and covering the skirts with the loose mould dug out of the trench ; also with that of a narrow trench, (a spade's width) dug for the purpose, on each side ; treading the mould firm to the roots of the faggots; which being sufficiently loaded, the trenchlets were shoveled and the banks smoothed.

One of the labourers says, he has set a furze-fence in this manner across Gresham-field (an exposed situation) which has stood one or two winters.

Calculate the expence thus:—One hundred and twenty faggots set about eight rods ; expence

pence of cutting two shillings and sixpence, or about fourpence a rod. Expence of setting about threepence a rod more: together sevenpence a rod.

The value of the furze, after having stood a year, will be about six shillings a hundred; or ninepence a rod.

Furze-faggots, thus placed, are a fence against every kind of stock; even hogs and hares; and, in a country over-stocked with the latter, might frequently be used, as a temporary fence, with great advantage.

136.

OCTOBER 31. Yesterday, procured the following particulars of the expences upon Norwich marl, brought round by Yarmouth, and landed at the staiths, at Wood-Bastwick.

Cost of a chaldron *(weighing a chaldron of coals)* at Thorp, and putting it on board the lighters eightpence; lighterage to Wood-Bastwick, round by Yarmouth, fifty miles, sixteen-pence; together, two shillings a chaldron. Two chaldrons make a middling cart-load; two chaldrons and a half a good load: seven or eight large loads are esteemed sufficient for an acre: the expence upon which stands thus:

The

		£.	s.	d.
The marl, (fuppofe eighteen chal- drons) at two fhillings	- - -	1	16	0
Filling it at the ftaith; carting to a medium diftance, and fpreading about, fifteen-pence a load,	-	1	2	6
Expence per acre,	- -	£.2	18	6

With the marl ought to be, and frequently is, laid on a quantity of Yarmouth muck, equal, in expence, to the marl.

After this dreffing, for about ten years, the foil (a fandy loam, but ftronger and deeper than the Norfolk foil in general) throws out very great crops; and, with the ufual teathe and ordinary dungings, will feel the effect of the marl for ten years longer.

Before the ufe of marl (which has not been brought by water, I apprehend, above ten or fifteen years) the farmers could grow no turneps; the land letting for ten or twelve fhillings an acre: now, the turneps upon it are remarkably fine; and the land lets at full twenty fhillings an acre: a rent the occupiers could not pay, were it not for marl.

The diftance between Wood-Baftwick and the marl-pits at Thorp next Norwich, is not,

by

by land, more than fix or feven miles; yet, the farmers find it cheaper to fetch their marl fifty miles by water, and then carry it, perhaps, half a mile from the ftaith to the ground, than fetch it thefe fix or feven miles by land. What an advantage, *in fome cafes*, is water-carriage to a farmer; and, confequently, to an eftate.

1 37.

OctobeR 31. I have lately obtained the following particulars refpecting the recent *inclofure.at Felbrigg.*

Some feven or eight years ago, Mr. Wyndham, who is Lord of the Manor, was alfo (in effect) the fole proprietor of this parifh; excepting one fmall farm, of feventy pounds a year, belonging to a young man, a yeoman, juft come of age.

An extenfive heathy wafte, and fome common-field lands, were defirable objects of inclofures: confequently, the poffeffion of this young man's eftate became an object of importance to Mr. Wyndham.

Steps were accordingly taken * towards obtaining the defired poffeffion: not, however, by

* Through the mediation of Mr. Kent; whofe ability, as an eftate-agent, is defervedly applauded in this Diftrict.

threats

threats and fubterfuges, too commonly but very impoliticly made ufe of upon fuch occafions; but by open and liberal proposals to the young man, the joint proprietor; who was made fully acquainted with the intention; and frankly told, that nothing could be done without his eftate. He was, therefore, offered, at once, a fpecific and confiderable fum, over and above its full value to any other perfon: and, to enfure the object in view, he had, at the fame time, an offer made him of a confiderable farm, on advantageous terms.

The young man, being enterprifing, and his little eftate being, I believe, fomewhat encumbered, accepted the offer, fold his eftate, and agreed for a farm; — confifting partly of old inclofure; — in part of common-field land; and, in a ftill greater proportion, of the heath to be inclofed.

Mr. Wyndham (whofe virtues and abilities are publicly known) having thus (*in effect as to this inclofure*) got the entire parifh into his poffeffion, and having fet out the leaft fertile part of the heath, as a common, for the poor to collect fireing from, — he parcelled out the remainder to different tenants, — laid out roads and driftways, and divided the whole, whether heath or common-field, into inclofures of eight to twelve acres each; or agreeably to the defire, or conveniency, of the intended occupiers.

A principal part of the heath-land was laid to the farm of Mr. Prieft, the young man above-mentioned; and was let to him on the following terms.

Landlord agreed to raife fences, hang gates, build a new barn upon a large fcale, make other alterations, and put the whole of the buildings into thorough repair.

The tenant agreed to marl twenty acres every year, until the whole fhould be marled, at the rate of twenty cart-loads an acre.

The rent agreed upon was this. Nothing until it has been marled three years. The fourth year, after marling, the rent to commence at three fhillings an acre: at which to continue four years; and then (namely, the eighth year after being marled) to rife to feven fhillings and fixpence an acre: and at this rent to remain until the expiration of the term of twenty-one years.

It was alfo further agreed that the tenant fhould be paid for the carriage of the materials of the new barn; but fhould do that for the repairs and alterations, gratis; as alfo for the

fubfequent

subsequent repairs during the term. Also that tenant should pay half the expence of workmen's wages for the subsequent repairs; provided that such moiety do not exceed five pounds in any one year.

This was a liberal agreement on the part of the landlord, and, on a cursory view, may seem to give extravagant encouragement to the tenant. The following calculation, however, will shew that, in the end, the plan will turn out highly advantageous to the landlord.

Suppose, for the sake of calculation, the quantity of heath-land, let to this tenant, to be exactly three hundred acres: and that these three hundred acres are divided into thirty inclosures of ten acres each; with a public road, or a driftway, between each line of inclosures. This is sufficiently near, if not exactly, the fact upon Felbrigg-Heath.

In this case, every inclosure required to be fenced on three sides.

Ten acres contain one thousand six hundred statute rods. The square root of one thousand six hundred is forty; consequently each inclosure, supposing them to be exactly square, required one hundred and twenty statute rods of fencing.

The

The price given for ditching, planting the quick, and hedging, was eighteen pence each long rod, of feven yards. An hundred and twenty ftatute rods contain about

95 long rods, which, at 18*d.* is - 7 2 6
4,500 quickfets, at 3*s.* 6*d.*—15*s.* 9*d.*
—furze-feed, 4*s.* 3*d.* - - 1 0 0

£. 8 2 6

For fencing 30 inclofures, at 8*l.* 2*s.* 6*d.*
  each, reckon - - 250 0 0
— 50 gates, with pofts, irons and
  hanging - - - 50 0 0
— the barn (very fpacious) fuppofe - 200 0 0
— additions, alterations and repairs 100 0 0

£. 600 0 0

— compound intereft on this fum, in
  21 yearly payments, at 4 per cent. 700 0 0

£. 1300 0 0

.The rents to be received, during the term, fuppofing twenty acres to be marled yearly, would be thefe :

Vol. II. B b 1 year

137.
INCLOSURES

1 year	-	0	0	0	Forward	1,53	0	0	
2 ———	-	0	0	0	12 year -	49	10	0	
3 ———	-	0	0.0		13 ——— -	57	0	0	
4 ———	-	3	0	0	14 ——— -	64	10	0	
5 ———	-	6	0	0	15 ——— -	72	0	0	
6 ———	-	9	0	0	16 ——— -	79	10	0	
7 ———	-	12	0	0	17 ——— -	87	0	0	
8 ———	-	19	10	0	18 ——— -	94	10	0	
9 ———	-	27	0	0	19 ——— -	99	0	0	
10 ———	-	34	10	0	20 ——— -	103	10	0	
11 ———	-	42	0	0	21 ——— -	108	0	0	

              153 0 0   967 10 0

As the compound interest of the
above receipts set down - - 232 10 0

£. 1200 0 0

Thus it appears, from this calculation, that, on the suppofition of the articles of agreement being ftrictly adhered to, the landlord will be paying at the expiration of the term one hundred pounds as the purchafe-money of three hundred acres of *improved land*, worth from ten to fifteen fhillings an acre; the principal part of this allotment being a good loam, lying on the defirable fubfoil, an abforbent brick earth.

But

But the fact is, and was probably forefeen,
that the tenant, inftead of marling twenty acres
annually, according to the letter of the agreement, marled, I think he told me, upwards
of one hundred the firft year, and has now
nearly finifhed the whole.

Therefore, fuppofing the original fix hundred pounds, and the firft feven years intereft,
to have been taken up, the landlord would,
at the end of the term, have cleared off the
incumbrance, and have found fome hundred
pounds in his pocket; befide the fee-fimple
of one hundred and fifty to two hundred
pounds a year, from this allotment only;
befide the advantages arifing from the remainder of the heath, and the inclofure of the
common field; and befides having done away
a nuifance, and planted induftry and plenty
upon an almoft ufelefs wafte: and this, too,
without rendering himfelf odious, or his tenants
miferable. IMPROVEMENTS like this are *real*,
and bring a *permanent* increafe to the rent-roll
of an eftate.

END OF THE MINUTES.

P R O-

PROVINCIALISMS

RURAL ECONOMY OF NORFOLK.

THE languages of Europe are not more various, or scarcely more different from each other, than are the dialects of husbandmen in different Districts of this Island.

The practice of a given District, therefore, can only be studied in the dialect of that District. No conversation can be carried on without its assistance. And although a man of observation may, by observation alone, make himself master of the outline and principal features of practice; yet for the minutiæ, he will find it convenient, and frequently necessary, to have recourse to *conversation*.

But a mere practitioner will not communicate with a man who does not speak his lan-

B b 3   guage

guage in its provincial purity : taking for
granted, that he is as ignorant of the subject
in general, as he happens to be of *his* merely
provincial terms. One word awry is capable
of putting an end to the moſt intereſting converſation; and of giving the practitioner ſuch
an opinion of the obſerver, as to conſider him
in future, either beneath his notice, or above
his comprehenſion.

The firſt ſtep, therefore, to be taken by a
man who is deſirous of ſtudying the practice
of a Diſtrict is to gain a knowledge of its provincial language : for until this be obtained,
in ſome certain degree, he cannot join profit-
ably in converſation with thoſe who are beſt
able to clear up his doubts, and lead him on
to freſh diſcoveries.

To acquire with greater readineſs, and retain with greater eaſe and certainty, this neceſſary knowledge; and to indulge, at the ſame
time, an inclination to an enquiry into the ori-
gin and progreſs of the Engliſh language; I
regiſtered the provincialiſms of the Diſtrict with
the ſame aſſiduity I did its practice; and find
myſelf poſſeſſed of near a thouſand deviations
from the eſtabliſhed language.

But

But the major part of thofe provincialifms do not relate efpecially to rural affairs; but belong to the ordinary dialect of the country; and cannot, with propriety, be introduced here. I have therefore felected fuch, only, as pertain to the fubject of thefe volumes. I have, however, made the felection as ample as this line of conduct would admit of—for feveral reafons.

Such a felection will, in the inftant, ferve to throw additional light upon the prefent volumes; and may, hereafter, be found ufeful to thofe who may have occafion to ftudy on the fpot, the rural economy of the Diftrict.

Other more material benefits may arife from a collection of Gloffaries of the provincial terms of different and diftant Diftricts: fuch Gloffaries may ferve to elucidate paffages in the EARLY WRITERS, on rural fubjects, which, without their affiftance, might remain inexplicable. And, above all, they may be ferviceable in afcertaining the particular Diftricts in which they feverally wrote: a circumftance, at prefent, little known; though moft effentially neceffary in fixing the degree of credit which is due to their refpective works.

Bb 4

A.

A - LADY. ' Lady-day (in common ufe).

ANBURY. A difeafe incident to turneps.
See vol. ii. p. 33.

B.

BARNED. Houfed in the barn (a fimple proper term).

BATTONS. Strong broad fencing rails. See vol. i. p. 85.

BARN-YARD. Straw-yard; fold-yard (a good term).

BECK. A rivulet (invariable).

BEGGARY. Land let down, through a want of proper
manure and tillage, is faid to be "run to beggary."

To BESTOW. To ftow away.

BINS. Applied, provincially, to the receptacles of
ftraw in a farm-yard; cow-cribs.

BLUNK OF WEATHER. A fit of fqually tem-
peftuous weather.

BOKE LOAD. A large top-heavy, bulky load.

BRAND. Smut (in common ufe).

BRANDY. Smutty (alfo common).

BRANK. Buck (ufed only in the fouthern hundreds).

BRECK. A large new-made inclofure (a Break).

BROADS. Frefh-water lakes (that is, *broad waters*;
in diftinction to *narrow waters*, or rivers).

BUCK. *Polygonum fagopyrum.* See vol. i. p. 126.

BUCKSTALLING. Cutting hedge-thorns fence-
height. See vol. i. p. 101.

BUDDLE. *Chryfanthemum fegetum*; corn-marigold.

BUDS. Yearling cattle.

BULLOCKS. See vol. i. p. 337.

BULLS.

BULLS. The ſtems of hedge-thorns.

BURGOT, or BEERGOOD. Yeaſt.

BUSH-DRAINING. Underdraining (being done with buſhes).

C.

CANKERS. Caterpillars.

CANKERWEED. *Senecio jacobæa*; common rag-wort.

CANSEY. Cauſeway.

CANSH. A ſmall mow.

CAST. Yield; applied to corn-crops.

CAULK. Hard chalk; or, perhaps, chalk in general.

CHEARY. Careful; ſparing; choice.

CHICKED. Sprouted; began to vegetate, as ſeed in the ground, or corn in ſwath or " ſhuck."

CHINGLE. Gravel, free from dirt.

CHOAKED. Blown up, or ſufflated, with a turnep in the throat.

CLOTE. *Tuſſilago farfara*; coltsfoot.

COBS. Sea-gulls.

COCKEY. The grate over a common ſewer. Hence, probably, Cockey-lane, in Norwich.

COCKSHEADS. *Plantago lanceolata*; plantain-rib-wort; rib-graſs.

COLDER. See STOVER.

COOMB. Four buſhels; half a quarter.

COSH. The huſk or chaff of wheat and oats.

COTTS. Lambs brought up by hand; cades.

COVEY. A cover of furze, &c. for game.

COW-

COW-PAR. Straw-yard; fold-yard.

A CRINGLE. A with, or rope, for faftening a gate.

To CRINGLE UP. To faften with a cringle.

CROFT, or CRAFT. A fmall common field. See
vol. i. p. 8.

CRONES. Old ewes. See vol. ii. p. 28.

CROOM, or CROME. Any thing hooked; as
muck-croom, turnep-crome.

To CROWD. To wheel in a wheel-barrow.

CROWDING-BARROW. A wheel-barrow.

D.

DABBING. Dibbling.

DANNOCKS. Hedging-gloves.

DAUBING. Plaiftering with clay.

DAUBY. Clammy, fticky: fpoken of land when wet.

DAVYING. See vol. ii. p. 257.

DICK. The mound, or bank of a ditch.

DICK-HOLL. The excavation, or ditch itfelf.

DINDLES. *Sonchus oleraceus & arvenfis*; common
and corn fow-thiftles: alfo, the taller hawkweeds.

DITCHING. A general term for fencing with hedge
and ditch.

DODMAN. A fnail.

DOGGEDLY. Badly; fhamefully done.

DOLE, or SEVERAL. A piece of land upon a
heath or common, off which only one particular perfon
hath a right to cut fuel.

DOLE-STONE. A landmark, or boundary-ftone.

To DOSS. To ftrike with the horn, or gore flightly, as cattle frequently do each other.

DOW, or DOO. A dove, or pigeon (common).

DOWLER. A dumplin (common).

DRAINS. Brewers' grains.

DRUG. A four-wheeled timber carriage.

DRY. Drought: " the crop was caught in the dry."

DYDLE. A kind of mud-drag.

F.

FALL-GATE. A gate acrofs a public road.

FAT-HEN. See MUCKWEED.

To FEY, or FAY. To cleanfe,—whether a well, a pit, or corn.

FICKELTOW. The fore-tackle, or carriage, which fupports the plowbeam.

FLAG. The furrow turned.

FLAGS. Turves, or fods.

FLIGHT,—of BEES,—the proper term for a *fwarm* of bees.

To FLITCH. To move from place to place; as from farm to farm.

FLUE. The coping of a gable or end-wall of a houfe.

FOLLOWERS. Lean ftore-cattle or fheep, which *follow* the fatting-bullocks. See vol. i. p. 29c.

FORCING. Fattening.

FOREIGNER. A ftranger; one of another county; not of the neighbourhood.

To FORGIVE. To thaw.

FOUR-

FOURINGS. An afternoon-meal in harveſt.

FULL-PITCH. Plowing the full depth of the ſoil is called " taking it up a full-pitch."

FURLONG. The line of direction of plowed lands. See vol. i. p. 131.

FURS. Furzes.

G.

GAIN. Handy; convenient; docile. *Ungain,* the reverſe (much in uſe).

GARGUT, or GARGET. A diſeaſe incident to calves. See vol. ii. p. 125.

GARGUT-ROOT. The root of *Helleborus fœtidus;* bear's-foot.

GATHERING. Rolling corn-ſwath into cocks or bundles.

GAY. Gaudy; as ſpeckled, light-coloured cattle.

GEER. Stuff; thing (a general term).

GILL. A pair of timber-wheels.

GLADDON, or GLADDEN. *Typha latifolia & anguſtifolia;* large and ſmall cats-tail.

GOOSE-TANSEY. *Potentilla anſerina;* ſilverweed.

GOTCH. A jug or pitcher (in common uſe).

To GRAZE. To fat.

GRAZIERS. Fatters of cattle; whether their food be graſs, turneps, or oil-cake.

GREASY. Foul; graſſy: ſpoken of fallows or other plowed grounds.

The GRISSONS. The ſtairs, or ſtair-caſe.

GROWERS. Farmers. *Great growers,* capital farmers.

GRUB-

GRUB-FELLING. The common method of taking down timber-trees. See vol. i. p. 123.

GULPH. A mow, or bay-full, in a barn.

GULPH - STEAD, GOAFSTEAD, or GO-STEAD. A bay, or divifion of a barn.

H.

To HAIN. To raife, or heighten ; as, " to hain the rent, the rick, or the ditch."

HAKES. The copfe or draught-irons of a plow. Alfo pot-hooks.

HARDS, or HURDS. Tow.

HARVEST-BEEF. A general term for butchers meat eaten in harveft, whether it be beef or mutton.

HAUGHTY WEATHER. Windy weather.

A HAY. A clipt hedge (common).

HEAD. Bullocks are faid *to go at head*, when they have the firft bite ; in diftinction to thofe which *follow*.

HEAD-KEEP. The firft bite : the beft the farm will afford.

HECK. A half door.

HECKFOR. Heifer.

HELVE. Applied to handles in general.

HIGHLANDERS. Scotch cattle of the Highland breed.

HILD. Lees or fediment of beer.

HILDER. Elder.

HOBBIDY. A man-boy (ufed in common).

HOBBY. A hack (in common ufe).

HOGWEED. *Polygonum aviculare* ; knotgrafs. . .

HOLL,

HOLL, or HOL. The hollow of the ditch, in distinction to the " dick" or bank of the ditch.

HOMEBREDS. Cattle of the Norfolk breed.

To HORN. To gore, or wound with the horns.

HORSE-BRAMBLES. Briars; wild rose.

HORSE-TREE. Whippin; or swingletree.

HULVER. Holly.

A HURRY. A small load of hay or corn.

I. & J.

A JAM. A vein or bed of marl or clay.

To JAM. To render firm by treading; as cattle do land they are foddered on.

JIMMERS. Door-hinges (common).

INWARDS. Intrails; intestines.

To JOLL. To job with the beak; as rooks *joll* for worms; or for corn recently sown.

JOURNEY. Half a day's work at plow or harrow.

K.

KEEPING-ROOM. A sitting-room.

KERNELS. Grains of wheat, &c.

KIDS, or KID. Faggots; bavins.

KILLER. A small shallow tub; a small cooler.

KNACKER. Used in common for collar-maker.

L.

LAID. Just frozen. When water is slightly frozen over, it is said to be *laid*.

LANNIARD. The thong of a whip.

LASH,

LASH, or LASHY. Very wet; as "cold lashy weather."

LAYER. Plants of hedgewood; quick.

To LATCH. To catch as water, &c.

To LECK-ON. To add more liquor; as in brewing.

LEGGET. A tool used by reed-thatchers.

LIFT-GATE. A gate without hinges, being lifted into notches in the posts.

LIFTING. (Corn in swath.) See vol. i. p. 242.

LOBSTER. A stote.

LOKE. A close narrow lane (common).

LOWER. A lever.

LUMPS. Barn-floor bricks.

M.

MANNER. Rich mould of any kind collected for the purpose of mixing with dung.

MARRAM, or MAREM. *Arundo arenaria*; sea-reed-grass.

MARSHES. Fens and swamps come under that denomination in Norfolk. See vol. i. p. 320.

MARSHLANDERS. Cattle of the marshland or short-horned breed.

MAVISH, or MAVIS. The thrush.

MAUL. A mallet.

MAUTHER. A little girl (in common use).

MEADOWS. Low, boggy, rotten grassland.

MEATY. Fleshy, but not "right fat."

MERGIN. The mortar or cement of old walls. See vol. i. p. 30.

To MOYS. To thrive: fpoken of crops and ftock; alfo in a general fenfe; as, "he muddles on but does not moys."

MUCK. The provincial and proper name of what is more commonly, but lefs properly, called dung.

MUCK-WEED, or FAT-HEN. *Chenopodium album*; common goofe-foot.

MUDCROOM. A tool ufed by water-workers. See vol. ii. p. 79.

MURRAIN. See GARGUT.

N.

NEEDLEWEED. *Scandix pecten Veneris*; fhepherd's needle.

A NIP. A near, fplit-farthing houfe-wife.

A NOCKLE, or KNOCKLE. A mallet or beetle.

NOGG. Strong beer (common).

NONSUCH, *black*. Trefoil-feed.

———— *white*. Rye-grafs-feed. See vol. ii. p. 179.

NOONINGS. Workmen's dinner-time.

O.

OAMY. Light, porous, floury; fpoken of plowed land.

OLLAND. Lay-ground (old land).

OPEN. Not fpayed; fpoken of a heifer, or a fow.

OVER-YEAR. Bullocks which are not finifhed at three years old, if homebreds—or the firft winter after
buying

buying, if purchased—but are kept through the enfuing fummer, to be fatted the next winter, are faid to
be kept *over-year*; and are termed *over-year* bullocks.

OUTHOLLING. Shovelling out a ditch for the manure it contains. See vol. i. p. 76, and 101. and
vol. ii. p. 76.

OWLSCROWN. *Gnaphalium fylvaticum*; wood-
cudweed.

P.

PACK-WAY. A bridle road (common).

PADS. See PEDS.

PAN. The flooring on which the cultivated foil lies.
See vol. i. p. 11.

PAR-YARD. Straw-yard; fold-yard.

PAVEMENTS. Square paving-bricks; flooring-bricks;
paving-tiles.

PEDS, or PADS. Panniers.

PETMAN. The laft of the fare.

PETTY SESSIONS. See vol. i. p. 40.

PICKPURSE, or SANDWEED. *Spergula arvenfis*; common fpurrey.

PIGHTLE, or PYKLE. A fmall inclofure; a croft.

PLANSHER, or PLANCHER. The chamber-ficor.

PLAT. The mould-board of a plow.

PLOWJOGGER. A plowman.

PLOWS. Plowed ground; whether clofes, or pieces
in open fields.

POLLARDS. Trees headed down to the ftem, and
cropped or polled, from time to time, for fire-wood.
A term general to the fouthern and eaftern counties.

POLLER, or POLLEN, or HEN POLLEN. The hen-roost.

PULK. A puddle.

PUTT. A mole-hill (in common use).

To PUT. To stumble, as a horse.

Q.

QUARTERS. The inn a farmer uses at market, &c. is called his *Quarters*: and he is said to *quarter* at such an inn.

QUICKS. *Triticum repens*; couch-grass.

R.

RANNY. The little field-mouse.

RAFTY. Damp and musty; as corn or hay in a wet season.

REDWEED. *Papaver rheas*; round-smooth-headed poppy.

To REAVE. To unroof or disturb the roof.

RED-ROW. When the grains of ripening barley are streaked with red, the crop is said to be in the *red-row*.

REED-RONDS. Plots, or beds of reed: or, the swamps which reed grows in.

RICEBALKING. A particular method of plowing. See vol. i. p. 142.

A RIDE. A common name for a saddle-horse.

RIGG. Ridge.

RIN. Brine.

RINGES. Rows, of hay, quicks, &c.

ROADING. Running races with teams, upon the road. See vol. i. p. 44.

ROKE.

ROKE. Mist, or fog.

ROOFING. The ridge-cap of thatched roofs.

To ROPE. To tedder; as a horse.

ROWEN. After-grass; latter-math.

S.

SANDWEED. See PICKPURSE.

SCAITHFUL. Given to breaking pasture. Also, liable to be over-run by stock; as open fields, &c.

SCALDS. Patches of land which are more liable to be *scorched*, *burned*, or *scalded* in a hot season, than the remainder of the piece they are situated in.

To SCALE-IN. To plow in with a shallow furrow.

SCORING; or, SCOWRING. See vol. i. p. 139.

SCOTCHES. Scores, or notches.

SCOTS. Scotch cattle.

SEEL, or SEAL. Time or season; as, "hay-feel," hay-time; "barley-feel," barley feed-time; wheat-feel," wheat feed-time: " bark-feel," the barking season. Also, used sometimes in common conversation; as, " what feel of day is it?"

SEVERAL. See DOLE.

SHACK. Stock turned into the stubbles after harvest are said to be at *shack*. Grounds lying open to common fields are said to " lie quite shack."

SHACKING. A shabby rambling fellow (living at shack).

To SHEAR. To reap; as wheat.

SHELLED.

SHELLED. Pied; party-coloured.

SHIFTS. Parts of a farm allotted for the reception of stock or crops. See vol. i. p. 131.

SHOTS. Young store-swine.

SHUD. Shed.

To SHUG. To shake; as hay, &c.

SHUGGINGS. That which is shed or scattered, as corn at harvest.

SHY. Harebrained; high-mettled; head-strong; as wild colts, &c.

SINGULAR. Lone or single; as a singular house, or farm.

SKEP. A coarse round farm-basket; also a bee-hive.

SLADE. Sledge.

To SLADE DOWN. To draw back part of the mould into the interfurrow, with the plow dragging, or *slading* upon its side.

SLAKE. Leisure: " to be at slake," to be at leisure.

SLOBBERERS. Slovenly farmers.

SLOB-FURROWING. A particular method of plowing. See vol. i. p. 142.

SLUSS. Mud; mire.

SMARTWEED. *Polygonum hydropiper et Pennsylvanicum*; biting and pale-flowered persicarias; arsmart.

SNAIL-HORNED. Having short down-hanging horns, with blunt points, and somewhat bent, in the usual form of the snail; spoken of cattle.

To SOL. To pull by the ear, as a dog pulls a sow.

SPARKLING. Claying between the spars to cover the thatch of cottages (spar-claying).

SPIRKET.

SPIRKET. A hook to hang things on.

SPOULT. Brittle; spoken of wood, &c.

SPURWAY. Bridle-road.

SQUALLY. A crop of turneps, or of corn, which is broken by vacant unproductive patches, is said to be squally.

To SQUINDER. To burn inwardly; as charcoal and the ashes of fern, &c. are burnt.

STANDS. Young timber-trees under six inches timber girt, or twenty-four inches in circumference.

STARK, or STUCK. Tight, or stiff.

STATESMEN. Yeomen; small owners.

STOCK. Species of a crop. See article TURNEPS, &c.

STONDLE. A bearing tub.

STOPS. Small well-buckets.

STOVER. A general term for the different species of fodder arising from thrashed corn, whether it be straw, chaff, or " colder ;" a provincial term for the short straws, ears, and rough chaff, which are separated from the corn-in-chaff, by the rake and the riddle, after the straw is shook off the floor; and which, in every country, has a provincial term assigned it; but totally different in different Districts.

To STOW. To confine; as cattle in a yard or pound.

STUBWOOD. All wood which grows in hedgerows and does not come under the denomination of " timbers," "pollards," or "thorns," is called " stubwood."

STULP. A post of any kind.

SUCKLING.

SUCKLING. *Trifolium repens*; white clover.

SUMMERLY. A turnep fallow. *A backward sum-merly*; an autumnal wheat-fallow: *a right-out sum-merly*; a whole year's fallow.

SWALE. Shade.

SWAYS. Rods, or fwitches.

SWINGLE. A crank.

T.

TACK. Subftance, folidity, proof; fpoken of the food of cattle and other ftock.

TAR-ROPE. Rope-yarn; the thread of old cables, &c.

TASKER. A thrafher.

TEAMER. A team of five horfes.

TEAMERMAN. A waggoner, carter, or driver of a teamer.

TEATHE. The dung, &c. of cattle. See vol. i. p. 33.

THAPES. Goofeberries.

THIGHT. Applied to turneps or other crops,—clofe, thickfet: applied to roofs or veffels,—impervious—op-pofed to leaky.

THACK. Thatch: *thackfter*, thatcher.

THONE, or THONEY. Damp, limber, as under-dried hay.

To TOP-UP. To finifh highly; as fatting bullocks.

TRIP. Of fheep;—a fmall flock.

TURF. Peat.

TWO-FURROWING. Double plowing; trench-plowing; fod-burying.

VALLEY.

V.

VALLEY. Any small hollow or channel; as a gutter in a roof.

VANCE-ROOF. The garret.

VARDLE. A common eye or thimble of a gate, with a spike only.

U.

UNCALLOW. The earth which covers a jam of marl.

UNDER-CORN. Short, weak, underling corn, over-hung by the crop.

W.

WALLACE. The withers of a horse.

WARBEETLES. The large maggots which are bred in the backs of cattle.

WARPS. Flat wide beds of plowed land.

WATER-WORKERS. Makers of meadow-drains and wet ditches.

WELL. A chimney or vent-hole in a rick or mow.

WINTER-DAY. The winter season.

WINTER-WEED. *Veronica hederifolia*; ivy-leaved speedwell.

WISP. A rowel, or seton.

WOODBOUND. Land which is encumbered with tall woody hedgerows, so as to hinder a free admission of sun and air, and thereby prevent it from exerting its natural strength and fertility, is said to be wood-bound.

WOOD-LAYER. Young plants of oak, or other tim-ber, laid into hedges among " white-thorn-layer."

WRECK.

WRECK.　Dead undigefted roots and ftems of graffes and weeds in plowland.

WRETWEED.　(That is, wart-weed).　*Euphorbia belioſcopia*; ſun-ſpurge.

WRONGS. Crooked arms, or large boughs, of trees, when the faggot-wood is cut off.

I N D E X.

GENERAL INDEX

TO THE

TWO VOLUMES.

Note, M. 38. 51. refer to MINUTES 38 and 51. i. 121.
to VOL. I. PAGE 121.